THE GUILD SHAKESPEARE™

Romeo and Juliet

Titus Andronicus

THE GUILD

Shakespeare

ROMEO AND JULIET
TITUS ANDRONICUS

BY

WILLIAM SHAKESPEARE

EDITED BY
JOHN F. ANDREWS

Forewords by
Julie Harris and Brian Bedford

GuildAmerica Books™
Doubleday Book & Music Clubs, Inc.
Garden City, New York

Cover Painting: Juliet, from Romeo and Juliet.
Painting, frontispiece, endpapers, and book design by Barry Moser.
Text is in Baskerville, with display calligraphy by
Reassurance Wunder. Binding design by Barry Moser
and Hideo Ietaka.

Art Director: Diana Klemin, with Rhea Braunstein.
Project Editor: Mary Sherwin Jatlow.

The Guild Shakespeare™
GuildAmerica Books™
Trademark registration pending on behalf of Doubleday Book &
Music Clubs, Inc.

Quality Printing and Binding by
Horowitz/Rae Book Manufacturers, Inc.
300 Fairfield Road
Fairfield, NJ 07006 U.S.A.

CONTENTS

Foreword to *Romeo and Juliet* by Julie Harris vii

Foreword to *Titus Andronicus* by Brian Bedford xi

Editor's Introduction to *Romeo and Juliet*
and *Titus Andronicus* xvii

ROMEO AND JULIET 1

TITUS ANDRONICUS 297

FOREWORD

to

ROMEO AND JULIET

by Julie Harris

I grew up in Michigan, and never saw a production of *Romeo and Juliet* on stage when I was young. I did see the movie starring Norma Shearer and Leslie Howard with John Barrymore as Mercutio. Those actors were not in their teens when they acted in the film, and I supposed that the roles should always be played by grown-ups. Later I attended a production of the play in England; it was in the early 1950s when I first went to visit London and traveled to Stratford-upon-Avon to see Shakespeare's home and the theatre where his plays are produced. Romeo was Laurence Harvey, and Zena Walker was Juliet. But for me it was still a play about older young people.

JULIE HARRIS has performed such diverse roles as Emily Dickinson in *The Belle of Amherst,* Blanche du Bois in *A Streetcar Named Desire,* and Mary Lincoln in *The Last of Mrs. Lincoln,* for which she won the Tony Award in 1972. Her Shakespearean roles include Juliet in *Romeo and Juliet,* Blanche in *King John,* Ophelia in *Hamlet,* and the Third Witch in *Macbeth.*

When Michael Langham asked me to play Juliet in 1960 at the Stratford Festival Theatre founded by Tyrone Guthrie in Stratford, Canada, I was terrified. Other than playing the Third Witch in the "Scottish" play (a production of *Macbeth* starring Michael Redgrave and Flora Robson), I had no experience acting in Shakespeare's plays.

Michael Langham came to New York City where I lived, and with great sensitivity and patience he guided me through the play scene by scene. He gave me a copy of the old Italian legend of Romeo and Juliet by Luigi da Porto. The legend found its way to England *and* to Shakespeare, for *Romeo and Juliet* was based on an English reworking of da Porto's story.

No matter how frightened I was of playing Juliet, I was challenged too: by the part, by the miraculous play itself, by the genius of the poetry, and by the uniqueness of the feelings expressed by a girl not yet fourteen—and I was thirty-five years old!

With Michael leading me through the play, my understanding increased and my terrors fell away—well, a little way away. But I did wonder how I could ever play the scene in which Juliet's Nurse comes to Juliet and tells her that her kinsman Tybalt is dead. And killed by Romeo. *And* Romeo banished! Juliet must go from shock at the news of Tybalt's death, to relief that Romeo is alive, to despair at knowing that Romeo has been banished and she has lost him! All these feelings tumble out in a cascade of emotion.

After the period of rehearsals at Stratford I was prepared to play Juliet, and I longed to be able to fill every moment with truth. But I didn't really realize what strength it would take to carry those three hours. Fortunately I had so much help: Kate Reid as the Nurse, Christopher Plummer as Mercutio, Douglas Rain as Tybalt, Eric Christmas as Peter, Bruno Gerussi as my Romeo, Jack Creley as my father, and Leo Ciceri as Paris. We were all helped by a brilliant vocal coach and a beautiful human being, Iris Warren.

I will always remember that season in Canada: my mountain-climbing expedition, my ascent to Mount Everest. I hardly ever reached the summit, but when I did, Oh, Glory! And even to try was a rich experience.

I had a lovely English friend, Caroline D. Hewitt, born near Shakespeare's home in Warwickshire, who headed a girl's school in New York City and was a great Shakespearean scholar. When "Miss Hew" learned I was to play Juliet that season of 1960, she told me about the great Ellen Terry's performance of Juliet long ago. In the final scene, when Juliet wakes in the tomb to find Romeo dead, she holds Romeo for the last time, kisses him, and says "Thy lips are warm!" Miss Hew told me that when Ellen Terry spoke those words she whispered them; they went right to your heart as you realized that if Juliet had woken a few moments earlier she would have found her Romeo alive. In the old Italian legend, she *does* wake before Romeo dies—but he has already drunk the poison, and so there is between them the terror that Romeo knows that he must die and Juliet must witness her lover's death!

I wondered why Shakespeare didn't use that part of the story in his play. I spoke about it to Michael Langham when we were in rehearsal, and he decided that we would use a moment of that part of the old legend. As Romeo raised the vial of poison to his lips to drink, my fingers trembled and my arms moved ever so slightly. Bruno (Romeo) was looking away from me as he drank and didn't see that I had moved. It became an exciting moment.

Eventually, I did see two *young* actors, Leonard Whiting and Olivia Hussey, portray Romeo and Juliet in Franco Zeffirelli's film. I also saw the glorious work of the great choreographer John Cranko, when he produced *Romeo and Juliet* for the Stuttgart Ballet with Marcia Haydée and Richard Cragun—heartbreakingly beautiful that work is.

So my dream has come true. I have seen the play done perfectly and had the great good fortune myself to work with an inspired director who gave me the opportunity to play one of the greatest parts ever written in a play of Divine inspiration.

> . . . when he [Romeo] shall die,
> Take him and cut him out in little Stars,
> And he will make the Face of Heav'n so fine
> That all the World will be in love with Night
> And pay no Worship to the garish Sun.

Has language ever been used more beautifully?

x

FOREWORD

t o

TITUS ANDRONICUS

by Brian Bedford

A great experience is possible from simply reading a play, but it's only half of what the author had in mind. Possibly *less* than half in the case of Shakespeare, because he was first and foremost an actor, and I suspect that in the Elizabethan theatre the *actor,* not the play, was the thing. Actors need material in which to dazzle, of course, and fortunately for us Will Shakespeare, player, also had the knack of throwing together a few "enterludes and pastoralls." Thanks to a couple of his fellow actors, who said he was a "happie imitator of Nature" who penned his plays at the speed of thought and with such ease that there was scarcely an inkblot on

BRIAN BEDFORD's first stage appearance was in *Julius Caesar,* in the part of Decius Brutus. He has directed a production of *Titus Andronicus,* and his numerous Shakespearean credits include the title roles in *Hamlet* and *Richard III,* Ariel in *The Tempest,* and Malvolio in *Twelfth Night.* In 1971 he won the Tony Award for his role as Arnolphe in *School for Wives.*

his original manuscripts, we have a record of what we now consider Shakespeare's *literary* works.

I was introduced to these at the age of eight when, on a rainy afternoon in the north of England, my brother cajoled me into memorizing "Friends, Romans, Countrymen" by the promise of a cigarette! The ensuing smoking habit I eventually overcame, but I'm afraid the Shakespeare dependence, instigated on that claustrophobic afternoon, has proved insurmountable. To this day I remain in the grip of the "happie imitator," as passionate admirer, actor, audience member, and director.

It was in this last capacity that I eventually got involved with *Titus Andronicus* in 1980 at Stratford, Ontario. As *Titus* was Shakespeare's first tragedy and this was to be its first-ever production at Stratford, it seemed, although potentially a baptism of fire, an appropriate choice.

Before he starts working with his cast and designers, a director must first evolve a clear idea of the overall effect intended by the playwright; he must then navigate all the elements of his production in that direction. In attempting to formulate what *I* thought an appropriate direction for *Titus Andronicus,* I studied the text at great length. I found it tremendously exciting and could envisage, given the right emotional commitment by the actors, a really powerful theatre experience. Yes, the play was a minefield due to occasional overwriting and a certain naiveté of effect, but I thought that with careful pruning I could negotiate a clear and dramatic path through this fascinating, complex piece. I did not, however, have a unifying concept that would give the production substance and prevent it from being, however histri-

onically thrilling, just a catalogue of horrors until I came across a
prophecy made by the Sibylline oracle in 6 A.D.:

> Inexorable wrath shall fall on Rome;
> A time of blood and wretched life shall come.
> Woe, woe to thee, O land of Italy,
> Great, barbarous nation . . .
> And no more under slavish yoke to thee,
> Will either Greek or Syrian put his neck,
> Barbarian or any other nation.
> Thou shalt be plundered and shalt be destroyed
> For what thou didst, and wailing aloud in fear,
> Thou shalt give until thou shalt repay.

This prophecy seemed to me to have been written (or bel-
lowed) with *Titus Andronicus* in mind, and it immediately inspired
me to place the tragedy (its characters and events having no
historical authenticity) at the very end of the 4th century, a few
years before the Barbarian conquest of Rome. By doing so, I was
able to approach this amazing product of Shakespeare's appren-
ticeship years not only as a superior version of the then-popular
Revenge play but as a metaphor for the demise of the greatest
civilization the world had yet known.

Thanks to the Sibyl, I now saw *Titus Andronicus* as an account
of the moral disintegration of a golden age as it gives way to
bestial anarchy. Historically this happened gradually, over centuries, but Shakespeare, in the business of creating great theatre,
compacts the process and produces the metamorphosis before
our very eyes. We see in Titus' exhausted nobility the grandeur

xiii

that was Rome, but almost immediately (the play is like one long superimposition effect in the movies) his image tarnishes, and the theme of the play emerges, as he endorses the mutilation and sacrifice of the Gothic Queen's heir. Through this barbarous act Titus unwittingly contributes to the "out-of-jointness" of a time for which, like Hamlet and Richard II later, he is tragically unprepared.

For forty years Titus has been a loyal soldier, and as the play opens, his conservative principles and his commitment to an outdated code of honour lead him, respectively, to two disastrous actions: the patently inappropriate choice of Saturninus for Emperor, and the impetuous killing of his own son. It is important to remember that the opening sequence is scrutinized by, and to a great extent staged expressly for, the hoi-polloi. This lends an appropriate reality to the dialogue, which would otherwise seem stiff and stilted. It also strengthens the motivation of certain key actions. For example, Titus's murderous reaction to being dishonoured by Mutius stems in part from his being publicly embarrassed.

After the long first scene, Aaron's words in the second have a fresh, audacious charisma. We sense a keenly focused vitality that will eventually bring Rome to its knees. Aaron is a political catalyst, and at the close of his introductory speech he spells out the Gothic manifesto: the annihilation of the Roman emperor *and his empire.* All Aaron's machinations are motivated by subversive intent. He is a Machiavellian revolutionary ("Blood and Revenge are hammering in my Head"), and the final image of my production would be Aaron's solitary black figure standing aloft, looking purposefully into the future, the lifeless victims of his strategies scattered beneath him. Simultaneously the audience would hear (replacing the lengthy eulogies after Titus' death) the Sibylline oracle's ominous prediction.

A careful look at Titus' volte-face—his amazing emotional journey from blinkered patriot, embodiment of Rome's greatest values, to diabolically inspired butcher—is essential to an appreciation of his tragedy and of the play itself. Titus' killing of Mutius, within minutes of his first appearance, establishes him as a martinet who has no respect for human life (not even his youngest son's) when honour is at stake. It also suggests that he has been infected by the disease of violence, which often assumes epidemic proportions at the inception of a nation and during its decline. Thus it is particularly surprising that the accumulation of horrifying experiences (and I think the realization that Rome, his raison d'être, is a "wilderness of tigers" is almost as shattering to him as seeing his mutilated daughter) releases a previously untapped *spiritual* resource in this war-machine of a man. When he is exhorted to temper his passionate, mind-threatening lament with *reason,* he replies:

> If there were Reason for these Miseries,
> Then into Limits could I bind my Woes.
> When Heav'n doth weep, doth not the Earth o'erflow?
> If the Winds rage, doth not the Sea wax mad,
> Threat'ning the Welkin with his big swoll'n Face?
> And wilt thou have a Reason for this Coil?
> I am the Sea.

xv

And later, passionately rebuking his brother for killing a fly:

Out on thee, Murderer! Thou kill'st my Heart.

Hitherto an unquestioning logistician committed to the annihilation of Rome's enemies, Titus glimpses (a) a cosmic perspective on his agonized existence, and (b) the intrinsic value of *all* life. In conjunction with these insights, he is engulfed by the conflicting, ignoble instinct for revenge; and it is the latter that splits his mind and provides the play with its chilling coup-de-théâtre of a climax.

Titus is the first of many Shakespeare characters who, when they have lost everything, begin to assemble true values. Unfortunately his obsessively violent nature forces him to reject his newfound enlightenment in favour of a spectacularly horrifying revenge. In doing so, he finally succumbs to the moral anarchy he has spent his life opposing, and thus helps usher his beloved civilization another step towards its own extinction.

Editor's Introduction to

ROMEO AND JULIET
and
TITUS ANDRONICUS

℞

The two plays in this volume provide us our first glimpse of the young Shakespeare as a writer of tragedy. *Romeo and Juliet* is the earliest major English play to accord full tragic stature to the trials of youthful love. Its characters are among the most vivid in the entire Shakespearean canon, and the sympathy with which the protagonists are depicted has made their story a point of reference for lovers the world over. *Titus Andronicus* is a work that marks the playwright's initial foray into Roman antiquity, a subject of great interest during Shakespeare's time. As a work focusing on revenge and on the problems of reconciling a belief in divine justice with a recognition of human suffering, it anticipates a number of themes in the two later tragedies that many consider to be Shakespeare's greatest.

Romeo and Juliet probably dates from around 1594–95, and it was almost certainly conceived in tandem with *A Midsummer Night's Dream.* Like the Mechanicals' play in Shakespeare's comedy, it derives from the story of Pyramus and Thisbe in Ovid's narrative poem, the *Metamorphoses.*

But even more than its comic counterpart, *Romeo and Juliet* has itself been a prolific source for later works of art. Of these the best known are lyrical ballets by Peter Ilyich Tchaikovsky and Sergei Prokofiev, an evocative film by Franco Zeffirelli, and a riveting Broadway musical, *West Side Story,* by Leonard Bernstein, Jerome Robbins, and Stephen Sondheim. Nor should we fail to note the dozens of parodies that have made Juliet's first question in the Balcony Scene the most familiar, and undoubtedly the most widely misunderstood, line in literary and theatrical history.

Yes, *Romeo and Juliet* is so deeply embedded in our culture that we run the danger either of overlooking it entirely or of failing to pause long enough to perceive it for what it is: a work of immense tragic power, and one that takes anything but a sentimental view of the love relationship that stands at its core.

Before we ever see the lovers together we learn something about the social contexts that will constrain their movements. We discover that Romeo belongs to a hot-blooded male world that lives by the code of the duel. In this setting tempers are always near the boiling point, and even well-meaning young gentlemen like Romeo and his friend Benvolio must be prepared to defend themselves at any time, particularly when irascible types like Tybalt are cruising in search of occasions to assert their "honor."

Meanwhile, we observe that Juliet, who at thirteen is probably several years younger than Romeo, has led a sheltered life under the tutelage of an earthy Nurse who functions, among other things, as a buffer between her charge and a set of parents whose primary objective is to use Juliet as an instrument to advance the family's "hopes" in society. Hence the Capulets' eagerness to have her marry a Count such as the youthful Paris.

Fittingly, the first words Romeo and Juliet speak to each other at the Capulet feast comprise a love sonnet. Romeo has already established a reputation for himself as a devotee of Petrarchan love-melancholy, and Juliet takes to "the Book" with an alacrity that shows her to be an equally ardent romantic. After their initial exchange of Love's courtesy, they immediately launch into a second sonnet. But in what will turn out to be a prophetic moment, their dialogue is abruptly interrupted by the Nurse with a call from Juliet's mother. Meanwhile, in what proves to be another ominous moment, Tybalt recognizes Romeo's voice as that of a Mountague and has to be restrained lest he immediately avenge what he considers a scornful intrusion on Capulet "solemnity."

Thus Shakespeare plants the seeds of an action in which "violent Delights" will bear fruit in "violent Ends." These words are Friar Lawrence's, and he plays a role that is best described as equivocal. On the one hand, he speaks for a tradition of "Learning," "good Counsel," and "Philosophy" that is several times invoked to remind the lovers, and especially Romeo, that they must use their heads if they hope to advance the desires of their hearts. On the other hand, in an effort to forge an "Alliance" that will turn their "Households' Rancor to pure Love," he agrees to marry the lovers secretly and, when things go wrong, to assist them with expedients to preserve their marriage and buy time until they can emerge in public as man and wife. At the end of the play it can be said of the Friar, as of Romeo in his well-intended intervention to stop the duel between Mercutio and Tybalt, that he "meant all for the best." But if some of the Friar's "Sentences" eventually prove applicable to Romeo's behavior, it may well be that Shakespeare also expected his audience to notice that many of them seem equally pertinent to the actions of the Friar himself.

What we generally remember most vividly from *Romeo and Juliet* is the scene in Capulet's Orchard when Romeo looks up to Juliet's window and the two lovers exchange the most eloquent vows ever spoken. This tableau is echoed in a later scene when Romeo descends from their one night together and Juliet has a premonition of him standing in a grave. But it is a more public moment in between these two that proves to be the point of crisis in the play. This is the pivotal instant when Romeo decides to draw his sword and avenge the death of his friend Mercutio.

Just a few minutes earlier, Romeo has turned the other cheek in response to the insults of his new cousin by marriage. Now, with Mercutio's "plague" ringing in his ears, the hero can only hear the promptings of "fire-ey'd Fury." We cannot help identifying with Romeo's plight. But as soon as the deed is done, we recognize, with the protagonist, that he has acted impulsively and is now "Fortune's Fool."

From this point on, the course of the action is downward. Once Romeo learns that he is banished, he becomes suicidal. Meanwhile, Juliet's parents decide to cure her supposed grief over the death of her cousin by marrying her to Paris. Shortly thereafter, the Nurse, who had been so endearingly loquacious in her earlier scenes, and in her own way so supportive of Juliet, displays a shocking incapacity to understand the meaning of Juliet's wedding vows. Eventually the heroine finds herself completely alone, and the fortitude she displays in her own moment of crisis is one of the most moving displays of courage in all of Shakespeare.

Similarly touching is the conviction with which Juliet responds to the situation she discovers when she awakens in the Capulet tomb. In their final moments both lovers prove equal to the highest demands on their fidelity, and the statues to be raised in their honor by their reunited fathers echo the sentiments of four centuries of Shakespearean audiences: if ever two lovers deserved to be canonized for their devotion, those two are "Juliet and her Romeo."

Lest we assume too quickly that the playwright meant for them to be regarded as "Sacrifices" in a more conventional theological sense, however, we should note that the words with which Romeo describes his mental and spiritual state at the moment of his suicide are images that recall the Friar's earlier warnings about "damned Hate." As such, they suggest that an Elizabethan audience in the 1590s might have attached more significance than we normally do to the Prince's observation that the action concludes with a "glooming Peace."

As a tragedy, *Romeo and Juliet* is unusual in the amount of comedy it contains. The Nurse is one of the most amusing characters in the canon. And Mercutio is so quick-witted, and so engaging, that some of his admirers have found it difficult to forgive Shakespeare for killing him off. But in a sense that is how the play itself is structured; up to the death of Mercutio, it functions in many respects as a comedy. Only then do the playwright's notes

xxi

turn tragic. To be sure, there have been tragic foreshadowings prior to that moment, such as Romeo's expressions of apprehension before and after Mercutio's celebrated Queen Mab speech (which is delivered, in fact, to exorcise Romeo's fear of his bad dreams). And there are moments of comedy after that point, such as the exchanges between Peter and the Musicians on the morning of Juliet's scheduled wedding to Paris. But it nevertheless holds true that *Romeo and Juliet* is in many respects a comedy gone sour. That may not account for all its power to enthrall us, but it certainly has a great deal to do with the pathos the play has always evoked in performance.

Recent productions have demonstrated that *Titus Andronicus* is also a tragedy that can move audiences. It was undoubtedly a popular work with the playgoers of its own day, so much so indeed that in 1614 Ben Jonson took it upon himself to ridicule the taste of those who still admired a play that by then struck many people as crude. Subsequent critics and producers tended to share Jonson's low estimate of the play, and for a while in the early years of this century it was even fashionable to deny that a work so "primitive," and so melodramatic in its wanton displays of blood and mayhem, could have been written by the same dramatist who gave us *Hamlet* and *King Lear*. Happily, those days are now behind us, and what is now emerging is a consensus that *Titus Andronicus* is worthy of attention both for its own merits and for a number of qualities in which it anticipates some of the finer moments of precisely those later tragedies.

Just when the play was written is still a subject of debate. It was on the boards by at least 1592, if not late 1591, and it may have been composed as early as 1589, in response to the fashion for revenge plays initiated by Thomas Kyd's notoriously popular *Spanish Tragedy* and the now-lost precursor to Shakespeare's *Hamlet*. In 1594 the *Titus Andronicus* text appeared in a good quarto printing that probably earned it the distinction of being the first of Shakespeare's plays to be published.

Notwithstanding its reputation for excessive stage violence, *Titus Andronicus* is in some ways the most "literary" of Shakespeare's tragedies. It contains several quotations from Latin sources the dramatist wished to invoke; and when the mutilated Lavinia finally discovers a way to tell her story, she does so by pointing to the passage in the *Metamorphoses* where Ovid describes the rape of Philomela.

A number of other details in the play also derive from Ovid. But another source, not only for items of plot and imagery but for the very concept of tragedy embodied in the play, was Seneca. His *Troades* may well have been Shakespeare's source for the sacrifice of Alarbus in the opening scene. And his *Thyestes* was surely one of the sources for the grotesque banquet at the end of the play.

For the story of the title character, Shakespeare probably drew from a prose history that now survives only in an eighteenth-century reprint. So far as we know, there was no actual Titus Andronicus in fourth-century Rome. The Titus of the play was therefore a fictional character whom Shakespeare seized upon as a means of dramatizing an episode in the decline of the Roman Empire.

In all likelihood the opening act of *Titus Andronicus* was

largely, if not entirely, Shakespeare's invention. As such, it demonstrates an interest in some of the same concerns that dominate the dramatist's other plays about the uses and abuses of political power. The Titus who returns victorious from his wars with the Goths is in many ways an anticipation of the Coriolanus who returns from combat in Shakespeare's later tragedy: for all his successes on the battlefield, he is anything but prepared for the challenges that now face him in the supposedly peaceful landscape of his mother city. With a touch of insensitivity, if not arrogance, he alienates Tamora by the brusqueness with which he sacrifices the Gothic Queen's oldest son to appease the spirits of the Roman dead he has brought back in coffins for the Andronicus tomb. With a singlemindedness that suggests inflexibility, he disregards the hints that Bassianus might be a better choice than his older brother and gives his vote for Emperor to Saturninus instead. With a blind loyalty to the new Emperor that makes him disregard the fact that his daughter is already betrothed to Bassianus, he accedes to Saturninus' request and promises Lavinia to him as his new Queen. And then with a stubbornness that anticipates King Lear's treatment of Cordelia, he slays his youngest son after Mutius tries to bar Titus from the exit through which Bassianus, Titus' brother Marcus, and Titus' other three sons have carried Lavinia away.

So much happens so quickly in this long opening scene that it is difficult to absorb it all at once. But the end result is clear enough: the Titus who returned from battle as "Rome's best Champion" is now maneuvered from the center of power to the periphery. Scorned by the Emperor he has placed on the throne, subject to the Machiavellian schemes of the Gothic Queen who has just been elevated to Empress, and only with difficulty reconciled to the brother and sons he feels have dishonored him, the old man now finds himself adrift in a world so alien from anything he has experienced before that he is at a loss for a way to regain his bearings.

And what is worse is that his troubles have only begun. In the scenes that follow, Titus and family suffer so much anguish that the protagonist comes desperately close to losing his sanity. As the play ends, Titus' brother Marcus is once again the People's Tribune he had been in the opening scene. Only this time the People's Choice accepts the crown when it is offered, and there is reason to hope that the chaos soon to engulf the Roman Empire can be forestalled for at least a few more years.

Just how the Elizabethan audience was meant to view Titus Andronicus is uncertain. Like Lear, he is clearly to be seen as a man "more sinned against than sinning." On the other hand, like most of the avengers depicted on the Elizabethan stage, he is driven to extremes that might be expected to taint his own character in the eyes of the shocked audience. If so, the concluding moments of the play would seem calculated to restore to the protagonist at least some of the sympathy he may have forfeited by his previous actions.

Except for "the Fly scene" (III.ii) and a few scattered lines elsewhere in the play, which first appeared in the 1623 First Folio, the authoritative text for *Titus Andronicus* is the 1594 First Quarto, which survives in a single copy now in the Folger Shakespeare Library. In general, the best text for *Romeo and Juliet* is the 1599

Second Quarto, which seems to have been printed from a manu-
script close to the author's own text. At times, however, superior
readings are to be found in the 1597 First Quarto, a text probably
reconstructed from memory by actors who had appeared in the
play. And occasionally there are corrections to be incorporated
from later quarto printings in 1609 and 1622 and from the First
Folio, whose text of the play was set primarily from the 1609
Third Quarto.

ROMEO AND JULIET

NAMES OF THE ACTORS

ESCALUS, Prince of Verona
PARIS, a young Count, kinsman to the Prince

MOUNTAGUE, Head of the Veronese family feuding with the
    Capulets
MOUNTAGUE'S WIFE
ROMEO, Son of the Mountagues
BENVOLIO, Nephew to Mountague and Friend to Romeo
MERCUTIO, Kinsman to the Prince and Friend to Romeo

CAPULET, Head of the Veronese family feuding with the
    Mountagues
CAPULET'S WIFE
JULIET, Daughter of the Capulets
TYBALT, Nephew to Capulet's Wife
PETRUCHIO, Friend to Tybalt
CAPULET'S COUSIN, an old Gentleman
NURSE to Juliet

FRIAR LAWRENCE, Franciscan Confessor to Romeo and
    Juliet
FRIAR JOHN, another Franciscan Friar
APOTHECARY, a Druggist of Mantua
PAGE to Paris
ABRAM, Servant to Mountague
BALTHASAR, Servant to Romeo
PETER, a Capulet Servant attending on the Nurse

CLOWN
SAMPSON
GREGORY   Servingmen of the Capulet household
ANTHONY
POTPAN

                  Simon Catling
MUSICIANS   Hugh Rebeck
                  James Soundpost

CHORUS

MEMBERS OF THE WATCH, CITIZENS OF VERONA,
    MASKERS, PAGES, SERVANTS

S.D.   **Prologue** *The Chorus is normally played by an actor who enters to speak his lines and then exits. On rare occasions, the Chorus remains in view of the audience as an observer throughout. Fittingly, in a play whose atmosphere stems from the world of the love sonnet popularized by the fourteenth-century Italian poet Petrarch, this and the Chorus' other speech at the beginning of Act II are both sonnets. The verse form, however, is Shakespearean rather than Petrarchan, with three quatrains (rhyming* abab cdcd efef) *and a concluding couplet (*gg) *rather than the octave (rhyming* ab-baabba) *and sestet (rhyming* cdecde) *used by Petrarch.*

1   **Dignity** *social standing, rank.*

3   **Mutiny** *This word carries the implication of both a violent outburst and an insurrection against authority.*

4   **Civil Blood . . . Civil Hands** *The primary meaning of* Civil *in both phrases is "of the city" (that is, pertaining to citizen blood and citizen hands); but there is also the suggestion that hands that should be "civil" (well-mannered, civilized) have instead become both bloody and morally stained ("unclean").*

6   **Star-cross'd** *thwarted by influences from the "Stars" (a term loosely applied to both the stars and the planets, and alluding to a complex system of astrology familiar to any well-educated Elizabethan).*

14   **What . . . mend** *What you miss here, our dramatic efforts will try to repair (make clear to you).*

4

Prologue

Enter Chorus.

CHORUS Two Households, both alike in Dignity,
  In fair Verona, where we lay our Scene,
  From ancient Grudge break to new Mutiny,
  Where Civil Blood makes Civil Hands unclean;
  From forth the fatal Loins of these two Foes   5
  A pair of Star-cross'd Lovers take their Life,
  Whose misadventur'd, piteous Overthrows
  Doth with their Death bury their Parents' Strife.
  The fearful Passage of their Death-mark'd Love,
  And the Continuance of their Parents' Rage,   10
  Which, but their Children's end, nought could
    remove,
  Is now the two Hours' Traffic of our Stage,
  The which, if you with patient Ears attend,
  What here shall miss, our Toil shall strive to
    mend.   *Exit.*

I.i   *The setting for the opening scene is a street in Verona.*

1   carry Coals   *hold in one's anger, submit to insults.*

2   Colliers   *coal workers or coal dealers, proverbially grimy.*

3   and   *if. This construction is quite frequent among lower-class characters in Shakespeare's plays.*
Choler   *anger.*

4–5   out of Collar   *out of the hangman's noose. Gregory pretends to understand "in Choler" as "in collar," or in the noose.*

6

Act One

Scene 1

Enter Sampson and Gregory of the House of Capulet
(with Swords and Bucklers).

SAMPSON Gregory, on my word, we'll not carry Coals.
GREGORY No, for then we should be Colliers.
SAMPSON I mean, and we be in Choler we'll draw.
GREGORY Ay, while you live, draw your Neck out of
  Collar.   5
SAMPSON I strike quickly being mov'd.
GREGORY But thou art not quickly mov'd to strike.
SAMPSON A Dog of the House of Mountague moves me.
GREGORY To move is to stir, and to be Valiant is
  to stand: therefore if thou art mov'd, thou   10
  runn'st away.

12   move me to stand *Sampson rejects Gregory's assumption that "to move" and "to stand" are necessarily opposites. When he is "mov'd" (aroused) to anger, he stands up to the Mountague men rather than running; meanwhile, he stands up for the Mountague maids, using his male "weapon" to "thrust" them (lines 19–20).*

13   take the Wall *In Shakespeare's time, when sewage ditches flowed down the center of many streets, the pathway close to the wall was usually the cleanest place to walk; it was thus considered a sign of superiority, and frequently of social rank, to "Take the wall."*

16   goes to the Wall *backs up to the wall, cowers.*

17–18 Women . . . Weaker Vessels *a proverbial expression deriving from 1 Peter 3:7 in the New Testament.*

24–25 civil with the Maids *Sampson uses the word* civil *ironically, implying that the maids whose "heads" are cut off (that is, the maids who lose their "Maidenheads," or virginity, to him) will derive pleasure from his "pretty piece of Flesh" (line 31–32) and thus consider his tyranny "civil."*

28   Sense *Gregory plays on two implications of the word: (a) meaning, and (b) physical sensation.*

34   Poor John *dried hake, a cheap form of salted fish. Gregory's bawdy joke is based on two characteristics of Poor John: (a) its stiffness, and (b) its having had its roe (sperm or eggs) removed in the "drying" or curing process. Benvolio and Mercutio engage in similar wordplay in II.iv.41–43.*

8

SAMPSON   A Dog of that House shall move me to stand:
   I will take the Wall of any Man or Maid of
   Mountague's.

GREGORY   That shows thee a weak Slave: for the   15
   weakest goes to the Wall.

SAMPSON   'Tis true, and therefore Women, being the
   Weaker Vessels, are ever thrust to the Wall:
   therefore I will push Mountague's Men from the
   Wall and thrust his Maids to the Wall.   20

GREGORY   The Quarrel is between our Masters, and us
   their Men.

SAMPSON   'Tis all one. I will show myself a Tyrant:
   when I have fought with the Men, I will be civil
   with the Maids; I will cut off their Heads.   25

GREGORY   The Heads of the Maids?

SAMPSON   Ay, the Heads of the Maids, or their
   Maidenheads; take it in what Sense thou wilt.

GREGORY   They must take it in Sense that feel it.

SAMPSON   Me they shall feel while I am able to   30
   stand, and 'tis known I am a pretty piece of
   Flesh.

GREGORY   'Tis well thou art not Fish: if thou hadst,
   thou hadst been Poor John. Draw thy Tool: here
   comes two of the House of Mountagues!   35

Enter two other Servingmen,
Abram and another,
of the House of Mountague.

9

---

36   naked Weapon   *This reference to an unsheathed sword provides an apt transition from talk of aggression with sexual "tools" to action involving real aggression with tools of combat. That the two kinds of "Weapon" are associated is one of the recurring themes of this play about the relationships between love and hate.*

40   marry   *a mild oath, originally referring to the Virgin Mary, which had a meaning more or less equivalent to "in faith" or "indeed."*

44   as they list   *as they will.*

45   bite my Thumb   *an insulting gesture made with a flick of the thumbnail against the back of the upper row of teeth.*

50–51   Is the Law of our side . . . ?   *Are we within our legal rights . . . ?*

57   for you   *ready for you, prepared to take you on.*

60   Well, Sir.   *an expression equivalent to "Fine, sir."*

SAMPSON My naked Weapon is out. Quarrel! I will
back thee.

GREGORY How? Turn thy back and run?

SAMPSON Fear me not.

GREGORY No marry, I fear thee.   40

SAMPSON Let us take the Law of our sides: let them
begin.

GREGORY I will frown as I pass by, and let them
take it as they list.

SAMPSON Nay, as they dare; I will bite my Thumb at   45
them, which is Disgrace to them if they bear it.

ABRAM Do you bite your Thumb at us, Sir?

SAMPSON I do bite my Thumb, Sir.

ABRAM Do you bite your Thumb at us, Sir?

SAMPSON [*Aside to Gregory*] Is the Law of our side   50
if I say ay?

GREGORY [*Aside to Sampson*] No.

SAMPSON No Sir, I do not bite my Thumb at you,
Sir; but I bite my Thumb, Sir.

GREGORY Do you Quarrel, Sir?   55

ABRAM Quarrel, Sir? No Sir.

SAMPSON But if you do, Sir, I am for you: I serve
as good a Man as you.

ABRAM No better.

SAMPSON Well, Sir.   60

Enter Benvolio.

11

66   Washing   *an alternative form for* swashing *(dashing, smashing).*

69   hartless Hinds   *literally, young or female deer ("hinds") without a "hart" (antlered stag) to guide and protect them. Most editors print* heartless *(as the word is spelled in the 1623 First Folio printing), but the spelling in the 1599 Second Quarto more faithfully conveys Tybalt's primary accusation: that Benvolio is taking unfair advantage of the metaphorical equivalent of "Weaker Vessels" by drawing on Capulet servants at a time when they are undefended by a Capulet master.*

72   manage it   *Benvolio means two things here: (a) use it, and (b) control it (employ it with restraint and sound judgment).*

76   Clubs, Bills, and Partisans!   *The citizens who intervene here are members of the Watch (the city's volunteer guard).* Bills *were long shafts with hooked concave blades;* partisans *were spears with broad double-edged blades.*

GREGORY   [*Aside to Sampson*] Say "better": here
   comes one of my Master's Kinsmen.
SAMPSON   Yes, better, Sir.
ABRAM   You lie.
SAMPSON   Draw if you be Men. —Gregory, remember   65
   thy Washing Blow!   *They fight.*
BENVOLIO   Part, Fools!
   Put up your Swords! You know not what you do!

Enter Tybalt.

TYBALT   What? Art thou drawn among these Hartless
   Hinds?
   Turn thee, Benvolio: look upon thy Death!   70
BENVOLIO   I do but keep the Peace: put up thy Sword,
   Or manage it to part these Men with me.
TYBALT   What, drawn and talk of Peace? I hate the
   word
   As I hate Hell, all Mountagues, and thee!
   Have at thee, Coward!   *They fight.*   75

Enter three or four Citizens
with Clubs or Partisans.

CITIZENS   Clubs, Bills, and Partisans! Strike! Beat
   them down! Down with the Capulets! Down with
   the Mountagues!

S.D.   in his Gown   *Capulet's dressing gown introduces an image of dignity and domesticity comically incompatible with the occasion and with the old man's impulsive determination to join the fray. Both wives emerge here as strong-willed proponents of common sense in their restraint of their husbands' childish irascibility.*

82   flourishes   *brandishes, waves flamboyantly.*
in spite of me   *to spite or challenge me.*

86   Neighbor-stained Steel   *steel weapons stained with the blood of neighbors. The Prince calls his subjects "Profaners" because they are desecrating what should be instruments of peace by using them against fellow citizens rather than reserving them for protection of the city against its external enemies.*

89   purple Fountains   *"fountains" of blood (which is frequently referred to as "purple" in Shakespeare's plays) rather than the beautiful water fountains for which Verona was well known. Usually called "conduits," they featured sculptured figures of gods, men, and animals.*

90   On pain of   *on penalty of.*

91   mistemper'd Weapons   *weapons made by tempering steel (heating and rapidly cooling the metal while beating it into the desired shape), but now profaned by intemperate (uncontrolled) violence. It takes the Prince until the end of this sentence (line 92) to quell the brawl so that he can address the crowd without shouting.*

14

Enter old Capulet (in his Gown) and his Wife.

CAPULET   What Noise is this? Give me my Long Sword,
    ho!
CAPULET'S WIFE   A Crutch, a Crutch! Why call you for
    a Sword!   80

Enter old Mountague and his Wife.

CAPULET   My Sword, I say! Old Mountague is come,
    And flourishes his Blade in spite of me.
MOUNTAGUE   Thou Villain, Capulet! —Hold me not!
    Let me go!
MOUNTAGUE'S WIFE   Thou shalt not stir one Foot to
    seek a Foe!

Enter Prince Escalus with his Train.

PRINCE   Rebellious Subjects, Enemies to Peace,   85
    Profaners of this Neighbor-stained Steel!
    —Will they not hear? —What ho! You Men, you
        Beasts,
    That quench the Fire of your pernicious Rage
    With purple Fountains issuing from your Veins:
    On pain of Torture, from those Bloody Hands   90
    Throw your mistemper'd Weapons to the Ground
    And hear the Sentence of your moved Prince!
    —Three Civil Brawls, bred of an airy Word

15

97   grave beseeming Ornaments   *ornaments suitable for persons of gravity and sobriety. The syntax in the original texts hovers between "grave-beseeming" and "grave, beseeming" in modern usage.*

99   Cank'red   *decayed, eaten away, diseased.*

101   Forfeit of the Peace   *penalty for breaking the peace.*

102   For this time   *for now.*

108   Who set . . . new abroach?   *Who opened up this old quarrel again?*

113   prepar'd   *drawn.*

116   nothing hurt withal   *not at all hurt thereby.*
       hiss'd him in Scorn   *Benvolio's phrasing imitates the sound of the sword's swipe while at the same time personifying that hiss as a gust of wind ridiculing Tybalt's ineffectual blustering.*

118   on Part and Part   *on one side and the other.*

By thee, old Capulet and Mountague,
Have thrice disturb'd the Quiet of our Streets 95
And made Verona's ancient Citizens
Cast by their grave beseeming Ornaments
To wield old Partisans in Hands as old,
Cank'red with Peace, to part your cank'red Hate.
If ever you disturb our Streets again, 100
Your Lives shall pay the Forfeit of the Peace.
—For this time all the rest depart away.
—You, Capulet, shall go along with me,
And Mountague, come you this afternoon,
To know our farther Pleasure in this Case, 105
To old Freetown, our common Judgment-place.
—Once more, on pain of Death, all Men depart.
                Exeunt all but the Mountagues and Benvolio.
MOUNTAGUE   Who set this ancient Quarrel new
    abroach?
Speak, Nephew: were you by when it began?
BENVOLIO   Here were the Servants of your Adversary 110
    And yours close fighting ere I did approach.
    I drew to part them; in the instant came
    The fiery Tybalt with his Sword prepar'd,
    Which, as he breath'd Defiance to my Ears,
    He swung about his Head and cut the Winds, 115
    Who, nothing hurt withal, hiss'd him in Scorn.
    While we were interchanging Thrusts and Blows
    Came more and more, and fought on Part and Part,
    Till the Prince came, who parted either Part.

124   drave   *drove.*

125   Sycamour   *a tree often associated with lovesick youth, proba-*
bly by way of a pun on the name ("sick-amour"). Shake-
speare's spelling of Romeo's surname may contain a related
pun: Mount *is a word for intercourse, and* ague *means*
"fever."

126   That . . . City-side   *that grows to the west of the city.*

128   Towards   *here pronounced as a one-syllable word.*
ware   *both "aware" and "wary."*

129   Covert   *cover, seclusion.*

131   most sought . . . found   *most desired to be where most*
people would not be (that is, most desired solitude). Benvolio
plays on the idea of seeking and not finding, and he here uses
sought *in two senses: (a) desired, and (b) searched for.*

133   humour   *disposition, mood. This edition uses the* -our *spell-*
ing to distinguish "humour" in its psychological sense (the
four "humours" believed to control human behavior) from the
modern term relating to wit and mirth. In line 145 "Hu-
mour" refers to a settled state of melancholic depression,
thought in Shakespeare's time to be the result of an excess of
black bile in the body.

140   Aurora   *Goddess of the Dawn.*

145   portendous   *portentous, ill-omened.*

MOUNTAGUE'S WIFE   O where is Romeo? Saw you him 120
    today?
    Right glad I am he was not at this Fray!
BENVOLIO   Madam, an hour before the worshipp'd Sun
    Peer'd forth the golden Window of the East,
    A troubled Mind drave me to walk abroad,
    Where underneath the Grove of Sycamour 125
    That westward rooteth from this City-side,
    So early walking did I see your Son;
    Towards him I made, but he was ware of me
    And stole into the Covert of the Wood.
    I, measuring his Affections by my own, 130
    Which then most sought where most might not be
        found,
    Being one too many by my weary Self,
    Pursu'd my Humour, not pursuing his,
    And gladly shunn'd who gladly fled from me.
MOUNTAGUE   Many a Morning hath he there been seen, 135
    With Tears augmenting the fresh Morning's Dew,
    Adding to Clouds more Clouds with his deep Sighs.
    But all so soon as the all-cheering Sun
    Should in the farthest East begin to draw
    The shady Curtains from Aurora's Bed, 140
    Away from light steals home my heavy Son
    And private in his Chamber pens himself,
    Shuts up his Windows, locks fair Daylight out,
    And makes himself an artificial Night.
    Black and portendous must this Humour prove 145

149   importun'd   *pleaded with. The metrical position of* impor-
           tun'd *calls for a stress on the word's second syllable.*

154   Sounding   *having his depth gauged (a nautical term).*

155   envious   *destructive, malicious. The "Worm" referred to is the*
           cankerworm, a type of larva feeding on the buds of flowers.

157   to the same   *to the air. Most editors emend to "to the sun."*
           But the sense preserved in the Quarto and First Folio printings
           seems quite adequate to the context.

163   true Shrift   *true confession. In lines 162–63, Mountague*
           says "I hope you'll be so lucky by your delay as to get the true
           story."

165   strook   *a frequent Elizabethan spelling and pronunciation for*
           struck.

Unless good Counsel may the Cause remove.

BENVOLIO   My noble Uncle, do you know the Cause?

MOUNTAGUE   I neither know it nor can learn of him.

BENVOLIO   Have you importun'd him by any Means?

MOUNTAGUE   Both by my self and many other Friends.   150
But he his own Affection's Counselor
Is to himself (I will not say how true);
But to himself so secret and so close,
So far from Sounding and Discovery,
As is the Bud bit with an envious Worm   155
Ere he can spread his sweet Leaves to the Air
Or dedicate his Beauty to the same.
Could we but learn from whence his Sorrows grow,
We would as willingly give Cure as know.

Enter Romeo.

BENVOLIO   See where he comes. So please you, step
aside: 160
I'll know his Grievance or be much denied.

MOUNTAGUE   I would thou wert so happy by thy Stay
To hear true Shrift. —Come, Madam, let's away.

Exeunt.

BENVOLIO   Good morrow, Cousin.

ROMEO   Is the Day so young?

BENVOLIO   But new strook nine.

ROMEO   Ay, sad Hours seem long.   165
Was that my Father that went hence so fast?

173   in his View   *in appearance, in prospect.*

174   in Proof   *in reality, once experienced.*

175   whose View is muffled still   *whose eyes are always covered. In lines 175–76 Romeo alludes to the traditional image of Cupid, the God of Love, as a blindfolded boy. Throughout this dialogue, Romeo personifies Love, speaking of an abstraction as if it were a deity. This was a convention of what is known as Courtly Love poetry, and it served as a convenient means of describing an emotional condition that seemed at times to have a mind and will of its own. By Shakespeare's time poets had developed a tradition that permitted Love to be spoken of as if it were a religion, with all the rituals and symbols normally associated with Christianity. Whether such a religion was ever taken literally is subject to debate. The lovers depicted as practicing it take it quite seriously, but the way they are portrayed suggests that many poets, if not all, took an ironic (albeit sympathetic) view of the state of "being in love."*

180–   brawling Love . . . Still-waking Sleep   *The oxymorons*
85   *(self-contradictory images) in these lines are typical expressions of the love-sickness depicted in romantic literature of the Renaissance. The oxymoron was an apt way of describing a lover's "betwixt and between" condition.*

BENVOLIO   It was; what Sadness lengthens Romeo's
    Hours?

ROMEO   Not having that which, having, makes them
    short.

BENVOLIO   In love?

ROMEO   Out.   170

BENVOLIO   Of love?

ROMEO   Out of her Favor where I am in love.

BENVOLIO   Alas that Love, so gentle in his View,
    Should be so tyrannous and rough in Proof!

ROMEO   Alas that Love, whose View is muffled still,   175
    Should without Eyes see pathways to his Will!
    Where shall we dine? O me, what Fray was here?
    Yet tell me not, for I have heard it all.
    Here's much to do with Hate, but more with Love.
    Why then, O brawling Love, O loving Hate,   180
    O anything of Nothing first create!
    O heavy Lightness, serious Vanity,
    Misshapen Chaos of well-seeming Forms!
    Feather of Lead, bright Smoke, cold Fire, sick
      Health;
    Still-waking Sleep, that is not what it is!   185
    This Love feel I, that feel no love in this.
    Dost thou not laugh?

BENVOLIO   No, Coz, I rather weep.

ROMEO   Good Heart, at what?

BENVOLIO   At thy good Heart's Oppression.

ROMEO   Why, such is Love's Transgression.

191   press'd   *oppressed, burdened.*

195   **Being purg'd . . . Eyes**   *Romeo is saying that if the smoke is removed ("purg'd") from the air, Love becomes an unimpeded fire, resulting in "sparkling" (brightly burning) eyes.*

196   **Being vex'd . . . Tears**   *If the smoke is stirred up ("vex'd"), the eyes will overflow with tears.*

197   discreet   *intelligent, discerning.*

198   choking **Gall**   *a cloyingly sweet ("choking") bitterness.*
        preserving **Sweet**   *a salty sweetness (an allusion to the use of salt as a preservative). Both word combinations are oxymorons. The opposition between* Gall *and* Sweet *will recur in a more ominous context in I.v.94.*

199   **Coz**   *Cousin.*
        Soft   *here, a term more or less equivalent to "Hush."*

201   my **Self**   *spelled as two separate words throughout the Quarto and First Folio texts. Most editors modernize to* myself *(and similarly to* thyself *and* yourself*). In some instances this practice results in no shift of meaning; often, however, it does. In Elizabethan usage the word* self *retains a more objective dimension than it has today when merged with* my *or* thy.

203   in **Sadness**   *in all seriousness. In the next line,* groan *alludes to the other sense of "sadness" (mourning or melancholy), preserved in the usual modern usage.*

211   fair **Mark**   *clear or easy target, but with a pun on other senses of* fair: *(a) blond, (b) attractive, and (c) just.*

24

Griefs of mine own lie heavy in my Breast,   190
Which thou wilt propagate to have it press'd
With more of thine. This Love that thou hast
    shown
Doth add more Grief to too much of mine own.
Love is a Smoke made with the fume of Sighs;
Being purg'd, a Fire sparkling in Lovers' Eyes;   195
Being vex'd, a Sea nourish'd with Loving Tears.
What is it else? A Madness most discreet,
A choking Gall, and a preserving Sweet.
Farewell, my Coz.
BENVOLIO   Soft, I will go along,
And if you leave me so, you do me wrong.   200
ROMEO   Tut, I have lost my Self; I am not here!
This is not Romeo: he's some other where.
BENVOLIO   Tell me in Sadness, who is't that you
    love?
ROMEO   What, shall I groan and tell thee?
BENVOLIO   Groan? Why no;
But sadly tell me who.   205
ROMEO   Bid a Sick Man in Sadness make his Will:
A Word ill urg'd to one that is so Ill.
In Sadness, Cousin, I do love a Woman.
BENVOLIO   I aim'd so near when I suppos'd you lov'd.
ROMEO   A right good Markman, and she's fair I love.   210
BENVOLIO   A right fair Mark, fair Coz, is soonest
    hit.

213 Dian's Wit *the cunning of Diana, the Goddess of Chastity. Diana was the earthly manifestation of a goddess called "triple Hecate" in V.i.388 of* A Midsummer Night's Dream. *In her role as Goddess of the Moon she was usually called Cynthia or Phoebe, and in her role as Goddess of Hades she was normally referred to as Persephone.*

215 uncharm'd *unaffected by Love's magic spell.*

218 Nor ope . . . Gold. *Romeo seems to be implying that he has tried to buy Rosaline's favors. It is more likely, however, that he is simply saying that gold is one of the things against which her chastity is proof (shielded). Shakespeare probably expected his audience to recognize an allusion to one of Jove's sexual exploits, when he disguised himself as a shower of gold to seduce the maiden Danae.*

222 Sparing . . . Waste *Romeo argues that in this instance thrift ("Sparing") is actually wasteful, because what is saved will be lost, resulting in a famine for future generations.*

226 Bliss . . . Despair *Here and elsewhere Romeo uses religious terminology to compare the states of a lover to those of a soul seeking salvation. His complaint is that Rosaline's route to bliss (the blessings of Heaven) through chastity leaves her suitor in despair (without hope of redemption).*

227 forsworn to love *renounced love.*

233 To call hers . . . in question more *to bring hers to mind even more (in ways illustrated by the lines that follow).*

26

ROMEO   Well, in that Hit you Miss: she'll not be
  hit
  With Cupid's Arrow. She hath Dian's Wit,
  And in strong Proof of Chastity well arm'd
  From Love's weak, childish Bow she lives
    uncharm'd.   215
  She will not stay the Siege of loving Terms,
  Nor bide th' Encounter of assailing Eyes.
  Nor ope her Lap to Saint-seducing Gold.
  O she is rich in Beauty; only poor
  That, when she dies, with Beauty dies her Store. 220
BENVOLIO   Then she hath sworn that she will still
  live Chaste?
ROMEO   She hath, and in that Sparing makes huge
  Waste:
  For Beauty, starv'd with her Severity,
  Cuts Beauty off from all Posterity.
  She is too fair, too wise, wisely too fair,   225
  To merit Bliss by making me Despair.
  She hath forsworn to love, and in that Vow
  Do I live dead that live to tell it now.
BENVOLIO   Be rul'd by me: forget to think of her.
ROMEO   O teach me how I should forget to think!   230
BENVOLIO   By giving Liberty unto thine Eyes:
  Examine other Beauties.
ROMEO   'Tis the way
  To call hers—exquisite—in question more.
  These happy Masks that kiss fair Ladies' Brows,

236   **strooken**   *stricken.*

238   **passing Fair**   *surpassing fair (even more lovely than all that the word* fair *conveys).*

239   **Note**   *written reminder.*

240   **pass'd that passing Fair**   *surpassed even that beauty that was beyond fair.*

242   **I'll pay that Doctrine . . . Debt.**   *Either I'll buy that doctrine from you (and replace it with the one I've been preaching), or I'll die a bankrupt trying to do so.*

I.ii   *The setting for this scene appears to be a street outside Capulet's house.*

1   **bound**   *under bond to keep the peace.*

4   **Reck'ning**   *reputation, standing.*

6   **Suit**   *request. Paris, a young Count, has just initiated negotiations with Capulet for Juliet's hand in marriage.*

9   **Change**   *passage.*

10   **wither in their Pride**   *see their glory subside with the seasons' change.*

28

Being Black, put us in mind they hide the Fair: 235
He that is strooken Blind cannot forget
The precious Treasure of his Eyesight lost.
Show me a Mistress that is passing Fair:
What doth her Beauty serve but as a Note
Where I may read who pass'd that passing Fair!   240
Farewell; thou canst not teach me to forget.

BENVOLIO   I'll pay that Doctrine, or else die in
    Debt.   *Exeunt.*

Scene 2

Enter Capulet, County Paris, and Servingman.

CAPULET   But Mountague is bound as well as I,
    In Penalty alike; and 'tis not hard, I think,
    For Men as old as we to keep the Peace.

PARIS   Of Honorable Reck'ning are you both,
    And pity 'tis you liv'd at odds so long.   5
    But now, my Lord, what say you to my Suit?

CAPULET   But saying o'er what I have said before:
    My Child is yet a Stranger in the World;
    She hath not seen the Change of fourteen Years;
    Let two more Summers wither in their Pride   10

12 Younger than she *maids younger than she. Shakespeare frequently uses ellipses (word omissions) to compress normal syntax.*

14–15 Earth . . . Earth. *Capulet says he has buried all his offspring ("Hopes") but Juliet, so she stands to inherit all his wealth. These two lines differ from the rest of the surrounding verse in two ways: (a) they are "headless" (lacking the initial unstressed syllable usual in iambic pentameter), and (b) they do not rhyme. Some editors assume that they are non-Shakespearean lines and omit them, but they are of a piece with the rest of the speech and with the play in general, and are in no way uncharacteristic of the playwright.*

18 scope of Choice *range of options.*

19 according Voice *voice of agreement, accord.*

26 lusty *robust, vigorous (as distinguished from "lustful").*

29 Fennel *a flowering herb whose buds were thrown at the feet of brides in the marriage ceremony.*

30 Inherit *Here the word simply means "have," but it keeps us mindful that Capulet's inheritance is on the minds of both participants in the conversation.*

32–33 Which one more View . . . none. *This passage can be paraphrased roughly as follows: A further look at many maidens, my daughter being one, will establish which one is the fairest—although in "Reck'ning" (numerical calculations) we must bear in mind the old proverb that one is no number ("none").*

30

Ere we may think her ripe to be a Bride.

PARIS   Younger than she are happy Mothers made.

CAPULET   And too soon marr'd are those so early
made.
Earth hath swallow'd all my Hopes but she;
She's the hopeful Lady of my Earth.   15
But woo her, gentle Paris, get her Heart;
My Will to her Consent is but a Part;
And she agreed, within her scope of Choice
Lies my Consent and fair according Voice.
This Night I hold an old accustom'd Feast,   20
Whereto I have invited many a Guest
Such as I love; and you among the Store
One more most welcome makes my Number more.
At my poor House look to behold this Night
Earth-treading Stars that make dark Heaven light.   25
Such Comfort as do lusty Young Men feel
When well-apparel'd April on the Heel
Of limping Winter treads, ev'n such Delight
Among fresh Fennel Buds shall you this Night
Inherit at my House. Hear all, all see,   30
And like her most whose Merit most shall be:
Which one more View of many, mine being one,
May stand in Number, though in Reck'ning none.
Come go with me.   *He hands a List to the Servant.*
                —Go, Sirrah, trudge about
Through fair Verona; find those Persons out   35
Whose Names are written there, and to them say

38–45   "Find . . . Learned. *Introduced in the Second Quarto stage direction as "the Clown," the Servant who speaks these lines is probably identical to Peter, the Nurse's man. He was evidently played by Will Kempe (whose name actually appears in a later stage direction), a comic actor who also performed such roles as Bottom in* A Midsummer Night's Dream. *Here, in a Bottom-like manner, he associates each workman with a tool that actually belongs to another workman on his list.*

46   In good time!   *Just in time! Benvolio and Romeo, two of "the Learned" the Servant needs, appear precisely when he invokes them.*

47–52   one Fire . . . will die.   *All of Benvolio's prescriptions illustrate what is known as homeopathic medicine ("fighting fire with fire"); thus, for example, the solution to giddiness (dizziness) from turning is to whirl in the opposite direction, and the cure for one infection is another that will kill the first one.*

49   holp   *helped.*

53   Plantan   *plaintain, a broad-leafed plant used to treat superficial cuts and scratches.*

My House and Welcome on their Pleasure stay.

Exeunt Capulet and Paris.

SERVANT   "Find them out whose Names are written
here." It is written that the Shoemaker should
meddle with his Yard, and the Tailor with his   40
Last, the Fisher with his Pencil, and the Painter
with his Nets. But I am sent to find those
Persons whose Names are here writ, and can never
find what Names the Writing-person hath here writ.
I must to the Learned.   45

Enter Benvolio and Romeo.

In good time!

BENVOLIO   Tut, Man, one Fire burns out another's
     Burning;
One Pain is lessen'd by another's Anguish:
Turn Giddy and be holp by backward Turning.
One desp'rate Grief cures with another's
     Languish: 50
Take thou some New Infection to thy Eye,
And the rank Poison of the Old will die.

ROMEO   Your Plantan Leaf is excellent for that.

BENVOLIO   For what, I pray thee?

ROMEO   For your broken Shin.

BENVOLIO   Why Romeo, art thou mad?   55

ROMEO   Not mad, but bound more than a Madman is:
Shut up in Prison, kept without my Food,

33

58   God-den   *good evening.*

59   God gi'god-den.   *God give you good e'en (evening), a greet-
      ing to be used any time after noon. The expression was also
      used as a mild expletive (as at IV.i.173).*

61   Perhaps . . . without Book.   *The Servant's meaning
      seems to be that Romeo could well have learned to "read"
      (understand) his misery without knowing how to read (in the
      literal sense of the word). Another meaning of "without Book"
      (memorized, so as not to require a text to refer to) occurs in
      I.iv.7.*

64   rest you merry   *fare you well.*

71   Rosaline   *This is the same Rosaline that Romeo loves, and it is
      of some interest that she is never mentioned in I.v, the scene
      devoted to Capulet's feast.*

74   whither should they come?   *To where are they to come?*

Whipp'd and tormented and— —God-den, good
Fellow.

SERVANT God gi'god-den. I pray, Sir, can you read?

ROMEO Ay, mine own Fortune in my Misery. 60

SERVANT Perhaps you have learned it without Book.
But I pray, can you read anything you see?

ROMEO Ay, if I know the Letters and the Language.

SERVANT You say honestly; rest you merry.

He turns to leave.

ROMEO Stay, Fellow: I can read. *He reads the Letter.* 65
"Signior Martin and his Wife and Daughters;
County Anselm and his beauteous Sisters; the
Lady Widow of Utruvio, Signior Placentio and
his lovely Nieces; Mercutio and his Brother
Valentine; mine Uncle Capulet, his Wife and 70
Daughters; my fair Niece Rosaline; Livia;
Signior Valentio and his Cousin Tybalt; Lucio
and the lively Helena."
A fair Assembly: whither should they come?

SERVANT Up. 75

ROMEO Whither? To Supper?

SERVANT To our House.

ROMEO Whose House?

SERVANT My Master's.

ROMEO Indeed, I should have ask'd you that before. 80

SERVANT Now I'll tell you without asking: my
Master is the great rich Capulet; and if you be
not of the House of Mountagues, I pray come and

35

84 crush *a colloquial term for "drink."*

85 ancient Feast *Earlier (I.ii.20) Capulet has described the occasion as "an old, accustom'd Feast." It was probably a traditional family gathering, and recognized as such throughout Verona.*

87 admired *wondered at; here treated as a three-syllable word.*

88 unattainted *untainted, able to perceive objectively.*

93 these *Romeo's eyes. Romeo probably points to them as he speaks this line.*

93–94 who, often drown'd . . . Liars *Romeo alludes to the practice whereby suspected disbelievers who did not start to drown when dunked to test their fidelity were thereby "proved" to be heretics; having been "rejected" by the water, these poor souls were then burned at the stake. Romeo says that if his eyes should prove false to Rosaline, the tears in which they have "often drown'd" should turn to fire and consume them.*

99– in that Crystal Scales . . . Maid *Benvolio compares Ro-*
100 *meo's eyes to a pair of balance scales and suggests that instead of having Rosaline "pois'd with her Self" (line 98) on both sides of the point of balance, Romeo should weigh her opposite "some other Maid."*

crush a cup of Wine. Rest you merry.   *Exit.*

BENVOLIO   At this same ancient Feast of Capulet's   85
　　Sups the fair Rosaline, whom thou so loves,
　　With all th' admired Beauties of Verona;
　　Go thither and with unattainted Eye
　　Compare her Face with some that I shall show,
　　And I will make thee think thy Swan a Crow.   90
ROMEO   When the devout Religion of mine Eye
　　Maintains such Falsehood, then turn Tears to
　　　　Fire;
　　And these who, often drown'd, could never die,
　　Transparent Heretics, be burnt for Liars.
　　One fairer than my Love? Th' all-seeing Sun   95
　　Ne'er saw her Match since first the World begun!
BENVOLIO   Tut, you saw her Fair none else being by,
　　Her Self pois'd with her Self in either Eye.
　　But in that Crystal Scales let there be weigh'd
　　Your Lady's Love against some other Maid   100
　　That I will show you shining at this Feast,
　　And she shall scant show well that now seems
　　　　best.
ROMEO   I'll go along, no such Sight to be shown
　　But to rejoice in Splendor of mine own.   *Exeunt.*

I.iii   *This scene is set in one of the rooms of Capulet's house.*

3   Lamb . . . Ladybird   *the Nurse's pet nicknames for Juliet. "Lamb" is apparently derived from "Lammastide" (August 1, a holiday to celebrate the first-fruits of summer harvest), on the eve of which Juliet was born.*

9   thou s' hear   *a contraction for "thou shalt hear."*

10   Thou . . . a pretty Age.   *Juliet's mother seems to mean that Juliet is approaching the age when she should think about marriage.*

12   o' my   *of my*

13   t' my Teen   *possibly a colloquial contraction for "to my teeth" (to be spoken in two syllables, as should the phrase "be 't spok'n"), which would provide a verbal link between "four teen" and Juliet's age. But teen also meant "grief," and that may be the Nurse's meaning.*

Scene 3

Enter Capulet's Wife and Nurse.

CAPULET'S WIFE   Nurse, where's my Daughter? Call
    her forth to me.
NURSE   Now by my Maidenhead, at twelve year old
   I bade her come. —What, Lamb? What, Ladybird?
   —God forbid, where is this Girl? —What, Juliet?

Enter Juliet.

JULIET   How now? Who calls?
NURSE   Your Mother.   5
JULIET   Madam, I am here. What is your Will?
CAPULET'S WIFE   This is the Matter. —Nurse, give
    leave a while:
   We must talk in secret. Nurse, come back again.
   I have rememb'red me: thou s' hear our Counsel.
   Thou know'st my Daughter's of a pretty Age.   10
NURSE   Faith, I can tell her Age unto an Hour.
CAPULET'S WIFE   She's not fourteen.
NURSE   I'll lay fourteen o' my Teeth
   (And yet t' my Teen, be 't spok'n, I have but
    four),

39

14   Lammastide   *August 1.*

17   Lammas Eve   *July 31. It is fitting that Juliet's birthday is at the end of July (a date Shakespeare may have chosen with her name in mind), and the association with an early harvest feast is in accord with the play's many references to her premature ripening.*

        sh' be   *A contraction for "she be," introduced here for metrical purposes. The Quarto and Folio texts spell the words out. A similar metrical elision is introduced in line 36 with "sh' could."*

19   of an Age   *the same age.*

26   Wormwood to my Dug   *The Nurse had put wormwood oil (proverbially bitter) on her nipple in order to wean Juliet.*

27   under the Dovehouse Wall   *beside the wall of the house where the Capulets' doves were kept. In lines 33–34 the Nurse personifies the Dovehouse.*

29   Nay . . . Brain!   *Evidently the Nurse is pleased with her ability to recall that the Capulets were at Mantua; she may also be responding to Lady Capulet's reaction.*

32   tetchy   *upset.*

33   trow   *assure you (usually pronounced to rhyme with* snow*).*

36   stand high 'lone   *stand up by herself.*
        by the Rood   *by the Cross.*

38   broke her Brow   *hurt her forehead in a fall.*

She's not fourteen. How long is't now to
    Lammastide?
CAPULET'S WIFE   A Fortnight and odd Days.   15
NURSE   Ev'n or odd, of all Days in the Year,
    Come Lammas Eve at Night shall sh' be fourteen;
    Susan and she, God rest all Christian Souls,
    Were of an Age. Well, Susan is with God:
    She was too good for me. But as I said,   20
    On Lammas Eve at night shall sh' be fourteen,
    That shall she, marry; I remember 't well.
    'Tis since the Earthquake now eleven years,
    And she was wean'd. I never shall forget it:
    Of all the days o' th' Year, upon that Day!   25
    For I had then laid Wormwood to my Dug
    Sitting in the Sun under the Dovehouse Wall.
    My Lord and you were then at Mantua
    (Nay, I do bear a Brain!). But as I said,
    When it did taste the Wormwood on the Nipple   30
    O' my Dug, and felt it bitter, pretty Fool,
    To see it tetchy and fall out wi' th' Dug!
    "Shake," quoth the Dovehouse! 'Twas no need, I
      trow,
    To bid me trudge.
    And since that time it is eleven years,   35
    For then sh' could stand high 'lone; nay, by the
      Rood,
    She could have run and waddled all about.
    For ev'n the Day before, she broke her Brow,

40 'A *here and elsewhere, "he."*

43 by my Holydam *an oath that was commonly thought to refer to the Virgin, though it probably originated as a reference to "halidom" (holiness), and by extension to any holy relic.*

44 left *ceased.*

45 come about *be fulfilled, prove prophetic.*

46 I warr'nt and I *I guarantee that if I.*

48 stinted *stopped.*

52 it *its. At this time it was still the normal form.*

53 Cock'rel's Stone *rooster's testicle.*

54 per'lous *perilous, fearful. In all likelihood the Nurse pronounces this word in the way it was often spelled:* parlous. *As in modern British usage for words like* clerk *(pronounced "clark"), -er combinations were frequently pronounced with an r sound in Shakespeare's time.*

59 God . . . Grace *God bless you.*

And then my Husband (God be with his Soul,
'A was a merry Man!) took up the Child;   40
"Yea," quoth he, "dost thou fall 'pon thy Face?
Thou wilt fall backward when thou hast more Wit,
Wilt thou not, Jule?" And by my Holydam,
The pretty Wretch left crying and said "Ay"!
To see now how a Jest shall come about!   45
I warr'nt and I should live a thousand years,
I never should forget it. "Wilt thou not, Jule?"
Quoth he. And, pretty Fool, it stinted and said
   "Ay."
CAPULET'S WIFE   Enough of this; I pray thee hold
   thy peace.
NURSE   Yes, Madam. Yet I cannot choose but laugh   50
   To think it should leave crying and say "Ay"!
   And yet I warr'nt it had upon it Brow
   A Bump as big as a young Cock'rel's Stone:
   A per'lous Knock, and it cried bitterly.
   "Yea," quoth my Husband, "fall'st upon thy Face?   55
   Thou wilt fall backward when thou com'st to Age,
   Wilt thou not, Jule?" It stinted and said "Ay."
CAPULET'S WIFE   And stint thou too, I pray thee,
   Nurse, say I!
NURSE   Peace, I have done. —God mark thee to his
   Grace,
   Thou wast the prettiest Babe that e'er I nurs'd.   60
   And I might live to see thee married once,
   I have my Wish.

67–68   "An Honor" . . . thy Teat!   *Assuming that the 1597 First Quarto reading here is correct (the 1599 Second Quarto reads "an hour," which is more difficult to connect with the Nurse's response to what Juliet says), Juliet's reply impresses the Nurse as one so elevated as almost to require a special explanation. It seems most likely that* thy *here refers to Lady Capulet. If so, the Nurse is toying with the fiction that Juliet must have been nursed by Lady Capulet, from whom alone she could have "suck'd Wisdom" enough to say "an Honor."*

69–71   younger than you . . . already Mothers.   *Lady Capulet's phrasing is so similar to that used earlier by Paris (I.ii.12) as to suggest that Capulet has quoted Paris' words verbatim to his wife and instructed her to speak to Juliet of Paris' suit.*

72   much upon these Years   *at about the same age.*

76   Man of Wax   *The Nurse means "the very model of a man."*

80   This Night . . . Feast.   *Just as there is no reference to Romeo's seeing Rosaline at the feast in I.v, there is no reference to Juliet's meeting Paris there.*

83   ev'ry married Lineament   *every harmonious feature.*

84   how . . . Content   *how one complements another.*

86   Margent   *margin, where notes (called "glosses") were supplied to explain the text of the volume.*

44

CAPULET'S WIFE   Marry, that "marry" is the very theme
    theme
    I came to talk of. Tell me, daughter Juliet,
    How stands your disposition to be married?   65
JULIET   It is an Honor that I dream not of.
NURSE   "An Honor": were not I thine only Nurse,
    I'd say thou hadst suck'd Wisdom from thy Teat!
CAPULET'S WIFE   Well, think of Marriage now: younger than you
    younger than you
    Here in Verona, Ladies of esteem,   70
    Are made already Mothers. By my count,
    I was your Mother much upon these Years
    That you are now a Maid. Thus then in brief:
    The valiant Paris seeks you for his Love.
NURSE   A Man, young Lady! Lady, such a Man   75
    As all the World! Why he's a Man of Wax!
CAPULET'S WIFE   Verona's Summer hath not such a Flower.
    Flower.
NURSE   Nay, he's a Flow'r, i'faith, a very Flower!
CAPULET'S WIFE   What say you? Can you love the Gentleman?
    Gentleman?
    This Night you shall behold him at our Feast.   80
    Read o'er the Volume of young Paris' Face
    And find Delight writ there with Beauty's Pen;
    Examine ev'ry marri'd Lineament
    And see how one another lends Content;
    And what obscur'd in this fair Volume lies,   85
    Find written in the Margent of his Eyes.

89   Fish . . . Sea *In a variation on Lady Capulet's elaborate conceit about Paris as an "unbound" volume (line 87), the young Count here becomes the fish who needs a sea (here represented by Juliet) to hold him. As his wife, Juliet will be able to take "much Pride" in being the "Fair Without" (line 90) that hides "the Fair Within" (that is, Paris).*

92   Gold Clasps . . . Golden Story *Lady Capulet says that if Paris is the "fair Volume" (line 85), "the Golden Story," Juliet will be the "Gold Clasps" designed to enclose and ornament that volume.*

95   Women grow by Men! *The Nurse's earthy translation of Lady Capulet's concluding line is a characteristic touch of homespun realism, the effect of which is to render all the more ludicrous the overwrought metaphors in Juliet's mother's speech. The Nurse means that women grow "bigger" by becoming pregnant.*

97   if Looking Liking move *if looking prompts liking.*

98   endart mine Eye *Juliet is likening her eye to a dart or arrow.*

102   Nurse curs'd in the Pantry *The Servant, probably Peter, is complaining that the Nurse is not helping with the preparations.*

103   to wait *to be of service to the guests.*

104   straight *immediately.*

105   stays *awaits your arrival.*

46

This precious Book of Love, this unbound Lover,
To beautify him only lacks a Cover.
The Fish lives in the Sea, and 'tis much pride
For Fair Without the Fair Within to hide: 90
That Book in many's Eyes doth share the Glory
That in Gold Clasps locks in the Golden Story.
So shall you share all that he doth possess,
By having him making your self no less.
NURSE   No less? Nay, bigger! Women grow by Men! 95
CAPULET'S WIFE   Speak briefly: can you like of
    Paris' Love?
JULIET   I'll look to like, if Looking Liking move.
    But no more deep will I endart mine Eye
    Than your Consent gives strength to make it fly.

Enter Servingman.

SERVANT   Madam, the Guests are come, Supper serv'd 100
    up, you call'd, my young Lady ask'd for, the
    Nurse curs'd in the Pantry, and everything in
    Extremity. I must hence to wait; I beseech you
    follow straight.
CAPULET'S WIFE   We follow thee.   *Exit Servant.*
                        Juliet, the County stays. 105
NURSE   Go, Girl: seek happy Nights to happy Days!
                                Exeunt.

I.iv   *The scene shifts to a site just outside the Capulets' house. Romeo and his friends are prepared to don their masks and enter.*

1–2   **shall this Speech . . . Apology?**   *Romeo refers to a formal speech to be used as a courteous explanation or "excuse" for their presence. Such introductions were part of the traditional decorum for masked balls.*

3   **The Date . . . Prolixity**   *Such wordy prologues are now considered out of date.*

4   **Cupid hoodwink'd**   *blindfolded. Cupid, the God of Love, was conventionally represented as a boy with his eyes covered, thereby conveying the commonplace that "love is blind."*

6   **Crowkeeper**   *scarecrow.*

7   **without-book**   *memorized.*

9   **measure us by what they will**   *size us up without our telling them what characters we are impersonating.*

10   **measure them a Measure**   *dance a measure with them.*

11   **Give me a Torch**   *Romeo wants to carry the light because he feels "Heavy" (depressed) and is unwilling to take part in the "Ambling" (dancing). In lines 35–39 he says that his role in the masked party will be that of an onlooking "Grandsire" rather than a carefree "Wanton."*

17–18 **You are a Lover . . . Bound.**   *Mercutio says that Romeo should attend the Mask in his true character, as a disciple of hoodwinked Cupid.*

Scene 4

Enter Romeo, Mercutio, Benvolio,
with five or six other Maskers and Torchbearers.

ROMEO   What, shall this Speech be spoke for our
    Excuse?
    Or shall we on without Apology?
BENVOLIO   The Date is out of such Prolixity:
    We'll have no Cupid hoodwink'd with a Scarf,
    Bearing a Tartar's painted Bow of Lath,   5
    Scaring the Ladies like a Crowkeeper,
    Nor no without-book Prologue, faintly spoke
    After the Prompter, for our Entrance,
    But let them measure us by what they will.
    We'll measure them a Measure and be gone.   10
ROMEO   Give me a Torch: I am not for this Ambling;
    Being but Heavy, I will bear the Light.
MERCUTIO   Nay, gentle Romeo, we must have you
    dance.
ROMEO   Not I, believe me: you have Dancing Shoes
    With Nimble Soles; I have a Soul of Lead   15
    So stakes me to the Ground I cannot move.
MERCUTIO   You are a Lover: borrow Cupid's Wings
    And soar with them above a common Bound.
ROMEO   I am too sore enpierced with his Shaft

49

22   **Burthen**   *burden. Romeo plays on two senses of "Pitch" (line
      21) to yield two senses of "Burthen": (a) a load that keeps one
      from bounding to the highest pitch of a flight, and (b) the bass
      level (the lowest notes or pitch) in a musical composition.*

23   **burthen Love**   *Mercutio here initiates a series of exchanges
      with sexual innuendo. First, he suggests that Romeo "burthen
      Love" or be atop the one he loves. This leads to wordplay on
      genitalia in lines 24–30.*

31   **cote**   *quote, take note of.*

39   **The Game . . . I am done.**   *This is a proverbial expres-
      sion, conveying the advice to quit while you're ahead. Romeo
      seems to be saying that because he feels like a "Grandsire," he
      is now "done" with the "Game" (a term normally associated
      with gambling, but here applied to dancing), even though it
      was "ne'er so fair."*

40   **Dun's the Mouse**   *Mercutio picks up Romeo's use of "done"
      to cite a proverbial expression meaning "be quiet as a mouse,"
      thus casting Romeo momentarily in the role of a cautious old
      Constable. In lines 41–43 Mercutio goes on to play on the
      word* **Dun,** *a name for a beast of burden and a word that
      sounds like* dung. *He thus portrays Romeo as a horse mired in
      "Love."*

42   **save your Rever'nce**   *begging your pardon. The expression
      also picks up on the implications of "sir reverence," a euphe-
      mism for dung.*

To soar with his light Feathers, and so bound   20
I cannot bound a Pitch above dull Woe:
Under Love's heavy Burthen do I sink.

MERCUTIO   And to sink in it should you burthen
    Love:
Too great Oppression for a tender Thing.

ROMEO   Is Love a tender Thing? It is too rough,   25
    Too rude, too boist'rous, and it pricks like
    Thorn.

MERCUTIO   If Love be rough with you, be rough with
    Love:
Prick Love for pricking, and you beat him down!
Give me a Case to put my Visage in,
A Visor for a Visor: what care I   30
What curious Eye doth cote Deformities?
Here are the Beetle-brows shall blush for me.

BENVOLIO   Come, knock and enter; and no sooner in
    But ev'ry Man betake him to his Legs.

ROMEO   A Torch for me: let Wantons light of Heart   35
    Tickle the senseless Rushes with their Heels.
For I am proverb'd with a Grandsire Phrase:
I'll be a Candle-holder and look on.
The Game was ne'er so fair, and I am done.

MERCUTIO   Tut, Dun's the Mouse: the Constable's own
    Word.   40
If thou art Dun, we'll draw thee from the Mire
Or, save your Rever'nce, Love, wherein thou
    stickest

51

45 **Lights by Day!** *an expression for wasting one's resources.*

46 **good Meaning** *intended meaning.*

47 **five Wits** *five senses.*

48–49 **mean well . . . no Wit** *Romeo picks up on Mercutio's previous lines, to say that though we have good intentions in attending this Mask, we are not wise to do so.*

53 **Queen Mab** *The name is probably meant to play on* quean, *a word for slut, and thus to give facetious dignity to "Mab," a common name for a prostitute.*

57 **Atomi** *atoms, the tiniest of creatures.*

59 **long Spinners'** *daddy longlegs, long-legged spiders.*

61 **Traces** *harness.*

63 **Film** *gossamer (light cobweb).*

Up to the Ears. Come, we burn Daylight: ho!

ROMEO Nay, that's not so.

MERCUTIO I mean, Sir, in Delay.
We waste our Lights in vain: Lights, Lights by
Day! 45
Take our good Meaning, for our Judgment sits
Five times in that ere once in our five Wits.

ROMEO And we mean well in going to this Mask,
But 'tis no Wit to go.

MERCUTIO Why, may one ask?

ROMEO I dreamt a Dream tonight.

MERCUTIO And so did I. 50

ROMEO Well, what was yours?

MERCUTIO That Dreamers often lie.

ROMEO In Bed asleep while they do dream things
true.

MERCUTIO O then I see Queen Mab hath been with
you.
She is the Fairies' Midwife, and she comes
In Shape no bigger than an Agate Stone 55
On the Forefinger of an Alderman,
Drawn with a Team of little Atomi
Over Men's Noses as they lie asleep;
Her Wagon Spokes made of long Spinners' Legs,
The Cover of the Wings of Grasshoppers, 60
Her Traces of the smallest Spider Web,
Her Collars of the Moonshine's Wat'ry Beams,
Her Whip of Cricket's Bone, the Lash of Film,

66   Lazy Finger   *probably little finger. But an old wives' tale held that worms grew in the fingers of lazy girls. Largely for that reason, most editors prefer the First Quarto reading, "Lazy Finger of a Maid" (adopted here), to the Second Quarto reading, "lazy finger of a Man."*

68   joiner   *cabinetmaker. Because of the squirrel's sharp teeth and the grub's ability to bore, Mercutio assigns these creatures their roles as "Coachmakers."*

75   with Blisters plagues   *afflicts with blisters.*

76   Sweetmeats   *candies or other sweet delicacies.*

78   Suit   *a request for patronage to advance the Courtier's position at Court.*

79   Tithepig   *a pig given to a parson as part of the tithe (tenth of one's livestock) owed by a parishioner to the Church.*

80   'a   *he.*

81   Benefice   *position within the Church.*

84   Breaches   *penetrations of enemy defenses.*
        Ambuscados   *ambushes.*

85   Fadom   *fathoms, each equal to six feet in depth.*

87   being   *here pronounced glidingly so as to constitute one syllable metrically.*

54

Her Wagoner a small gray-coated Gnat
Not half so big as a round little Worm 65
Prick'd from the Lazy Finger of a Maid.
Her Chariot is an empty Hazelnut
Made by the joiner Squirrel or old Grub,
Time out o' mind the Fairies' Coachmakers.
And in this State she gallops Night by Night 70
Through Lovers' Brains, and then they dream of
    Love;
On Courtiers' Knees, that dream on Cur'sies
    straight;
O'er Lawyers' Fingers, who straight dream on
    Fees;
O'er Ladies' Lips, who straight on Kisses dream,
Which oft the angry Mab with Blisters plagues 75
Because their Breaths with Sweetmeats tainted
    are.
Sometime she gallops o'er a Courtier's Nose,
And then dreams he of smelling out a Suit;
And sometimes comes she with a Tithepig's Tail,
Tickling a Parson's Nose as 'a lies asleep, 80
Then he dreams of another Benefice.
Sometimes she driveth o'er a Soldier's Neck,
And then dreams he of cutting Foreign Throats,
Of Breaches, Ambuscados, Spanish Blades,
Of Healths five Fadom deep, and then anon 85
Drums in his Ear, at which he starts and wakes,
And, being thus frighted, swears a Pray'r or two

89   plats   *plaits, tangles, and mats.*

90   Elflocks   *clumps of hair that are matted and unkempt from lack of grooming.*

91   Which . . . bodes   *Since tangled hair was thought by peasants to be the work of elves (whence the name* elflocks*), it was also assumed that elves would take revenge if their handiwork were undone.*

94   Women of Good Carriage   *Mercutio puns on three senses of* carriage*: (a) erect, dignified posture, (b) bearing a sexual partner, and (c) bearing children.*

98   vain Fantasy   *empty make-believe.* Fantasy *was a term for the human capacity to extrapolate from ordinary experience and conceive of imaginary realms of being. It was roughly equivalent to imagination, and it was the root word for the more common term* fancy, *which was often used as a synonym for the state of being in love.*

102   puffs   *an aptly chosen word that personifies the Wind's gusts as the huffs of an offended suitor.*

106–   I fear . . . Gentlemen!   *Apart from the concluding sentence, which is delivered with a somewhat unconvincing bravado, this speech has a reflective quality suggestive of soliloquy. It may be that the actor playing Romeo is meant to hang back from the group for a moment and deliver the lines as if he were alone with his thoughts. Words like* Date, Term, *and* Forfeit *compare Romeo's lifespan to a loan whose contractual term is about to expire.*

And sleeps again. This is that very Mab
That plats the Manes of Horses in the Night,
And bakes the Elflocks in foul sluttish Hairs,   90
Which, once untangled, much Misfortune bodes.
This is the Hag, when Maids lie on their Backs,
That presses them and learns them first to
    bear,
Making them Women of Good Carriage: this
Is she—
ROMEO   Peace, peace, Mercutio, peace!   95
Thou talk'st of Nothing.
MERCUTIO   True: I talk of Dreams,
Which are the Children of an Idle Brain,
Begot of nothing but vain Fantasy,
Which is as thin of Substance as the Air
And more inconstant than the Wind, who woos   100
Ev'n now the frozen Bosom of the North,
And, being anger'd, puffs away from thence,
Turning his side to the Dew-dropping South.
BENVOLIO   This Wind you talk of blows us from our
    Selves:
Supper is done, and we shall come too late.   105
ROMEO   I fear too early: for my Mind misgives
Some Consequence, yet hanging in the Stars,
Shall bitterly begin his fearful Date
With this Night's Revels, and expire the Term
Of a despised Life clos'd in my Breast   110
By some vile Forfeit of untimely Death.

57

112   he . . . Course   *Romeo often uses navigational images (compare II.ii.83–85 and V.iii.116–18); here he seems to be thinking of Love as the pilot "that hath the Steerage of his Course."*

S.D.   They march about the Stage . . .   *The stage direction suggests that the Maskers are to remain in view of the audience while the Servingmen open the next scene, clearing away the dishes from the feast that has just been completed. But it is equally possible that the original staging called for Romeo and his friends to exit and then re-enter when the Capulets emerge to greet them at I.v.19. In any event, it is obvious that the action was continuous.*

I.v   *The setting now shifts to the interior of Capulet's house, initially to an anteroom and then to the large hall referred to in line 15 as the Great Chamber.*

2   Trencher   *wooden platter.*

7   Joinstools   *stools made by joiners; often called jointstools.*

8   Court-Cubbert   *court-cupboard, elaborate sideboard.* Plate   *silverware.*

9   Marchpane   *marzipan, a confection made with ground almonds, sugar, and egg-white.*

10–11   let . . . Nell   *Now that his evening's tasks are nearly over, the First Servant prepares to do a little entertaining of his own.* Grindstone *is a graphically apt name for the kind of woman whose companionship he seeks after a hard day's work.*

But he that hath the Steerage of my Course
Direct my Suit. —On, lusty Gentlemen!
BENVOLIO   Strike, Drum!

They march about the Stage, and Servingmen
come forth with Napkins.

Scene 5

FIRST SERVANT   Where's Potpan that he helps not to
take away? He shift a Trencher? He scrape a
Trencher?
SECOND SERVANT   When good Manners shall lie all in
one or two Men's Hands, and they unwash'd too,   5
'tis a Foul Thing.
FIRST SERVANT   Away with the Joinstools; remove the
Court-Cubbert; look to the Plate! —Good thou,
save me a piece of Marchpane; and, as thou loves
me, let the Porter let in Susan Grindstone and   10
Nell.

Enter Anthony and Potpan.

59

19–28 Welcome . . . play. *Capulet's greeting, in its graciously colloquial informality, is meant to put his new guests at ease. Capulet speaks first to the visiting Maskers, then to the Ladies, then to the Maskers again, and finally to the Musicians. Here as elsewhere, dashes are used to indicate interruptions or shifts in mode of address.*

20 walk about *dance a turn.*

22 makes dainty *coyly hesitates to join in.*

25 Visor *mask.*

29 A Hall, a Hall! *This order is directed to the Servants, who are being told to speed up their work in preparing the hall for dancing. In line 30 the Servants are jocularly called "Knaves."*

32 this unlook'd-for Sport *Capulet seems pleased to see that what had been planned merely as a family gathering will now feature "Sport" with some "unlook'd-for" visitors. This line is addressed to one of the servants. "Sirrah" is normally a term for a social inferior.*

33 Nay sit *Apparently Cousin Capulet is preparing to join the dancing. Or it may be that Capulet is assuring him that he is not expected to be able to keep up with the younger people.*

FIRST SERVANT   Anthony and Potpan.

ANTHONY   Ay Boy, ready.

FIRST SERVANT   You are look'd for, and call'd for,
    ask'd for, and sought for in the Great Chamber.   15

POTPAN   We cannot be here and there too. Cheerly,
    Boys, be brisk a while, and the Longer Liver
    take all!   *Exeunt.*

Enter the Capulets and all the Guests and Gentlewomen
to the Maskers.

CAPULET   Welcome, Gentlemen! Ladies that have their
    Toes unplagued with Corns will walk about with   20
    you. —Ah, my Mistresses, which of you all will
    now deny to dance? She that makes dainty, she
    I'll swear hath Corns. Am I come near ye now?
    —Welcome, Gentlemen; I have seen the Day that I
    have worn a Visor and could tell a whisp'ring   25
    Tale in a fair Lady's Ear such as would please.
    'Tis gone, 'tis gone, 'tis gone! You are welcome,
    Gentlemen. —Come, Musicians, play.
                        Music plays, and they dance.
    —A Hall, a Hall! —Give room and foot it, Girls!
    —More Light, you Knaves, and turn the Tables up!   30
    And quench the Fire: the Room is grown too hot.
    Ah Sirrah, this unlook'd-for Sport comes well!
    —Nay sit, nay sit, good Cousin Capulet:
    For you and I are past our Dancing Days.

61

39   Pentecost   *a holiday fifty days after Easter (also known as Whitsunday).*

43   a Ward   *a minor.*

50   shows   *appears.*
      Dove . . . Crows   *This imagery recalls Benvolio's pledge in I.ii.90 and proves him to have been a good prophet.*

52   her place of Stand   *where she stands.*

53   rude   *low, common.*

54   Forswear   *unswear, disavow.*

How long is't now since last your self and I   35
Were in a Mask?

SECOND CAPULET   By'r Lady, thirty years!

CAPULET   What Man, 'tis not so much, 'tis not so
    much!

'Tis since the Nuptial of Lucentio,
Come Pentecost as quickly as it will,
Some five and twenty years, and then we mask'd.   40

SECOND CAPULET   'Tis more, 'tis more! His Son is
    elder, Sir;

His Son is thirty.

CAPULET   Will you tell me that?

His Son was but a Ward two years ago.

ROMEO   [*To a Servant*] What Lady's that which doth
    enrich the Hand

Of yonder Knight?

SERVANT   I know not, Sir.   45

ROMEO   [*Aside*] O she doth teach the Torches to burn
    bright!

It seems she hangs upon the Cheek of Night
As a rich Jewel in an Ethiop's Ear:
Beauty too rich for Use, for Earth too dear!
So shows a snowy Dove trooping with Crows   50
As yonder Lady o'er her Fellows shows.
The Measure done, I'll watch her place of Stand,
And, touching hers, make blessed my rude Hand.
Did my Heart love till now? Forswear it, Sight;
For I ne'er saw true Beauty till this Night!   55

57   Fetch . . . Boy!   *Tybalt addresses this line to his Page, who exits to carry out his Master's order.*

58   Antic Face   *a face masked with a grotesque or fantastic visor (Antic is often spelled* antique *in English Renaissance texts).*

59   fleer   *grin mockingly.*
           Solemnity   *ceremonious occasion.*

68   'A   *he.*
           portly   *well-comported, well-mannered.*

79   goodman Boy   *By calling Tybalt both a goodman (that is, a yeoman, a man below the rank of gentleman) and a boy, Capulet delivers a double rebuke to the irascible young man's overweening dignity.*

TYBALT   This by his Voice should be a Mountague.
Fetch me my Rapier, Boy!   *Exit Page.*
                    —What dares the Slave
Come hither cover'd with an Antic Face
To fleer and scorn at our Solemnity?
Now, by the Stock and Honor of my Kin,   60
To strike him dead I hold it not a Sin.
CAPULET   Why how now, Kinsman? Wherefore storm
you so?
TYBALT   Uncle, this is a Mountague, our Foe:
A Villain that is hither come in Spite
To scorn at our Solemnity this Night.   65
CAPULET   Young Romeo is't?
TYBALT   'Tis he, that villain Romeo.
CAPULET   Content thee, gentle Coz, let him alone.
'A bears him like a portly Gentleman;
And to say truth, Verona brags of him
To be a virtuous and well-govern'd Youth.   70
I would not for the Wealth of all this Town
Here in my House do him Disparagement:
Therefore be Patient, take no Note of him.
It is my Will, the which if thou respect,
Show me a Fair Presence and put off these Frowns,   75
An ill-beseeming Semblance for a Feast.
TYBALT   It fits when such a Villain is a Guest:
I'll not endure him!
CAPULET   He shall be endur'd!
What, goodman Boy? I say he shall! Go to!

82   make a Mutiny   *create an unruly disturbance.*

83   You will set Cock-a-hoop   *Capulet is telling Tybalt that his behavior is like that of a strutting cock (the sound of the phrase perhaps echoing that of a crowing rooster). The phrase may also refer to the wild drinking bouts that occur when the "cock" (spigot) is removed and placed atop the "hoop" of a barrel of alcoholic drink.*

    you'll be the Man   *Capulet probably means that Tybalt is acting like the Master (line 80) rather than an obedient nephew.*

84   'tis a Shame   *Tybalt is saying that Romeo's unchallenged presence is an insult to the Capulets' honor.*

86   This Trick . . . scathe you   *Tybalt's unruly defiance may injure ("scathe") him if he doesn't mend his behavior.*

88   Well said   *well done.*

    Princox   *a name combining the words* prince *and* cock, *thus connoting a prancing audacity. Capulet's remarks in lines 88–90 are thrice interrupted by his shouts to the dancers and servants.*

91–92 Patience . . . Greeting.   *Tybalt allegorizes his conflict by depicting his "Choler" (anger) as having been impeded "perforce" (forcibly) by the "Patience" (forbearance) of his uncle.*

96   holy Shrine   *Romeo probably says these words while holding Juliet's hand. Throughout this scene he depicts himself as an unworthy supplicant for redemption at a religious sanctuary.*

Am I the Master here or you? Go to!   80
You'll not endure him! God shall mend my Soul,
You'll make a Mutiny among my Guests;
You will set Cock-a-hoop; you'll be the Man!
TYBALT   Why, Uncle, 'tis a Shame!
CAPULET   Go to, go to!
You are a saucy Boy! Is't so indeed?   85
This Trick may chance to scathe you, I know
    what!
You must contrary me! Marry 'tis Time:
—Well said, my Hearts! —You are a Princox, go!
Be quiet, or— More light! More light! —for
    shame,
I'll make you quiet! —What, cheerly, my Hearts!   90
TYBALT   [*Aside*] Patience perforce with willful
    Choler meeting
Makes my flesh tremble in their different
    Greeting.
I will withdraw, but this Intrusion shall,
Now seeming Sweet, convert to bitt'rest Gall.
                                              Exit.
ROMEO   If I profane with my unworthiest Hand   95
This holy Shrine, the gentle Sin is this:
My Lips, two blushing Pilgrims, ready stand
To smooth that rough Touch with a tender Kiss.
JULIET   Good Pilgrim, you do wrong your Hand too
    much,
Which mannerly Devotion shows in this,   100

102   **Palmers** *Palmers were pilgrims who had visited the Holy Sepulcher in Jerusalem and wore palm leaves to signify their devotion.*

107   **Saints . . . sake.** *Juliet seems to be saying that though saints do not take the initiative to intervene in human affairs, they do provide assistance when requested to do so by prayer. Here her implication is that she will "move not" to resist if the "Pilgrim" takes the kiss he prays for.*

112   **by th' Book** *by the rules. Though the idea of doing things by the book is ridiculed elsewhere in the play, Juliet appears to mean no criticism here. Her implication seems to be that everything about Romeo's behavior is in accordance with the rituals of "mannerly Devotion" (line 100). Appropriately, lines 95–108 take the form of a Shakespearean sonnet. Lines 109–12 constitute the first quatrain of a second sonnet—interrupted, significantly, by the Nurse's intrusion with a message from Juliet's mother. It could be said that these brief exchanges capture the play in epitome.*

For Saints have Hands that Pilgrims' Hands do
  touch,
And Palm to Palm is holy Palmers' Kiss.

ROMEO   Have not Saints Lips, and holy Palmers too?

JULIET   Ay, Pilgrim: Lips that they must use in
  Pray'r.

ROMEO   O then, dear Saint, let Lips do what Hands
  do: 105
  They pray. Grant thou, lest Faith turn to
  Despair.

JULIET   Saints do not move, though grant for
  Prayers' sake.

ROMEO   Then move not while my Prayer's effect I
  take.   *He kisses her.*
  Thus from my Lips by thine my Sin is purg'd.

JULIET   Then have my Lips the Sin that they have
  took.   110

ROMEO   Sin from my Lips? O Trespass sweetly urg'd!
  Give me my Sin again.   *He kisses her again.*

JULIET   You kiss by th' Book.

NURSE   Madam, your Mother craves a Word with you.
                              Juliet goes to her Mother.

ROMEO   What is her Mother?

NURSE   Marry, Bachelor,
  Her Mother is the Lady of the House,   115
  And a good Lady, and a wise and virtuous.
  I nurs'd her Daughter that you talk withal;
  I tell you, he that can lay hold of her

119   Chinks   *the coins, the money.*

120   dear Account   *Romeo continues the monetary metaphor by suggesting that he has just put his life in his "Foe's Debt." He fears that this will prove to be a costly ("dear") transaction ("Account") for him.*

121   The Sport is at the best.   *It was proverbial that one should leave gaming while ahead, an idea expressed earlier in I.iv.39. The "fear" Romeo expresses in the next line is that this moment at the heights can only lead to a downward turning of Fortune's wheel.*

124   Banquet   *a light refreshment of fruit, wine, and sweets. As we know from I.iv.105, the feast itself is now over.*
         towards   *in the offing. Here pronounced as a single syllable.*

128   by my fay   *by my faith. This line is evidently spoken to one of the servants.*

130   What   *who. What was often used to identify people in terms of their title, rank, or function in society.*

141   Too early . . . too late.   *Juliet says that she saw Romeo "too early," when his identity was "unknown" to her; now that she is in love, she realizes that it is "too late" to undo what might not have happened had she first known him to be a Mountague.*

142   Prodigious   *portentously abnormal. The word* prodigy *was often applied to deformed or freakish offspring, who were thought to signify Heaven's displeasure.*

70

Shall have the Chinks!

ROMEO [*Aside*] Is she a Capulet?

O dear Account! My Life is my Foe's Debt. 120

BENVOLIO Away! Begone! The Sport is at the best.

ROMEO Ay, so I fear: the more is my Unrest.

CAPULET Nay, Gentlemen, prepare not to be gone:

We have a trifling, foolish Banquet towards.

They whisper in his ear.

Is it e'en so? Why then I thank you all; 125

I thank you, honest Gentlemen; goodnight.

Romeo, Benvolio, Mercutio begin to leave.

—More Torches here! Come on then, let's to Bed.

Ah Sirrah, by my fay, it waxes late;

I'll to my Rest.

JULIET Come hither, Nurse. What is yond Gentleman? 130

NURSE The Son and Heir of old Tiberio.

JULIET What's he that now is going out of door?

NURSE Marry, that I think be young Petruchio.

JULIET What's he that follows there that would not

dance?

NURSE I know not. 135

JULIET Go ask his Name. [*Aside*] If he be married,

My Grave is like to be my Wedding Bed.

NURSE His Name is Romeo, and a Mountague:

The only Son of your great Enemy.

JULIET My only Love sprung from my only Hate: 140

Too early seen unknown, and, known, too late.

Prodigious Birth of Love it is to me

144   **Rime**   *rhyme. This spelling, derived from Italian, is used in all the original texts of the play.*

145   **withal**   *with. When* with *ends a sentence or clause, Shakespeare frequently lengthens it to* withal *for emphasis.*

146   **Anon**   *equivalent to "Right away!" or "Coming!"*

That I must love a loathed Enemy!

NURSE   What 'tis? What 'tis?

JULIET   A Rime I learnt ev'n now

Of one I danc'd withal.   145

One calls within: Juliet!

NURSE   Anon, anon!

—Come, let's away; the Strangers all are gone.

                                        Exeunt.

II.　Chorus　*Here the Chorus functions to effect a transition from the Mask scene inside the Capulet's house to the scenes that follow once Romeo, Benvolio, and Mercutio leave the party. A second role for the Chorus is to help the audience step outside the play for a brief but ostensibly more objective appraisal of what is happening.*

1–2　Now Old Desire . . . Heir.　*From the point of view of the Chorus, the only significant difference between Romeo's new "Affection" and his old "Desire" is that the new one is requited. There is nothing in the description of the two romantic states here to suggest that the Chorus considers what Romeo feels for Juliet to be superior in kind to what he felt for Rosaline.*

2　Young Affection gapes　*The image suggests a baby bird with its mouth eagerly open for food.*

6　Charm of Looks　*Together with the word* bewitched *earlier in the line, this phrase suggests that, from the point of view of the Chorus, what Juliet feels is merely a superficial infatuation similar to Romeo's. In Shakespeare's time* Charm *(a binding spell) is normally a word with negative connotations.*

8　fearful Hooks　*a reference to the feud, and to the parental disapproval it would evoke if the two lovers were to go public with their relationship. The "Hooks" image relates to "Bait" earlier in the line—suggesting that the lovers are at best unwitting victims (like unsuspecting fish), at worst risk-taking fools.*

74

Act Two

Enter Chorus.

CHORUS   Now Old Desire doth in his Deathbed lie,
And Young Affection gapes to be his Heir.
That Fair for which Love groan'd for and would
   die,
With tender Juliet match'd, is now not Fair.
Now Romeo is belov'd, and loves again,   5
Alike bewitched by the Charm of Looks;
But to his Foe suppos'd he must complain,
And she steal Love's sweet Bait from fearful
   Hooks.
Being held a Foe, he may not have Access

75

---

13   **Passion**   *a term suggesting that the relationship between the lovers is founded not on reason but on undisciplined ("extreme," line 14) emotions.*

II.i   *The setting for this scene is the wall surrounding the Capulets' Orchard. After line 2, Romeo stands just inside the wall, with Mercutio and Benvolio outside it, within earshot of Romeo. On the bare Elizabethan stage the wall could have been "presented" by something as simple as one of the pillars supporting the canopy above the main playing area.*

2   **dull Earth**   *Romeo is referring to his body.*
       Center   *Romeo refers both to his heart and to Juliet, to whom he has just surrendered his heart.*

3   **He's wise**   *Mercutio seems to mean "He's given us the slip."*

6   **I'll conjure**   *Mercutio pretends to summon Romeo as if he were a spirit subject to a magician's charms.*

76

To breathe such Vows as Lovers use to swear;   10
And she, as much in love, her Means much less
To meet her new Beloved anywhere.
But Passion lends them Pow'r, Time Means, to
   meet,
Temp'ring Extremities with extreme Sweet.   *Exit.*

Scene 1

Enter Romeo alone.

ROMEO   Can I go forward when my Heart is here?
   Turn back, dull Earth, and find thy Center out.
                             He retires.

Enter Benvolio with Mercutio.

BENVOLIO   Romeo! My Cousin Romeo! Romeo!
MERCUTIO   He's wise,
   And on my Life hath stol'n him home to Bed.
BENVOLIO   He ran this way and leapt this Orchard
   Wall.   5
   Call, good Mercutio.
MERCUTIO   Nay, I'll conjure too.

11   Goship   *Most modern editions read* gossip, *the spelling in the First Quarto text. But the Second Quarto spelling ("goship"), which is also found in the Folio, is probably a purposeful combination of "godship" and "gossip," an apt way of reducing the Goddess Venus to a garrulous old woman.*

12   purblind   *proverbially and completely blind.*

13   Abra'm   *here elided for metrical purposes. Cupid is so called, perhaps, because Mercutio thinks him no more dignified than the half-naked "Abraham-man" who was said to roam the country begging and stealing. If so, "Abra'm Cupid" is simply Mercutio's satirical name for "naked Cupid."*

14   King Cophetua   *an allusion to an old ballad about a king whom Cupid forced to love a beggar maiden at first sight.*

16   The Ape is dead   *apparently a reference to a trained ape who would feign death until he heard a designated magic word from his master.*

20   Demesnes   *domains.*

24   raise a Spirit . . . Circle   *Mercutio is trying to summon up "Old Desire" with an oblique sexual reference. Since conjurers normally invoked spirits to appear within a magic circle, Mercutio is perfectly orthodox in suggesting a "Mistress' Circle" for Romeo's "Spirit" to rise within.*

31   hum'rous Night   *Here* hum'rous *means both (a) damp, and (b) conducive to the moods of a person under sway of the humours.*

Romeo! Humours! Madman! Passion! Lover!
Appear thou in the likeness of a Sigh;
Speak but one Rime, and I am satisfied.
Cry but "Ay me"! Pronounce but "Love" and "Dove"!　10
Speak to my Goship Venus one fair Word,
One Nickname for her purblind Son and Heir,
Young Abra'm Cupid, he that shot so true
When King Cophetua lov'd the Beggar Maid.
—He heareth not, he stirreth not, he moveth not:　15
The Ape is dead, and I must conjure him.
—I conjure thee, by Rosaline's bright Eyes,
By her high Forehead, and her scarlet Lip,
By her fine Foot, straight Leg, and quiv'ring
　　Thigh,
And the Demesnes that there adjacent lie,　20
That in thy Likeness thou appear to us!
BENVOLIO　And if he hear thee, thou wilt anger him.
MERCUTIO　This cannot anger him! 'Twould anger him
　To raise a Spirit in his Mistress' Circle
　Of some strange nature, letting it there stand　25
　Till she had laid it and conjur'd it down?
　That were some Spite! My Invocation
　Is fair and honest: in his Mistress' Name
　I conjure only but to raise up him.
BENVOLIO　Come, he hath hid himself among these
　　Trees　30
　To be consorted with the hum'rous Night:
　Blind is his Love, and best befits the Dark.

79

36   Medlars   *small, apple-like fruits, eaten only when nearly rot-
      ten, and thought to resemble the female genitalia. The word-
      play on "medlars" relates to "meddlers," those who meddle
      around sexually.*

38   op'n Et-cet'ra   *This reading, from the First Quarto, suggests
      that Mercutio has a more bawdy word in mind.*
      Pop'rin Pear   *a fruit thought to resemble the male genitalia.*

39   Truckle-bed   *trundle bed, used primarily by children, and
      equipped with rollers to be stored under an adult's bed when
      not in use.*

40   Field-bed   *a portable bed used by soldiers on military cam-
      paigns.*

II.ii   *The setting shifts to the inside of the Orchard wall as Romeo
      emerges from where he has been listening to Mercutio and
      Benvolio's gibes. Almost immediately Romeo's focus shifts to a
      window above, where a light indicates Juliet's presence.*

3–9   It is . . . off!   *Romeo begins by likening Juliet to the Sun
      and thereby placing her above "the envious Moon," who is
      jealous because "her Maid" is "more fair than she." Romeo
      then prays that Juliet will cast off her allegiance to the Moon
      (that is, to Diana, Goddess of the Moon and patroness of
      virgins) and exchange the "Liv'ry" (uniform) of Diana for
      that of Venus (Goddess of Love).*

MERCUTIO   If Love be blind, Love cannot hit the
     Mark.
     Now will he sit under a Medlar Tree
     And wish his Mistress were that kind of Fruit   35
     As Maids call Medlars when they laugh alone.
     —O Romeo, that she were, O that she were
     An op'n Et-cet'ra, thou a Pop'rin Pear!
     Romeo, goodnight; I'll to my Truckle-bed:
     This Field-bed is too cold for me to sleep.   40
     —Come, shall we go?
BENVOLIO   Go then, for 'tis in vain
     To seek him here that means not to be found.
                         Exeunt Benvolio and Mercutio.

Scene 2

Romeo steps forward.

ROMEO   He jests at Scars that never felt a Wound.
     —But soft, what Light through yonder Window
        breaks?
     It is the East, and Juliet is the Sun.
     Arise, fair Sun, and kill the envious Moon,
     Who is already sick and pale with Grief   5

8   Vestal Liv'ry   *apparel of virgins dedicated to Vesta, Roman goddess of the Hearth. Here Vesta's attributes are merged with those of Diana, Goddess of Chastity.*
    sick and green   *characteristics associated with envy.*

9   none . . . wear it   *Court fools wore a motley uniform, with green as one of its dominant colors.*

10–11   It is . . . were!   *In the early texts these clauses are printed as a single line of sixteen syllables. It may be that the actor playing Romeo was to convey his excitement by speaking these words in a rush of ardor. Another possibility is that the actor was to pause after a second, short line to give Juliet a four-syllable moment to "speak" silently.*

17   Spheres   *Shakespeare refers to the Ptolemaic cosmology whereby the stars and planets were thought to revolve around the Earth in concentric crystalline spheres to the accompaniment of a celestial music too refined for mortal ears to hear.*

18   they   *the "Stars" referred to in line 15.*

That thou her Maid art far more fair than she.
Be not her Maid, since she is envious:
Her Vestal Liv'ry is but sick and green,
And none but Fools do wear it. Cast it off!

Enter Juliet above at the Window.

It is my Lady, O it is my Love!   10
O that she knew she were!
She speaks, yet she says nothing. What of that?
Her Eye discourses; I will answer it.
I am too bold: 'tis not to me she speaks.
Two of the fairest Stars in all the Heaven,   15
Having some Business, do entreat her Eyes
To twinkle in their Spheres till they return.
What if her Eyes were there, they in her Head?
The brightness of her Cheek would shame those
   Stars
As Daylight doth a Lamp; her Eyes in Heav'n   20
Would through the Airy Region stream so bright
That Birds would sing and think it were not
   Night.
See how she leans her Cheek upon her Hand:
O that I were a Glove upon that Hand!
That I might touch that Cheek!

JULIET   Ay me!

ROMEO   She speaks!   25
   O speak again, bright Angel, for thou art

33   **wherefore art thou Romeo?**   *Juliet's question is "why are you Romeo?" and not "where," as is commonly thought. We should also note that in most of their occurrences, the names* **Romeo** *and* **Juliet** *are pronounced as two-syllable words (Roám-yo and Joól-yet). Curiously, in this scene in which so much is made of Romeo's name, the hero never once speaks Juliet's name to her.*

39   **Thou . . . Mountague.**   *You would be the same self if you were not a Mountague.*

44   **By any other Name**   *This reading comes from the First Quarto; the Second Quarto (followed by the First Folio) reads "By any other word." That version of the line is equally acceptable. But because there are deficiencies in the Second Quarto rendering of this speech (for example, it does not supply the words "nor any other part / Belonging to a man", which must be supplied from the First Quarto), this edition departs from it in adopting the First Quarto's more familiar "name" in Juliet's famous meditation.*

46   **owes**   *owns.*

51   **Call . . . new baptiz'd**   *Romeo refers to the christening ceremony where infants are given their Christian names. He says that henceforth he will be called "Love" rather than "Romeo," and in that sense "new baptiz'd." The baptismal imagery also reinforces the suggestion that Romeo's new "religion," centered on Juliet, has resulted in his being newly born.*

As glorious to this Night, being o'er my Head,
As is a winged Messenger of Heav'n
Unto the white upturned wond'ring Eyes
Of Mortals that fall back to gaze on him   30
When he bestrides the lazy, puffing Clouds
And sails upon the Bosom of the Air.

JULIET   O Romeo, Romeo, wherefore art thou Romeo?
Deny thy Father and refuse thy Name;
Or if thou wilt not, be but sworn my Love   35
And I'll no longer be a Capulet.

ROMEO   Shall I hear more, or shall I speak at this?

JULIET   'Tis but thy Name that is my Enemy:
Thou art thy Self, though not a Mountague.
What's Mountague? It is nor Hand nor Foot,   40
Nor Arm nor Face, nor any other Part
Belonging to a Man. O be some other Name.
What's in a Name? That which we call a Rose
By any other Name would smell as sweet;
So Romeo would, were he not Romeo call'd,   45
Retain that dear Perfection which he owes
Without that Title. Romeo, doff thy Name,
And for thy Name, which is no part of thee,
Take all my Self.

ROMEO   [*To Juliet*] I take thee at thy Word: 50
Call me but Love, and I'll be new baptiz'd;
Henceforth I never will be Romeo.

JULIET   What Man art thou that, thus bescreened
in Night,

85

54   my Counsel   *my private musings.*

67   Love's light Wings   *another allusion to traditional portray-als of Cupid as a winged boy.*

68   Stony Limits   *a reminder of the wall separating Pyramus and Thisbe, whose story as told by Ovid was the ultimate source of the Romeo and Juliet legend. Their tragedy was treated comically in* A Midsummer Night's Dream, *Shakespeare's companion piece to* Romeo and Juliet. *There, of course, the "Stony Limits" that separate the lovers are represented by a character called Wall.*

72   Alack   *a mild intensifier, comparable to* alas *and generally more negative in implication than* indeed.

74   proof against   *protected from.*

86

So stumblest on my Counsel?

ROMEO   By a Name
I know not how to tell thee who I am!   55
My Name, dear Saint, is hateful to my Self
Because it is an Enemy to thee;
Had I it written, I would tear the Word.

JULIET   My Ears have yet not drunk a hundred Words
Of thy Tongue's utt'ring, yet I know the Sound.   60
Art thou not Romeo, and a Mountague?

ROMEO   Neither, fair Maid, if either thee dislike.

JULIET   How cam'st thou hither, tell me, and
wherefore?
The Orchard Walls are high and hard to climb,
And the place Death, consid'ring who thou art,   65
If any of my Kinsmen find thee here.

ROMEO   With Love's light Wings did I o'erperch
these Walls:
For Stony Limits cannot hold Love out,
And what Love can do, that dares Love attempt.
Therefore thy Kinsmen are no stop to me.   70

JULIET   If they do see thee, they will murder thee!

ROMEO   Alack, there lies more Peril in thine Eye
Than twenty of their Swords; look thou but sweet,
And I am proof against their Enmity.

JULIET   I would not for the World they saw thee
here!   75

ROMEO   I have Night's Cloak to hide me from their
Eyes;

87

79   prorogued   *postponed (here pronounced as a three-syllable word).*

82   Counsel   *instruction.*

83   Pilot   *ship captain, person responsible for a vessel's course.*

85   Marchandise   *merchandise, goods deriving from merchant ventures.*

86   Mask of Night   *a reminder of the masking just concluded. Juliet describes herself as a masker costumed as Night.*

89   Fain   *gladly.*
      dwell on Form   *insist on the rules of etiquette.*

90   Compliment   *compliance with socially accepted forms.*

93   Perjuries   *falsehoods, infidelities.*

100   light   *wanton, frivolous. Maidens who yielded too easily were referred to as "light." Juliet also plays on the distinction between "Light" and "Dark" in lines 106–7.*

And but thou love me, let them find me here.
My Life were better ended by their Hate
Than Death prorogued, wanting of thy Love.

JULIET By whose direction found'st thou out this
place?   80

ROMEO By Love, that first did prompt me to
inquire:
He lent me Counsel and I lent him Eyes.
I am no Pilot, yet wert thou as far
As that vast Shore wash'd with the farthest Sea,
I should adventure for such Marchandise.   85

JULIET Thou know'st the Mask of Night is on my
Face,
Else would a Maiden Blush bepaint my Cheek
For that which thou hast heard me speak tonight.
Fain would I dwell on Form; fain, fain deny
What I have spoke; but farewell, Compliment.   90
Dost thou love me? I know thou wilt say "Ay,"
And I will take thy Word. Yet if thou swear'st,
Thou may'st prove false; at Lovers' Perjuries
They say Jove laughs. O gentle Romeo,
If thou dost love, pronounce it faithfully.   95
Or if thou think'st I am too quickly won,
I'll frown and be perverse and say thee nay
So thou wilt woo; but else not for the World.
In truth, fair Mountague, I am too fond:
And therefore thou may'st think my 'havior light,   100
But trust me, Gentleman, I'll prove more true

102   Cunning to be Strange   *skill at seeming distant, aloof.*

104   ware   *aware, wary.*

106   Light Love   *love lacking in the weightiness of truth and sincerity.*

107   discovered   *disclosed.*

110   th' inconstant Moon   *The Moon was proverbial for inconstancy. Everything "sublunary" (that is, below, or within, the sphere containing the Moon) was thought to be subject to change.*

115   Idolatry   *It may be that Juliet speaks more than she realizes here, because in fact many members of Shakespeare's original audience would have interpreted her sentiments as verging on a kind of worship in the place of—if not indeed in opposition to—Christianity.*

118   Contract   *Juliet is thinking of the practice whereby vows exchanged in private by a man and a woman were considered binding in the eyes of the Church, tantamount to a kind of marriage, whether or not validated by a formal ceremony.*

122–   This Bud . . . meet.   *Juliet appears ready to step back from*
23   *what she and Romeo have said and wait for "Summer's ripening Breath" to determine whether a "Bud" will in fact "prove a beauteous Flow'r."*

Than those that have more Cunning to be Strange.
I should have been more Strange, I must confess,
But that thou overheard'st ere I was ware
My True-love Passion; therefore pardon me,   105
And not impute this yielding to Light Love
Which the Dark Night hath so discovered.

ROMEO   Lady, by yonder blessed Moon I vow,
    That tips with silver all these Fruit-tree
        Tops—

JULIET   O swear not by the Moon, th' inconstant
        Moon,   110
    That monthly changes in her circled Orb,
    Lest that thy Love prove likewise variable.

ROMEO   What shall I swear by?

JULIET   Do not swear at all;
    Or if thou wilt, swear by thy gracious Self,
    Which is the God of my Idolatry,   115
    And I'll believe thee.

ROMEO   If my Heart's dear Love—

JULIET   Well, do not swear. Although I joy in thee,
    I have no joy of this Contract tonight:
    It is too rash, too unadvis'd, too sudden;
    Too like the Lightning, which doth cease to be   120
    Ere one can say "It lightens!" Sweet, goodnight:
    This Bud of Love, by Summer's ripening Breath,
    May prove a beauteous Flow'r when next we meet.
    Goodnight, goodnight: as sweet Repose and Rest
    Come to thy Heart as that within my Breast.   125

127   What Satisfaction . . . tonight?   *What Juliet fears is that Romeo wants to go to bed with her right now. Courtly lovers in medieval and Renaissance poetry regularly complained of their need to be "satisfied."*

132   frank   *free, generous.*

134   My Bounty   *Juliet refers to her love. This expression serves to remind us that her other suitor, Paris, is at least as interested in the Capulet "Bounty" she represents (what the Nurse has called "the Chinks" in I.v.119) as he is in the qualities that draw Romeo to her. A concern for that kind of bounty never enters Romeo's mind.*

142   flatt'ring sweet   *deceptively sweet.*
       substantial   *based on substance rather than on the "nothing" to which Mercutio has reduced dreams in I.iv.96–98.*

144   bent   *inclination, intention.*

ROMEO   O wilt thou leave me so unsatisfied?

JULIET   What Satisfaction canst thou have tonight?

ROMEO   Th' Exchange of thy Love's faithful Vow for
mine.

JULIET   I gave thee mine before thou didst request
it;

And yet I would it were to give again.   130

ROMEO   Wouldst thou withdraw it? For what purpose,
Love?

JULIET   But to be frank and give it thee again.

And yet I wish but for the thing I have:

My Bounty is as boundless as the Sea,

My Love as deep; the more I give to thee   135

The more I have, for both are infinite.

Nurse calls within.

I hear some Noise within: Dear Love, adieu!

—Anon, good Nurse. —Sweet Mountague, be true.

Stay but a little; I will come again.   *Exit.*

ROMEO   O blessed, blessed Night! I am afeard,   140

Being in Night, all this is but a Dream,

Too flatt'ring sweet to be substantial.

Enter Juliet again.

JULIET   Three words, dear Romeo, and goodnight
indeed.

If that thy bent of Love be honorable,

Thy purpose Marriage, send me word tomorrow,   145

149   my Lord   *The Quarto and Folio texts do not set off "my Lord"*
        as a parenthetical phrase, so it may be that Juliet's meaning is
        "follow thee as my Lord." An alternative interpretation
        (which would be expressed by setting off "my Lord" in paren-
        thetical commas) is that she already regards him as her lord by
        virtue of the vows they have just exchanged.

152   By'n'by   *right away. Both the dramatic context and the metri-*
        cal position of the phrase suggest that it be pronounced glid-
        ingly as if it were a single syllable.

153   thy Strife   *your efforts.*

160   Tassel gentle   *gentle tercel, or male falcon. This noble pere-*
        grine could be called back to its master by a quiet signal similar
        to Juliet's "hist" (line 159).

161   Bondage is hoarse   *Feeling bound because of her need for*
        secrecy, Juliet metaphorically ascribes her whisper to hoarse-
        ness.

163   airy Tongue   *a reference to Echo's ability to cast her voice into*
        the air in reverberation. Juliet alludes to a nymph in classical
        mythology who fell in love with Narcissus; after she gave up
        her pursuit, she pined away until nothing was left of her but a
        lonely voice to be heard in caves. Ovid tells the story in Book
        III of the Metamorphoses.

94

By one that I'll procure to come to thee,
Where and what time thou wilt perform the Rite,
And all my Fortunes at thy Foot I'll lay
And follow thee my Lord throughout the World.

NURSE   [*Within*] Madam!   150

JULIET   I come, anon! —But if thou mean'st not
        well,
    I do beseech thee—

NURSE   [*Within*] Madam!

JULIET   By'n'by I come!
    —To cease thy Strife and leave me to my Grief.
    Tomorrow will I send.

ROMEO   So thrive my Soul.

JULIET   A thousand times goodnight.   *Exit above.*   155

ROMEO   A thousand times the worse to want thy Light.
    Love goes toward Love as Schoolboys from their
        Books,
    But Love from Love toward School with heavy
        Looks.   *He turns to leave.*

                Enter Juliet again.

JULIET   Hist, Romeo, hist! —O for a Falc'ner's
        Voice,
    To lure this Tassel gentle back again!   160
    Bondage is hoarse, and may not speak aloud;
    Else would I tear the Cave where Echo lies
    And make her airy Tongue more hoarse than mine

95

165–
67   It is my Soul . . . Ears.   *Romeo's reflection is apparently
      prompted by the softness of Juliet's voice, which makes it seem
      as if her words are an echo of his own thoughts, his own
      "Soul."*

168   My Niesse   *The Second Quarto and First Folio reading is
       "My Neece." This could be correct, because "niece" was a
       word that could be applied to any young woman, regardless of
       relationship. But the emendation "My Niesse," adopted here,
       picks up on Juliet's falcon imagery and provides a metrically
       superior two-syllable word. A* niesse *(often spelled* nyas *or*
       eyas*) was a young hawk approaching the age when it was
       ready to leave the nest, an image particularly apt for the
       youthful Juliet.*

175   still   *In this line, though not in line 173 (where it has its usual
       modern meaning),* still *apparently means "always."*

180   Gyves   *fetters, chain shackles for the legs and feet.*

96

With repetition of my Romeo's Name.

ROMEO   It is my Soul that calls upon my Name.   165
How silver sweet sound Lovers' Tongues by Night,
Like softest Music to attending Ears.

JULIET   Romeo—

ROMEO   My Niesse?

JULIET   What o'clock tomorrow
Shall I send to thee?

ROMEO   By the hour of nine.

JULIET   I will not fail. 'Tis twenty years till
then!   170
I have forgot why I did call thee back.

ROMEO   Let me stand here till thou remember it.

JULIET   I shall forget, to have thee still stand
there,
Rememb'ring how I love thy Company.

ROMEO   And I'll still stay, to have thee still
forget,   175
Forgetting any other Home but this.

JULIET   'Tis almost Morning: I would have thee gone,
And yet no farther than a Wanton's Bird,
That lets it hop a little from her Hand,
Like a poor Pris'ner in his twisted Gyves,   180
And with a silken Thread plucks it back again,
So loving jealous of his Liberty.

ROMEO   I would I were thy Bird.

JULIET   Sweet, so would I;
Yet I should kill thee with much cherishing.

189   ghostly   *spiritual. This Anglo-Saxon sense of* ghost *is the one preserved in the name "Holy Ghost," as the third person of the Trinity is normally called in the King James Version of the Bible published in 1611.*

190   dear Hap   *precious happening. The phrase carries the sense of the expression "great good fortune."*

II.iii   *The setting shifts to the garden outside Friar Lawrence's "close Cell."*

3   flecked   *dappled.*

4   From forth   *away from.*
        Titan's Wheels   *wheels of the chariot of the Sun God, and thus a metaphor for the Sun's course through the sky. The God of the Sun had various names: Helios, Phoebus, and Hyperion. Because he was a son of the Titans, the Gods who ruled the Universe before they were overthrown by Zeus and the Olympian Gods, the Sun God was often referred to simply as Titan.*

7   Osier Cage   *wicker basket, made from branches of the osier, a type of willow.*

8   baleful   *harmful.*

9   that's   *which is.* That *is commonly used by Shakespeare to introduce a nonrestrictive (parenthetical) clause; in modern usage such clauses are normally introduced by* which *and set off with commas.*

Goodnight, goodnight: Parting is such sweet
   Sorrow 185
That I shall say goodnight till it be Morrow.

ROMEO   Sleep dwell upon thine Eyes, Peace in thy
   Breast. *Exit Juliet.*
—Would I were Sleep and Peace, so sweet to rest.
Hence will I to my ghostly Friar's close Cell,
His Help to crave and my dear Hap to tell. *Exit.* 190

Scene 3

Enter Friar Lawrence alone, with a Basket.

FRIAR LAWRENCE   The gray-ey'd Morn smiles on the
   frowning Night,
Check'ring the Eastern Clouds with streaks of
   Light,
And flecked Darkness like a Drunkard reels
From forth Day's Pathway, made by Titan's Wheels.
Now ere the Sun advance his burning Eye, 5
The Day to cheer and Night's dank Dew to dry,
I must upfill this Osier Cage of ours
With baleful Weeds and precious juiced Flowers.
The Earth, that's Nature's Mother, is her Tomb;

15   mickle   *much.*
         Grace   *The Friar uses the term here to refer to any earthly manifestation of divine goodness.*

16   true Qualities   *In this passage (lines 11–22) the Friar is distinguishing between natural ("true") qualities and qualities resulting from abuse of those qualities.*

19   strain'd from that fair Use   *constrained, forced away from its natural use; perverted.*

20   Revolts from true Birth   *rebels against its natural state or use.*
         stumbling on Abuse   *This phrase could have either of two meanings: (a) finding ("stumbling on") a way to abuse its ordained use, or (b) falling ("stumbling") "on" (as a result of) such abuse.*

22   by Action dignified   *made virtuous by its action.*

23   Rind   *outer covering or layer.*

25   smelt   *smelled.*
         with that part cheers each part   *with its part that yields fragrance the flower brings pleasure to each part of our body.*

26   stays all Senses with the Heart   *stops all senses as it stops the heart from beating.*

30   Canker   *the cankerworm, a larva that fed on plants.*

What is her burying Grave, that is her Womb.   10
And from her Womb Children of divers kind
We sucking on her natural Bosom find:
Many for many Virtues excellent,
None but for some, and yet all different.
O mickle is the pow'rful Grace that lies   15
In Plants, Herbs, Stones, and their true
    Qualities:
For nought so vile that on the Earth doth live,
But to the Earth some special good doth give,
Nor ought so good but, strain'd from that fair
    Use,
Revolts from true Birth, stumbling on Abuse.   20
Virtue itself turns Vice, being misapplied,
And Vice sometime's by Action dignified.

Enter Romeo.

Within the infant Rind of this weak Flower
Poison hath residence, and Med'cine power:
For this, being smelt, with that part cheers
    each part;   25
Being tasted, stays all Senses with the Heart.
Two such opposed Kings encamp them still
In Man as well as Herbs: Grace and Rude Will.
And where the worser is predominant,
Full soon the Canker Death eats up that Plant.   30

31   Benedicite!   *God bless you! (Here it is used as a mild ejaculation of surprise.)*

33   distemper'd Head   *a disturbed head; a mind not governing itself properly.*

37   unbruised   *untouched with the cares that "stuff" the brains of older men and keep them from sleep.*

38   couch   *lay down, repose.*

40   Distemp'rature   *mental or emotional disturbance resulting from the bodily humours' being out of "temper" (lacking their proper balance or combination).*

43   Rest   *peace, contentment (with wordplay on the sense implied by the Friar's reference to "Bed" in the preceding line).*

49   feasting with mine Enemy   *probably an allusion to such New Testament teachings as Jesus' admonition to love rather than hate one's enemies (Matthew 5:43–44).*

50   wounded   *a reference to the commonplace that one who has fallen in love has been pierced by Cupid's golden arrow.*

52   Holy Physic   *"Physic" was the term normally used for the doctor's healing powers (whence our word "physician"); as a spiritual doctor, the Friar is now being asked to "heal" Romeo and Juliet's "wounds" by marrying the lovers.*

54   steads   *stands well; supports or aids.*

ROMEO   Good morrow, Father.

FRIAR LAWRENCE   *Benedicite!*
What early Tongue so sweet saluteth me?
Young Son, it argues a distemper'd Head
So soon to bid good morrow to thy Bed.
Care keeps his Watch in every Old Man's Eye,   35
And where Care lodges, Sleep will never lie;
But where unbruised Youth with unstuff'd Brain
Doth couch his Limbs, there golden Sleep doth
    reign.
Therefore thy Earliness doth me assure
Thou art uprous'd with some Distemp'rature.   40
Or if not so, then here I hit it right:
Our Romeo hath not been in Bed tonight.

ROMEO   That last is true: the sweeter Rest was mine!

FRIAR LAWRENCE   God pardon Sin! Wast thou with
    Rosaline?

ROMEO   With Rosaline, my ghostly Father, no;   45
I have forgot that Name, and that Name's Woe.

FRIAR LAWRENCE   That's my good Son, but where
    hast thou been then?

ROMEO   I'll tell thee ere thou ask it me again:
I have been feasting with mine Enemy,
Where on a sudden one hath wounded me   50
That's by me wounded; both our Remedies
Within thy Help and Holy Physic lies.
I bear no Hatred, blessed Man: for lo,
My Intercession likewise steads my Foe!

55 homely *unadorned, plainspoken.*
   thy Drift *the direction (literally, the drive) of your discourse.*

56 Shrift *absolution, forgiveness of sins confessed.*

65 Change *This word often means "exchange" in Shakespeare, and that may well be one of the Friar's implications here, echoing Romeo's use of the word in line 62 and suggesting that Romeo has simply exchanged Rosaline for Juliet in his affections.*

69 Brine *salt water; here referring to Romeo's tears.*

72 season *both (a) to flavor, and (b) to preserve with salt, as in pickling.*

75 here upon thy Cheek *At this moment the Friar probably puts his finger on Romeo's cheek.*

FRIAR LAWRENCE   Be plain, good Son, and homely in
    thy Drift: 55
    Riddling Confession finds but riddling Shrift.
ROMEO   Then plainly know, my Heart's dear Love is
    set
    On the fair Daughter of rich Capulet;
    As mine on hers, so hers is set on mine,
    And all combin'd save what thou must combine   60
    By Holy Marriage. When and where and how
    We met, we woo'd, and made exchange of Vow
    I'll tell thee as we pass; but this I pray,
    That thou consent to marry us today.
FRIAR LAWRENCE   Holy Saint Francis! What a Change
    is here!   65
    Is Rosaline, that thou didst love so dear,
    So soon forsaken? Young Men's Love then lies
    Not truly in their Hearts but in their Eyes.
    Jesu Maria, what a deal of Brine
    Hast wash'd thy sallow Cheeks for Rosaline!   70
    How much Salt-water thrown away in waste
    To season Love, that of it doth not taste!
    The Sun not yet thy Sighs from Heaven clears;
    Thy old Groans ring yet in mine ancient Years;
    Lo here upon thy Cheek the Stain doth sit   75
    Of an old Tear that is not wash'd off yet.
    If e'er thou wast thy self, and these Woes
    thine,
    Thou and these Woes were all for Rosaline.

105

79   Sentence   Sententiae *were maxims, pithy sayings to be mem-
      orized and stored for use in dealing with life's crises. Here the
      Friar's "Sentence" derives from the theological premise that
      men were divinely ordained to provide spiritual guidance for
      what St. Peter called "weaker vessels" (1 Peter 3:7).*

86   Grace   *favor, gift.*

88   by rote   *by memory, by following a prescribed "route" in a
      mechanical way.*

90   In one respect   *for one reason, in view of one consideration
      (*respect *stems from Latin and literally means "look" or
      "see").*

91   happy   *lucky, fortunate.*

93   stand on   *require, insist on. The expression* stand on sudden
      Haste *contains a paradox, of which Romeo may be unaware,
      in the contradictory meanings of* stand *and* Haste. *The
      phrase echoes Sampson's "shall move me to stand" (I.i.12),
      and Shakespeare probably expected some members of his audi-
      ence to recognize in it a variation on the Latin motto* festina
      lente *("make haste slowly"). The Friar's next line is another
      variation on the same theme.*

94   Wisely and slow   *Whether the Friar is heeding his own coun-
      sel at this moment is a question the audience may well be
      expected to ask.*

And art thou chang'd? Pronounce this Sentence
    then:
Women may fall when there's no Strength in Men.   80
ROMEO   Thou chid'st me oft for loving Rosaline.
FRIAR LAWRENCE   For doting, not for loving, Pupil
    mine!
ROMEO   And bad'st me bury Love.
FRIAR LAWRENCE   Not in a Grave
    To lay one in, another out to have.
ROMEO   I pray thee chide me not; her I love now   85
    Doth Grace for Grace and Love for Love allow.
    The other did not so.
FRIAR LAWRENCE   O she knew well:
    Thy Love did read by rote that could not spell!
    But come, young Waverer, come go with me.
    In one respect I'll thy Assistant be: 90
    For this Alliance may so happy prove,
    To turn your Households' Rancor to pure Love.
ROMEO   O let us hence: I stand on sudden Haste.
FRIAR LAWRENCE   Wisely and slow: they stumble that
    run fast.   *Exeunt.*

II.iv *The setting is a hot street at midday.*

4 pale *probably Mercutio's way of parodying the Petrarchan lover's insistence that his Lady is a goddess with pure white skin. Characteristically, Mercutio insists on referring to the object of Romeo's worship as a common "Wench."*

10–13 answer *Benvolio's first use of the word carries the implication that Romeo will accept the challenge and duel with Tybalt. Mercutio's reply allows only that Romeo will send back another letter in return. As the scene develops, we see that Mercutio's words prove prophetic, though for reasons of which he is unaware.*

18–19 blind Bow-Boy's Butt-shaft *a dismissive reference to Cupid and his arrow. The* butt *was the target, and in its center was a* pin *(line 17) or wooden peg. A butt-shaft, then, was an arrow aimed at the pin in the center of a target.*

21 Prince of Cats *Tybalt (spelled variously) was the name of the Prince of Cats in* Reynard the Fox, *a popular fable.*

21–22 he's . . . Compliments *He complies with all the rules of etiquette in the use of the rapier.*

Scene 4

Enter Benvolio and Mercutio.

MERCUTIO Where the devil should this Romeo be?
Came he not home tonight?

BENVOLIO Not to his Father's; I spoke with his Man.

MERCUTIO Why, that same pale, hard-hearted Wench,
that Rosaline, torments him so, that he will   5
sure run mad.

BENVOLIO Tybalt, the Kinsman to old Capulet, hath
sent a Letter to his Father's House.

MERCUTIO A Challenge, on my Life.

BENVOLIO Romeo will answer it.   10

MERCUTIO Any Man that can write may answer a
Letter.

BENVOLIO Nay, he will answer the Letter's Master,
how he dares, being dared.

MERCUTIO Alas, poor Romeo: he is already Dead,   15
stabb'd with a white Wench's black Eye, run
through the Ear with a Love Song, the very pin
of his Heart cleft with the blind Bow-Boy's
Butt-shaft. And is he a Man to encounter Tybalt?

BENVOLIO Why, what is Tybalt?   20

MERCUTIO More than Prince of Cats. O he's the

23   **Pricksong** *Mercutio refers here to printed music, which one followed with strict adherence to the notes (or "pricks") on the page. He also alludes to another meaning of "pricksong" as the descant or counterpoint augmenting a "plainsong" or simple melody. In addition, he plays on at least two other meanings of the word* prick*: (a) a verb, to puncture, and (b) a noun referring to the male member.*

24   **Minim Rests** *pauses equal to the shortest notes in music.*

27   **House** *probably a reference to a "school" of fencing.*

28   **Cause** *reason for defending one's honor.*
        Passado *forward thrust or "pass" with the sword, as distinguished from the "Punto Reverso" (lines 28–29) or backhanded thrust.*

29   **Hay!** *"Thou hast it!" (from Italian* hai*), marking a hit.*

43   **fishified** *a coinage alluding to Romeo's loss of his "Roe" (here, the sperm of a male herring). Mercutio assumes that when Romeo gave him and Benvolio "the Slip" (line 54) the previous night, he found a way to release his sexual tension.*

44   **flow'd in** *Mercutio continues the fish and water imagery, but he now relates it to "Numbers," or the syllable counts used in Renaissance metrical analyses of poetry. By "flow'd in" he probably also means the expression of passion, both poetic and erotic.*

46–48 **Dido . . . Harlots** *Mercutio reduces each heroine to a form of lowborn wench: a dowdy, a gipsy, a hilding, and a harlot.*

courageous Captain of Compliments. He fights as
you sing Pricksong: keeps Time, Distance, and
Proportion. He rests his Minim Rests: one, two,
and the third in your Bosom. The very Butcher of   25
a Silk Button: a Duelist, Duelist. A Gentleman
of the very First House, of the First and Second
Cause. Ah the Immortal Passado, the Punto
Reverso, the Hay!

BENVOLIO   The what?   30

MERCUTIO   The Pox of such antique, lisping,
affecting Fantasticos! These new Tuners of
Accent! "By Jesu, a very good Blade, a very tall
Man, a very good Whore!" Why, is not this a
lamentable thing, Grandsir, that we should be   35
thus afflicted with these strange Flies? These
Fashion-mongers? These Pardon-me's, who stand so
much on the new Form that they cannot sit at
ease on the old Bench? O their Bones, their
Bones!   40

Enter Romeo.

BENVOLIO   Here comes Romeo; here comes Romeo.

MERCUTIO   Without his Roe, like a dried Herring: O
Flesh, Flesh, how art thou fishified! Now is he
for the Numbers that Petrarch flow'd in. Laura,
to his Lady, was a Kitchen Wench (marry, she had   45
a better Love to be-rime her!), Dido a Dowdy,

111

50   French Slop   *This term often referred to a pair of baggy pants, and thus probably had a meaning similar to "baggage" (whore). But* slop *also meant "dung," and may have been used to refer to semen as well.*

51   Counterfeit   *If the first syllable of* Counterfeit *is here meant to allude to the female genitalia, the word as a whole probably refers to that which "fits" such a receptacle or "Case" (line 57).*

54   Slip   *A slip was a counterfeit coin, but it was also a term for the male member and for the fluid by which it was said to "conceive" (line 55).*

58   strain   *both (a) stretch, and (b) constrain (force, compel). Romeo and Mercutio are joking about the kind of "curtsy" a man performs when his "Business" is "great."*

72–73   O single-sol'd Jest . . . Singleness!   *This jest seems to be based on the fact that, among their other implications, both* sole *and* single *mean "standing alone." Mercutio and Romeo are probably thinking of the upright figure of the number 1. And in the word "Sole" (line 70, where its primary meaning has to do with a "Pump," or light slip-on shoe) they are probably also alluding once more to a type of fish and its roe.*

112

Cleopatra a Gipsy, Helen and Hero Hildings and
Harlots, Thisbe a gray Eye or so but not to the
purpose. —Signior Romeo, *bonjour!* There's a
French Salutation to your French Slop. You gave   50
us the Counterfeit fairly last night.

ROMEO   Good morrow to you both. What Counterfeit
did I give you?

MERCUTIO   The Slip, Sir; the Slip. Can you not
conceive?   55

ROMEO   Pardon, good Mercutio, my Business was
great, and in such a Case as mine a Man may
strain Courtesy.

MERCUTIO   That's as much as to say, such a Case as
yours constrains a Man to bow in the Hams.   60

ROMEO   Meaning to Cur'sy.

MERCUTIO   Thou hast most kindly hit it.

ROMEO   A most courteous Exposition.

MERCUTIO   Nay, I am the very Pink of Courtesy.

ROMEO   Pink for Flower.   65

MERCUTIO   Right.

ROMEO   Why then is my Pump well-flower'd.

MERCUTIO   Sure Wit! Follow me this Jest now till
thou hast worn out thy Pump, that when the
single Sole of it is worn, the Jest may remain,   70
after the wearing, solely singular.

ROMEO   O single-sol'd Jest: solely singular for the
Singleness!

74–75   **my Wits faints**   *Mercutio is saying that his "Wits" cannot "stand up" to Romeo's.*

76   **Swits and Spurs**   *Romeo pretends that he and Mercutio are in a horse race;* **swits** *are "switches," and Romeo's meaning is "keep it up."*

77   **cry "A Match!"**   *declare a victory.*

78   **Wild-Goose Chase**   *a hunting game; here a hunt for pleasure.*

81   **for the Goose**   *to chase a loose woman willing to be caught.*

84   **bite thee by the Ear**   *a phrase usually associated with the friendly nuzzling one animal gives to another.*

85   **good Goose**   *simpleton, perhaps with the suggestion that it takes a goose (that is, a wanton) to chase one.*

90   **Cheverel**   *kid leather, known for its ability to stretch, in this case from 1 inch to 45 (an ell). Mercutio uses the term to continue the innuendo on that which is expandable or stretchable (as in "my Business was great," lines 56–57, and "strain Courtesy," line 58).*

98–   **driveling Love . . . Hole**   *Love is depicted here as a drool-*
100   *ing idiot (a "Natural") sporting a long stick with a "Bauble" (an inflated bladder) dangling from its end. Court jesters were also called "naturals," and their baubles were topped with coxcombs. Mercutio's image reduces "Love" to a drooling personification of idiotic lust.*

MERCUTIO   Come between us, good Benvolio: my Wits
   faints. 75

ROMEO   Swits and Spurs, Swits and Spurs, or I'll
   cry "A Match!"

MERCUTIO   Nay, if our Wits run the Wild-Goose Chase,
   I am done: for thou hast more of the Wild-Goose
   in one of thy Wits than, I am sure, I have in my 80
   whole five. Was I with you there for the Goose?

ROMEO   Thou wast never with me for anything when
   thou wast not there for the Goose.

MERCUTIO   I will bite thee by the Ear for that Jest.

ROMEO   Nay, good Goose, bite not. 85

MERCUTIO   Thy Wit is a very bitter Sweeting; it is
   a most sharp Sauce.

ROMEO   And is it not then well serv'd in to a sweet
   Goose?

MERCUTIO   O here's a Wit of Cheverel, that 90
   stretches from an inch narrow to an ell broad!

ROMEO   Ay, stretch it out for that word "Broad,"
   which, added to the Goose, proves thee far and
   wide a Broad Goose.

MERCUTIO   Why, is not this better now than groaning 95
   for Love? Now art thou Sociable; now art thou
   Romeo; now art thou what thou art, by Art as
   well as by Nature. For this driveling Love is
   like a great Natural, that runs lolling up and
   down to hide his Bauble in a Hole. 100

BENVOLIO   Stop there, stop there!

115

102   **Tale**   *a pun on* **tail,** *yet another word that could be applied to the male member.*

103   **against the Hair**   *normally an expression for the friction caused by rubbing an animal or a person the wrong way. Here Mercutio uses* **against** *in a different sense, and he probably also intends a pun on* **Hair** *similar to that in line 140.*

107   **occupy the Argument**   *dwell on the theme, but with "Argument" here used to refer to a genital "case."*

109   **goodly Gear**   *a reference to the elaborate get-up of the Nurse, whose efforts to dress smartly subject her to ridicule.*

110   **A Sail**   *Some of the hats women wore actually resembled sailing ships.*

118   **God ye good-den**   *God give you good e'en (evening). Mercutio is reminding the Nurse that it is no longer morning.*

120–   **bawdy Hand . . . Prick of Noon**   *For Mercutio, even the*
21   *clock is engaged in wanton behavior. Here the "Prick" is the mark engraved on the clockface to indicate the hour of twelve.*

124   **himself to mar**   *In view of Mercutio's preceding line, Romeo is probably alluding to the view that sexual license is a form of self-abuse.*

126   **quoth 'a**   *said he.*

MERCUTIO   Thou desirest me to stop in my Tale
     against the Hair?
ROMEO   Thou wouldst else have made thy Tale large.
MERCUTIO   O thou art deceiv'd: I would have made it   105
     short, for I was come to the whole depth of my
     Tale, and meant indeed to occupy the Argument no
     longer.

Enter Nurse and her man Peter.

ROMEO   Here's goodly Gear.
MERCUTIO   A Sail, a Sail!   110
BENVOLIO   Two, two: a Shirt and a Smock.
NURSE   Peter!
PETER   Anon.
NURSE   My Fan, Peter!
MERCUTIO   Good Peter, to hide her Face: for her   115
     Fan's the fairer Face.
NURSE   God ye good morrow, Gentlemen.
MERCUTIO   God ye good-den, fair Gentlewoman.
NURSE   Is it good-den?
MERCUTIO   'Tis no less, I tell ye, for the bawdy   120
     Hand of the Dial is now upon the Prick of Noon.
NURSE   Out upon you! What a Man are you?
ROMEO   One, Gentlewoman, that God hath made for
     himself to mar.
NURSE   By my troth, it is well said: "for himself   125
     to mar," quoth 'a. Gentlemen, can any of you

117

131   **for fault of a Worse**   *Romeo is facetiously saying that owing to the "fault" (error or misstep) of a worse man of that name (that is, Romeo's father), he is "the Youngest of that Name."* **Fault** *was also a term for female genitalia, by analogy with another sense of* **fault** *(crack, as in the modern use of the term for a geological fault). As such, it reinforced the notion that a woman's sexual organs involved a deficiency (literally, no "thing") and related to the frequent bawdy wordplay on "nothing," "naught," and similar words.*

135   **some Confidence**   *some words in private.*

137   **endite**   *probably intended as a mock malapropism (for "invite") in imitation of the pretentious manner in which the Nurse says she wants to speak with Romeo privately.*

138   **So ho!**   *Mercutio evidently says this in such a way as to convey the message "Eureka!" Hence Romeo's reply in the next line.*

140   **Hare**   *The reference is to a rabbit discovered in a hunt, but Mercutio also picks up on "hair" as a pun on "whore."*

141   **Lenten Pie**   *a reference to a pie baked before the beginning of Lent (during which time meat was forbidden) and kept despite its becoming stale and "hoar" (white with mold). In the bawdy song that follows, Mercutio puns on "hoar" and "whore." A "Score" (line 147) is a bill.*

tell me where I may find the young Romeo?

ROMEO   I can tell you, but young Romeo will be
older when you have found him than he was when
you sought him. I am the Youngest of that Name,   130
for fault of a Worse.

NURSE   You say well.

MERCUTIO   Yea, is the Worst well? Very well took,
i'faith, wisely, wisely.

NURSE   If you be he, Sir, I desire some Confidence   135
with you.

BENVOLIO   She will endite him to some Supper.

MERCUTIO   A Bawd, a Bawd, a Bawd! So ho!

ROMEO   What hast thou found?

MERCUTIO   No Hare, Sir, unless a Hare, Sir, in a   140
Lenten Pie, that is something Stale and Hoar ere
it be spent.   *He walks by them and sings.*

> An old Hare hoar,
> And an old Hare hoar
> Is very good Meat in Lent;   145
> But a Hare that is hoar
> Is too much for a Score,
> When it hoars ere it be spent.

Romeo, will you come to your Father's? We'll to
Dinner thither.   150

ROMEO   I will follow you.

MERCUTIO   Farewell, ancient Lady; farewell [*singing*]
"Lady, Lady, Lady!"   *Exeunt Mercutio and Benvolio.*

NURSE   I pray you, Sir, what saucy Merchant was

155　Ropery　*indecent jesting (from "rope," a term for the male member).*

158　stand to　*make good on, defend. The sexual sense of the phrase is also pertinent. Subsequent phrases such as "against me" and "take him down" continue the wordplay inadvertently.*

159　And 'a　*if he.*

163　Flirt-gills　*flirting Jills (loose women), here used in connection with "Jacks" (line 161).*
　　　Skain's-mates　*usually explained as a reference to women who were companions to cutthroats (a skain was an Irish knife), but here more likely to refer to women who encouraged men to "lay Knife aboard" (line 211) them sexually.*

166　use you at his Pleasure　*Peter takes the Nurse to mean "use me sexually." The "Weapon" he refers to in the next line, however, is probably his sword.*

176　lead her in a Fool's Paradise　*deceive her into thinking you intend marriage when all you really want is to use her at your pleasure.*

this that was so full of his Ropery?   155

ROMEO   A Gentleman, Nurse, that loves to hear
himself talk, and will speak more in a Minute
than he will stand to in a Month.

NURSE   And 'a speak anything against me, I'll take
him down, and 'a were lustier than he is, and   160
twenty such Jacks! And if I cannot, I'll find
those that shall. Scurvy Knave! I am none of his
Flirt-gills; I am none of his Skain's-mates!
—And thou must stand by too, and suffer every
Knave to use me at his Pleasure!   165

PETER   I saw no Man use you at his Pleasure: if I
had, my Weapon should quickly have been out, I
warrant you. I draw as soon as another Man if I
see occasion in a good Quarrel and the Law on
my side.   170

NURSE   Now, afore God, I am so vex'd that every
part about me quivers! Scurvy Knave! —Pray you,
Sir, a Word. And as I told you, my young Lady
bid me inquire you out. What she bid me say I
will keep to my self; but first let me tell ye,   175
if ye should lead her in a Fool's Paradise, as
they say, it were a very gross kind of Behavior,
as they say. For the Gentlewoman is young; and
therefore if you should deal double with her,
truly it were an ill thing to be off'red to any   180
Gentlewoman, and very weak Dealing.

ROMEO   Nurse, commend me to thy Lady and Mistress,

183–85   I protest . . . Woman!   *The Nurse probably confuses "protest" (swear) with "profess" and assumes that this high-sounding language is Romeo's assurance that his intentions are honorable.*

187   mark me   *hear me out.*

192   shriv'd   *absolved.* Shriv'd *derives from* shrift, *confession.*

194   Go to   *roughly equivalent to our "go on" or "come on"; an indication to say no more and put up no further protest.*

198   Cords . . . tackl'd Stair   *rope ladder.*

199   Topgallant   *the platform atop a ship's mast, attainable by a rope ladder.*

200   Convoy   *means of conveyance.*

201   quit   *requite, reward.*

205   secret   *trustworthy to keep a secret.*

206   "Two . . . away"   *The point of the proverb is that only one may keep a secret.*

I protest unto thee—

NURSE   Good Heart, and i'faith I will tell her as
much: Lord, Lord, she will be a joyful Woman!   185

ROMEO   What wilt thou tell her, Nurse? Thou dost
not mark me.

NURSE   I will tell her, Sir, that you do protest,
which, as I take it, is a Gentleman-like Offer.

ROMEO   Bid her devise some means to come to Shrift
This afternoon.   190
And there she shall at Friar Lawrence' Cell
Be shriv'd and married. Here is for thy Pains.

NURSE   No, truly, Sir, not a Penny.

ROMEO   Go to, I say you shall.   *She accepts the money.*

NURSE   This afternoon, Sir; well, she shall be
there.   195

ROMEO   And stay, good Nurse, behind the Abbey Wall:
Within this hour my Man shall be with thee
And bring thee Cords made like a tackl'd Stair,
Which to the high Topgallant of my Joy
Must be my Convoy in the secret Night.   200
Farewell; be trusty, and I'll quit thy Pains.
Farewell; commend me to thy Mistress.

NURSE   Now God in Heaven bless thee! Hark you Sir—

ROMEO   What say'st thou, my dear Nurse?

NURSE   Is your Man secret? Did you ne'er hear say   205
"Two may keep Counsel, putting one away"?

ROMEO   I warrant thee, my Man's as true as Steel.

NURSE   Well, Sir, my Mistress is the sweetest Lady—

211   would fain lay Knife aboard   *would like to win her hand. This image picks up on Romeo's "true as Steel" (line 207) as well as on the nautical imagery introduced earlier, with Paris here presented as one who would mount an attack at sea.*

212   as lieve   *as lief, as willingly.*

215   Clout   *cloth. The phrase* as pale as any Clout *is roughly equivalent to "as white as a sheet."*

216   'versal World   *universal world (equivalent to "whole wide world").*
       Rosemary   *an herb thought to foster good memory, and hence proverbial as a symbol of remembrance.*

217   a Letter   *the same letter.*

219   Dog's Name   *The Nurse is alluding to the commonplace notion that the sound of the letter* R *resembles a dog's growl. She thus thinks that Romeo is simply a "Mocker" (making fun of her).*

221   prettiest sententious of it   *The Nurse is trying to say that Juliet has been composing "sentences" (her term for them seems to be a garbled version of the Latin word* sententiae) *or maxims linking "Romeo" and "Rosemary."*

227   apace   *quickly, at a fast pace.*

Lord, Lord, when 'twas a little prating thing!—
O there is a Nobleman in Town, one Paris, that   210
would fain lay Knife aboard; but she, good soul,
had as lieve see a Toad, a very Toad, as see him.
I anger her sometimes, and tell her that Paris
is the properer Man; but I'll warrant you, when
I say so, she looks as pale as any Clout in the   215
'versal World. Doth not "Rosemary" and "Romeo"
begin both with a Letter?

ROMEO   Ay, Nurse, what of that? Both with an *R*.

NURSE   Ah, Mocker! That's the Dog's Name! *R* is for
the—no, I know it begins with some other Letter.   220
And she hath the prettiest sententious of it, of
you and Rosemary, that it would do you good to
hear it!

ROMEO   Commend me to thy Lady.

NURSE   Ay, a thousand times! —Peter!   *Exit Romeo.*   225

PETER   Anon.

NURSE   Before, and apace!   *Exeunt.*

II.v   *The setting is Juliet's bedroom, where Juliet waits impatiently for the Nurse's return.*

1   strook   *struck.*

4   lame   *hobbled. (Juliet is presumably thinking about the Nurse's sore back, about which we are soon to hear a great deal.)*

6   low'ring   *lowering (louring), frowning, lurking threateningly (until their shadows are driven back by the ascending sunbeams).*

7   nimble-pinion'd   *nimble-winged (a pinion is the end joint of a bird's wing).*
        draw Love   *represent Love in drawings and other artistic renderings.*

14   bandy   *toss or bounce (as a tennis ball).*

16   feign as   *pretend as if.*

Scene 5

Enter Juliet.

JULIET The Clock strook nine when I did send the
     Nurse;
     In half an hour she promis'd to return.
     Perchance she cannot meet him. That's not so!
     O she is lame. Love's Heralds should be Thoughts,
     Which ten times faster glides than the Sun's
     Beams   5
     Driving back Shadows over low'ring Hills.
     Therefore do nimble-pinion'd Doves draw Love,
     And therefore hath the wind-swift Cupid Wings.
     Now is the Sun upon the highmost Hill
     Of this Day's Journey, and from nine till twelve   10
     Is three long Hours. Yet she is not come!
     Had she Affections and warm youthful Blood,
     She would be as swift in motion as a Ball:
     My Words would bandy her to my sweet Love
     And his to me.   15
     But Old Folks, many feign as they were dead:
     Unwieldy, slow; heavy and pale as Lead.

Enter Nurse and Peter.

---

22   News   *This word was often treated as plural in Shakespeare's time; it was understood to mean "new things."*

25   give me leave   *allow me to rest.*

26   Jaunce   *a jolting jaunt (probably colloquial in Shakespeare's time).*

36   stay the Circumstance   *wait till later to hear the details.*

38   simple   *foolish, naive.*

40–45 Though . . . Lamb.   *Despite her best efforts, the Nurse cannot maintain her pretense that Romeo is a bad choice for Juliet.*

O God, she comes! —O honey Nurse, what News?
Hast thou met with him? Send thy Man away.

NURSE Peter, stay at the Gate.   *Exit Peter.*   20

JULIET Now, good sweet Nurse—O Lord, why look'st
    thou sad?
    Though News be sad, yet tell them merrily.
    If good, thou sham'st the Music of sweet News
    By playing it to me with so sour a Face.

NURSE I am a-weary; give me leave a while.   25
    Fie, how my Bones ache! What a Jaunce have I!

JULIET I would thou hadst my Bones and I thy News!
    Nay come, I pray thee, speak! Good, good Nurse,
    speak!

NURSE Jesu, what Haste! Cannot you stay a while?
    Do you not see that I am out of Breath?   30

JULIET How art thou out of Breath when thou hast
    Breath
    To say to me that thou art out of Breath?
    Th' Excuse that thou dost make in this Delay
    Is longer than the Tale thou dost Excuse.
    Is thy News good or bad? Answer to that: 35
    Say either, and I'll stay the Circumstance.
    Let me be satisfied: is't good or bad?

NURSE Well, you have made a simple Choice: you
    know not how to choose a Man. Romeo, no not he!
    Though his Face be better than any Man's; yet   40
    his Leg excels all Men's; and for a Hand and a
    Foot and a Body, though they be not to be talk'd

45   **Go . . . serve God.** *The Nurse is implying that Juliet should forget about Romeo and serve God patiently until a better man is provided.*

51   **a' t'other side** *on the other side.*

52   **Beshrew** *curse.*

55   **Sweet . . . Love?** *Although this line has the requisite number of syllables (ten) for iambic pentameter, it is in fact an emphatic breach of the metrical norm, with long-voweled spondees (two equally stressed syllables) in the first two feet and a trochee (a stressed syllable followed by an unstressed) in the third, leaving iambs (feet comprised of an unstressed syllable followed by a stressed) in the fourth and fifth feet only: "Sweét, sweét, / sweèt Nurśe, / téll mĕ, / whăt sáys / mў Lóve?" In this play the verse is usually so regular that departures from the established pattern have a great deal of expressive emphasis.*

63   **Marry come up, I trow!** *an expression of disapproval, roughly similar to "Come on now!"* **I trow** *means "I declare."*

64   **Poultice** *a hot, moist paste, usually of mustard, to be applied to an aching muscle or an inflammation.*

66   **Coil** *turmoil.*

on, yet they are past compare. He is not the
flower of Courtesy, but I'll warrant him as
gentle as a Lamb. Go thy ways, Wench; serve God.   45
What, have you din'd at home?

JULIET   No, no. But all this did I know before.
What says he of our Marriage? What of that?

NURSE   Lord, how my Head aches! What a Head have I!
It beats as it would fall in twenty pieces!   50
My Back: *Juliet rubs Nurse's Back for her.*
a' t'other side! Ah, my Back, my Back!
Beshrew your Heart for sending me about
To catch my death with jauncing up and down!

JULIET   I'faith, I'm sorry that thou art not well.
Sweet, sweet, sweet Nurse, tell me, what says my
   Love?   55

NURSE   Your Love says, like an honest Gentleman,
An' a courteous, and a kind, and a handsome,
And I warrant a virtuous— Where is your
   Mother?

JULIET   Where is my Mother? Why, she is within.
Where should she be? How oddly thou repliest: 60
"Your Love says, like an honest Gentleman,
'Where is your Mother?' "

NURSE   O God's Lady, dear!
Are you so hot? Marry come up, I trow!
Is this the Poultice for my aching Bones?
Henceforward do your Messages your self!   65

JULIET   Here's such a Coil! Come, what says Romeo?

131

67   Shrift   *confession.*

69   hie   *hasten.*

72   in Scarlet straight   *scarlet immediately.*

75   Bird's Nest   *This homespun metaphor is the Nurse's variation on Romeo's "high Topgallant" (II.iv.199), and it also provides an amusing echo of the falcon imagery employed by Romeo and Juliet at the conclusion of the Balcony Scene (II.ii.159–83).*

76   Drudge   *slavish servant, one whose work is burdensome drudgery.*

77   bear the Burthen   *This phrase recalls I.iv.23 and I.iv.92–94.*

II.vi   *This scene is set in Friar Lawrence's cell.*

2   After-hours   *the future.*

4   countervail   *prevail against, undo.*

NURSE   Have you got leave to go to Shrift today?

JULIET   I have.

NURSE   Then hie you hence to Friar Lawrence' Cell:
    There stays a Husband to make you a Wife.   70
    Now comes the wanton Blood up in your Cheeks!
    They'll be in Scarlet straight at any News.
    Hie you to Church; I must another way
    To fetch a Ladder by the which your Love
    Must climb a Bird's Nest soon when it is dark.   75
    I am the Drudge, and toil in your Delight;
    But you shall bear the Burthen soon at Night.
    Go! I'll to Dinner; hie you to the Cell.

JULIET   Hie to High Fortune! Honest Nurse, farewell.

Exeunt.

Scene 6

Enter Friar Lawrence and Romeo.

FRIAR LAWRENCE   So smile the Heav'ns upon this Holy
    Act,
    That After-hours with Sorrow chide us not.

ROMEO   Amen, amen. But come what Sorrow can,
    It cannot countervail th' exchange of Joy

6   close   *join, seal in marriage.*

7   Love-devouring Death   *This image foreshadows V.iii.45–48.*

13   confounds   *overwhelms, destroys. The Friar's point in this line is that too much of a good thing is cloying and self-defeating.*

15   Too Swift . . . Too Slow.   *an allusion to Aesop's fable of the Hare and the Tortoise, and another variation on "Make haste slowly." (See II.iii.93–94.)*

16–17   so light a Foot . . . everlasting Flint!   *The Friar's initial observation of Juliet suggests that she enters with a delicate footstep incapable of leaving an impression on even the softest surface. His reference to "Vanity" (symbolic not only of lightness but also of that which is impermanent) would lead us to expect a spiritual appraisal from a man of his profession; however, the Friar's comments about Juliet are more poetic than moralistic. These lines (down to line 20) may be intended for delivery as an aside.*

18   Gossamours   *gossamers, delicate cobwebs. The spelling in the Quarto and Folio texts, retained here, suggests a purposeful weaving together of* gossamers *and* amour *(love).*

26   blazon   *display, as on a coat of arms.*

27   neighbor   *nearby.*

That one short Minute gives me in her Sight. 5
Do thou but close our Hands with holy Words,
Then Love-devouring Death do what he dare.
It is enough I may but call her mine.
FRIAR LAWRENCE   These violent Delights have violent
    Ends,
And in their Triumph die, like Fire and Powder, 10
Which as they kiss consume. The sweetest Honey
Is loathsome in his own Deliciousness
And in the Taste confounds the Appetite.
Therefore love moderately: long Love doth so.
Too Swift arrives as tardy as Too Slow. 15

Enter Juliet.

Here comes the Lady. O so light a Foot
Will ne'er wear out the everlasting Flint!
A Lover may bestride the Gossamours
That idles in the wanton Summer Air
And yet not fall, so light is Vanity. 20
JULIET   Good even to my ghostly Confessor.
FRIAR LAWRENCE   Romeo shall thank thee, Daughter,
    for us both.
JULIET   As much to him, else is his Thanks too much.
ROMEO   Ah Juliet, if the Measure of thy Joy
    Be heap'd like mine, and that thy Skill be more 25
    To blazon it, then sweeten with thy Breath
    This neighbor Air, and let rich Music's Tongue

28   Unfold   *disclose.*

29   dear   *precious, invaluable.*

30   Conceit   *understanding, the ability to conceive or think.*

32   count   *measure.*

34   sum up Sum   *sum up the total.*

36   by your leaves   *with your consent.*
      stay alone   *sleep together.*

37   incorp'rate two in one   *join two into one body, an image
      deriving ultimately from Genesis 2:24, where a husband and
      his wife are described as "one flesh."*

Unfold th' imagin'd Happiness that both
Receive in either by this dear Encounter.

JULIET   Conceit, more rich in Matter than in Words,   30
Brags of his Substance, not of Ornament;
They are but Beggars that can count their Worth,
But my true Love is grown to such Excess
I cannot sum up Sum of half my Wealth.

FRIAR LAWRENCE   Come, come with me, and we will
make short Work: 35
For by your leaves you shall not stay alone
Till Holy Church incorp'rate two in one.   *Exeunt.*

III.i   *The setting is a street in Verona.*

1   retire   *withdraw, go inside.*

2   Capels   *an abbreviated version of* Capulets, *probably used here for metrical purposes.*

4   Hot Days   *Elizabethans believed that warmer climates fostered more passionate, violent forms of behavior.*

6–7   claps me   *slaps down for me. The "me" construction in Shakespeare is frequently used to convey familiarity or to signal that the speaker is imitating the manner of the person being "presented" in a description.*

8–9   by the operation . . . Cup   *by the time the second cup has had its intoxicating effects.*

9   Drawer   *waiter.*

Act Three

Scene 1

Enter Mercutio, Benvolio, and Men.

BENVOLIO   I pray thee, good Mercutio, let's retire.
 The Day is hot, the Capels are abroad,
 And if we meet we shall not 'scape a Brawl:
 For now these Hot Days is the Mad Blood stirring.
MERCUTIO   Thou art like one of these Fellows that,   5
 when he enters the confines of a Tavern, claps
 me his Sword upon the Table and says "God send
 me no need of thee," and by the operation of the
 second Cup draws him on the Drawer, when indeed
 there is no need.   10
BENVOLIO   Am I like such a Fellow?
MERCUTIO   Come, come, thou art as hot a Jack in thy

13–14   moved to be Moody   *aroused to anger.*

14   moody to be Moved   *disposed to be aroused.*

16   and   *if*
two such   *Mercutio says "two" because he is pretending to misunderstand Benvolio's question "And what to?" in the previous line.*

22   Hazel   *Mercutio's point is that Benvolio is so "moody" that, to him, a man who cracks nuts is offending anyone whose eye color shares the same name as one kind of nut.*

24   Meat   *food.*

25   addle   *muddled, addled; with a play on the expression "addle-egg" or rotten egg.*

30   Doublet   *a close-fitting jacket worn by a gentleman of the period.*

31   Riband   *ribbon, in this case shoe laces or bands.*

34   Fee Simple   *total ownership. A fee simple was a title to an estate in which no conditions or restrictions applied to the inheritance.*

35   for an Hour and a Quarter   *for a fraction of its value, equivalent to the ratio between an hour and a quarter and a full lifetime.*

36   O simple!   *roughly equivalent to "O baloney!"*

Mood as any in Italy; and as soon moved to be
Moody, and as soon moody to be Moved.

BENVOLIO   And what to?   15

MERCUTIO   Nay, and there were two such we should
have none shortly: for one would kill the other.
Thou, why thou wilt quarrel with a Man that hath
a Hair more or a Hair less in his Beard than
thou hast. Thou wilt quarrel with a Man for   20
cracking Nuts, having no other reason but
because thou hast Hazel Eyes; what Eye but such
an Eye would spy out such a Quarrel? Thy Head is
as full of Quarrels as an Egg is full of Meat,
and yet thy Head hath been beaten as addle as an   25
Egg for Quarreling. Thou hast quarrel'd with a
man for Coughing in the Street, because he hath
waken'd thy Dog that hath lain asleep in the Sun.
Didst thou not fall out with a Tailor for
wearing his new Doublet before Easter? With   30
another for tying his new Shoes with old Riband?
And yet thou wilt tutor me from Quarreling!

BENVOLIO   And I were so apt to quarrel as thou art,
any Man should buy the Fee Simple of my Life
for an Hour and a Quarter.   35

MERCUTIO   The Fee Simple: O simple!

Enter Tybalt, Petruchio, and Others.

BENVOLIO   By my Head, here comes the Capulets.

141

48   Consort? *Mercutio takes offense at Tybalt's use of a verb ("consortest") that tends to be derogatory, either suggesting association with lowlife ne'er-do-wells or, as here, evoking the image of traveling musicians, the minstrels who depended for their livelihood on the patronage of courts or of privileged families like the Capulets. In either case, Mercutio assumes that Tybalt intends to insult Romeo and his friends by suggesting that their social status is lower than that of gentlemen such as himself. A* consort *was a group of minstrels.*

51   Fiddlestick *Mercutio gestures to his sword while referring to the bow of a violin or fiddle.*

52   'Zounds! *a contraction of "God's wounds."*

55   reason coldly *consider calmly. Benvolio shifts the dialogue to blank verse, itself an indication of his desire to restore a degree of measured control to a situation that is rapidly getting overheated.*

MERCUTIO By my Heel, I care not.

TYBALT Follow me close, for I will speak to them.
   —Gentlemen, good-den; a Word with one of you.   40

MERCUTIO And but one Word with one of us? Couple
   it with something: make it a Word and a Blow.

TYBALT You shall find me apt enough to that, Sir,
   and you will give me Occasion.

MERCUTIO Could you not take some Occasion without   45
   giving?

TYBALT Mercutio, thou consortest with Romeo.

MERCUTIO Consort? What, dost thou make us
   Minstrels? And thou make Minstrels of us, look
   to hear nothing but Discords. Here's my   50
   Fiddlestick: here's that shall make you dance!
   'Zounds! Consort!

BENVOLIO We talk here in the Public Haunt of Men.
   Either withdraw unto some Private Place,
   Or reason coldly of your Grievances,   55
   Or else depart. Here all Eyes gaze on us.

MERCUTIO Men's Eyes were made to look, and let
   them gaze;
   I will not budge for no Man's Pleasure, I.

Enter Romeo.

TYBALT Well, peace be with you, Sir; here comes my
   Man.

60   your Liv'ry   *Mercutio responds as if Tybalt had just called Romeo his servant ("my Man," line 59). A servant wore the "Livery" or uniform of his master.*

61   to Field   *to the place appointed for a duel.*

64   Villain   *originally a serf or peasant (villein); by extension, any man whose behavior is unworthy of a gentleman.*

66   appertaining Rage   *the anger that would normally pertain to a gentleman's response to such a challenge.*

69   Boy   *deliberately spoken as an insult.*

72   devise   *figure out, appreciate.*

73   the Reason of my Love   *Romeo alone knows that he is now wed to Juliet, and that they will be "one flesh" as soon as the marriage is consummated.*

77   Alla stucatho   *Mercutio's rendering of* alla stoccata, *an Italian phrase from fencing manuals, describing what to do "at the thrust." Mercutio is appalled that Romeo is allowing a villain who "fights by the Book of Arithmetic" (line 109) to dishonor him.*

78   Ratcatcher   *the first of several allusions to Tybalt as the fabled King of Cats.*

82   dry-beat   *thrash.*

84   Pilcher   *a leather outer garment; here used to personify Tybalt's sword as a coward who must be extracted by the ears.*

144

MERCUTIO   But I'll be hang'd, Sir, if he wear your
        Liv'ry.   60
    Marry, go before to Field, he'll be your
        foll'wer:
    Your Worship in that sense may call him "Man."
TYBALT   Romeo, the Love I bear thee can afford
    No better Term than this: thou art a Villain!
ROMEO   Tybalt, the Reason that I have to love thee   65
    Doth much excuse the appertaining Rage
    To such a Greeting. Villain am I none:
    Therefore farewell, I see thou know'st me not.
TYBALT   Boy, this shall not excuse the Injuries
    That thou hast done me: therefore turn and draw!   70
ROMEO   I do protest I never injur'd thee,
    But love thee better than thou canst devise
    Till thou shalt know the Reason of my Love;
    And so, good Capulet, which Name I tender
    As dearly as mine own, be satisfied.   75
MERCUTIO   O calm, dishonorable, vile Submission:
    Alla stucatho carries it away!   *He draws.*
    —Tybalt, you Ratcatcher, will you walk?
TYBALT   What wouldst thou have with me?
MERCUTIO   Good King of Cats, nothing but one of   80
    your Nine Lives, that I mean to make bold withal,
    and as you shall use me hereafter, dry-beat the
    rest of the eight. Will you pluck your Sword out
    of his Pilcher by the Ears? Make haste, lest
    mine be about your Ears ere it be out!   85

145

---

88   Passado   *the word for "lunge" or "pass" in the Italian fencing books. Mercutio is deriding Tybalt's emphasis on precise technique.*

92   Bandying   *exchanging blows.*

S.D.   Tybalt flies.   *Tybalt flees.*

96   sped   *sent away; probably an ironic reference to "Godspeed" (farewell).*

98   a Scratch   *another reference to Tybalt as a cat.*

105   Grave Man   *Even in the throes of death, Mercutio engages in wordplay, here suggesting that his "gravity" will be that of the earth itself as he lies in his grave.*

105–6   pepper'd . . . for this World   *dealt a death blow.*

TYBALT   I am for you!   *He draws.*
ROMEO   Gentle Mercutio, put thy Rapier up!
MERCUTIO   Come, Sir, your Passado.   *They fight.*
ROMEO   Draw, Benvolio, beat down their Weapons!
    —Gentlemen, for Shame! Forbear this Outrage!   90
    Tybalt, Mercutio: the Prince expressly hath
    Forbid this Bandying in Verona Streets!
    Hold, Tybalt! Good Mercutio!
              Tybalt, under Romeo's arm, thrusts Mercutio in.
PETRUCHIO   Away, Tybalt!   *Tybalt flies.*
MERCUTIO   I am hurt. A Plague a' both Houses: I am   95
    sped. Is he gone and hath nothing?
BENVOLIO   What, art thou hurt?
MERCUTIO   Ay, ay, a Scratch, a Scratch. Marry, 'tis
    enough. Where is my Page? —Go, Villain, fetch a
    Surgeon!   *Exit Page.*   100
ROMEO   Courage, Man: the Hurt cannot be much!
MERCUTIO   No, 'tis not so deep as a Well, nor so
    wide as a Church Door, but 'tis enough, 'twill
    serve. Ask for me tomorrow, and you shall find
    me a Grave Man. I am pepper'd, I warrant, for   105
    this World. A Plague a' both your Houses!
    'Zounds, a Dog, a Rat, a Mouse, a Cat, to
    scratch a Man to death! A Braggart, a Rogue, a
    Villain, that fights by the Book of Arithmetic!
    Why the devil came you between us? I was hurt   110
    under your Arm!
ROMEO   I thought all for the best.

115   Worm's-meat   *a decomposing corpse being eaten by earth-worms.*

117   near Ally   *close relative.*

123   Temper   *When steel was "tempered" (by a combination of heating and rapid cooling), it was made harder; in lines 122–23 Romeo is saying that by exercising a different kind of "temper" (self-control, restraint in the face of Tybalt's challenge to his honor), he has allowed his love of Juliet to make "Valor's Steel" soft and "Effeminate" (weak). Whether or not this is a true appraisal of how he responded to Tybalt's remarks, it reflects the way Romeo evaluates his earlier behavior now that he has Mercutio's "Plague" ringing in his ears.*

125   aspir'd the Clouds   *risen to the Heavens.*

127   moe   *more. Shakespeare probably uses* moe *here to rhyme with* woe, *which occupies the same position metrically in the next line.*

131   Away to Heav'n   *It was characteristic of revengers in tragedies of the Renaissance to recognize that personal vengeance was expressly forbidden by both Church and State, in keeping with the teachings in Romans 12:17–13:6.*
      respective Lenity   *heedful mildness, leniency, deliberation.*

132   Conduct   *guide.*

MERCUTIO   Help me into some House, Benvolio, or I
    shall faint. A Plague a' both your Houses! They
    have made Worm's-meat of me. I have 't, and   115
    soundly; to your Houses.

Exeunt Mercutio and Benvolio.

ROMEO   This Gentleman, the Prince's near Ally,
    My very Friend, hath got this mortal Hurt
    In my behalf, my Reputation stain'd
    With Tybalt's slander: Tybalt, that an hour   120
    Hath been my Cousin. —O sweet Juliet,
    Thy Beauty hath made me Effeminate,
    And in my Temper soft'ned Valor's Steel.

Enter Benvolio.

BENVOLIO   O Romeo, Romeo, brave Mercutio's dead!
    That gallant Spirit hath aspir'd the Clouds,   125
    Which too untimely here did scorn the Earth.
ROMEO   This Day's black Fate on moe Days doth
        depend:
    This but begins the Woe others must end.

Enter Tybalt again.

BENVOLIO   Here comes the furious Tybalt back again.
ROMEO   Alive in Triumph, and Mercutio slain!   130
    Away to Heav'n, respective Lenity,
    And fire-ey'd Fury be my Conduct now!

149

139   This   *Romeo refers to his drawn sword as he speaks this word.*

142   amaz'd   *bewildered, as if lost in a maze.*
      doom thee death   *condemn you to death.*

144   Fortune's Fool   *victim of blind Fortune. At this moment Romeo feels that he is at the mercy of forces beyond his control. In Shakespeare's time, Fortune, Fate, and the Stars were all referred to as ways of accounting for aspects of life that seemed subject to something other than a person's free will. There was a widespread conviction that what seemed like chance frequently had a pattern. To understand those aspects of "Fortune" (chance) that seemed "fated" (patterned), many turned to astrology, a system that sought to discern how various configurations of the stars and planets influenced human life. Even orthodox Christians were generally inclined to give astrology its due. But most thinkers of the period assumed that, though the "stars" might affect the body and its passions, they could not determine the fate of one whose actions were governed by reason. To be a fool of Fortune, then, was ultimately to be a victim of one's own failure to use reason in such a way as to rise above the sway of the Stars.*
      stay   *wait. Benvolio's line suggests that Romeo is to be played here as a man momentarily rapt in reflection on the consequences of what he has just done.*

147   Up, Sir   *This line is directed to Tybalt, with the arresting Citizen watchman not yet realizing that he is dead.*

—Now Tybalt, take the "Villain!" back again
That late thou gav'st me: for Mercutio's Soul
Is but a little way above our Heads,   135
Staying for thine to keep him Company.
Either thou or I or both must go with him.

TYBALT Thou, wretched Boy, that didst consort him
 here,
Shalt with him hence!

ROMEO   This shall determine that!

         They fight. Tybalt falls.

BENVOLIO Romeo, away be gone: 140
The Citizens are up, and Tybalt slain!
Stand not amaz'd; the Prince will doom thee
 death
If thou art taken. Hence! Be gone away!

ROMEO O I am Fortune's Fool!

BENVOLIO   Why dost thou stay?

           Exit Romeo.

    Enter Citizens.

FIRST CITIZEN Which way ran he that kill'd
 Mercutio?   145
Tybalt, that Murderer! Which way ran he?

BENVOLIO There lies that Tybalt.

FIRST CITIZEN   Up, Sir; go with me.
I charge thee in the Prince's Name. Obey!

151

150   discover   *disclose.*

151   Manage   *course, direction. As a term normally used to convey a sense of order and control,* Manage *has ironic connotations here.*

162   nice   *petty.*
          withal   *in addition.*

165   take Truce with   *achieve peace with.*

166   tilts   *points menacingly. We should notice that Benvolio's account of the altercation differs in some ways from what a theatre audience would have just seen.*

169–   with one Hand . . . aside   *Benvolio's imagery suggests*
70   *that Mercutio (and presumably Tybalt) had a smaller sword in his other hand with which to fend off blows while he sought an opening for his own thrusts.*

152

Enter Prince, old Mountague, Capulet,
their Wives, and all.

PRINCE   Where are the vile beginners of this Fray?
BENVOLIO   O noble Prince, I can discover all   150
    Th' unlucky Manage of this fatal Brawl:
    There lies the Man, slain by young Romeo,
    That slew thy Kinsman, brave Mercutio.
CAPULET'S WIFE   Tybalt, my Cousin, O my Brother's
    Child!
    —O Prince, O Husband, O the Blood is spill'd   155
    Of my dear Kinsman! Prince, as thou art true,
    For Blood of ours shed Blood of Mountague.
    —O Cousin, Cousin!
PRINCE   Benvolio, who began this bloody Fray?
BENVOLIO   Tybalt, here slain, whom Romeo's Hand did
    slay: 160
    Romeo, that spoke him fair, bid him bethink
    How nice the Quarrel was, and urg'd withal
    Your high Displeasure (all this uttered
    With gentle Breath, calm Look, Knees humbly
    bow'd),
    Could not take Truce with the unruly Spleen   165
    Of Tybalt, deaf to Peace, but that he tilts
    With piercing Steel at bold Mercutio's Breast,
    Who, all as hot, turns deadly Point to Point,
    And with a martial Scorn, with one Hand beats
    Cold Death aside, and with the other sends   170

172   Retorts   *returns, replies in kind.*

176   envious   *driven by enmity.*

179   entertain'd   *considered, welcomed.*

186   Some twenty . . . Strife   *Lady Capulet's reaction to Benvolio's account is so extreme in its partisanship as to make us disregard any minor distortions in what Romeo's friend has just said.*

It back to Tybalt, whose Dexterity
Retorts it. Romeo he cries aloud
"Hold, Friends! Friends, part!" and swifter than
  his Tongue
His agile Arm beats down their fatal Points
And twixt them rushes, underneath whose Arm   175
An envious Thrust from Tybalt hit the Life
Of stout Mercutio, and then Tybalt fled.
But by and by comes back to Romeo,
Who had but newly entertain'd Revenge,
And to 't they go like Lightning, for ere I   180
Could draw to part them was stout Tybalt slain;
And as he fell did Romeo turn and fly.
This is the Truth, or let Benvolio die.
CAPULET'S WIFE He is a Kinsman to the Mountague:
  Affection makes him False, he speaks not true!   185
  Some twenty of them fought in this black Strife,
  And all those twenty could but kill one Life!
  I beg for Justice, which thou, Prince, must give:
  Romeo slew Tybalt; Romeo must not live!
PRINCE Romeo slew him, he slew Mercutio: 190
  Who now the Price of his dear Blood doth owe?
MOUNTAGUE Not Romeo, Prince; he was Mercutio's
    Friend.
  His Fault concludes but what the Law should end,
  The life of Tybalt.
PRINCE   And for that Offense
  Immediately we do exile him hence.   195

198   amerce   *penalize; a contraction of "at the mercy of."*

201   purchase out   *buy absolution for.*

203   Hour   *here pronounced as a two-syllable word.*

204   attend   *pay attention to, heed.*

III.ii   *The setting is Juliet's bedroom.*

2   Phoebus' Lodging   *the home of the God of the Sun. Juliet is eager for the Sun to set so that she and Romeo can consummate their marriage.*
      Wagoner   *charioteer, driver.*

3   Phaeton   *son of the Sun God, who tried to drive Phoebus' chariot too fast and would have set the world on fire had not Zeus shot him down with a thunderbolt. Phaeton was an emblem of the moral embodied in the Friar's sentence "they stumble that run fast" (II.iii.94).*

5–6   Spread . . . wink   *One way to interpret this line is to assume that the "fiery-footed Steeds" of the Sun's chariot are the "Runaways" whose eyes would "wink" (be blindfolded or "hoodwink'd," as in I.iv.4). If so, the "close Curtain" of Night is the "hood" covering the Steeds' eyes and making it possible for the lovers to meet "unseen" (line 7).*

I have an interest in your Hate's proceeding:
My Blood for your rude brawls doth lie
    a-bleeding.
But I'll amerce you with so strong a Fine
That you shall all repent the loss of Mine.
I will be deaf to Pleading and Excuses: 200
Nor Tears nor Pray'rs shall purchase out Abuses,
Therefore use none. Let Romeo hence in haste,
Else when he's found that Hour is his last.
Bear hence this Body, and attend our Will:
Mercy but murders, pard'ning those that kill.   205

Exeunt.

Scene 2

Enter Juliet alone.

JULIET   Gallop apace, you fiery-footed Steeds,
        Towards Phoebus' Lodging! Such a Wagoner
        As Phaeton would whip you to the West
        And bring in cloudy Night immediately.
        Spread thy close Curtain, Love-performing Night,   5
        That Runaways' Eyes may wink, and Romeo
        Leap to these Arms untalk'd of and unseen.

10   civil Night   *"Love-performing Night" (line 5) is now invoked as an emblem of propriety and sobriety.*

12   learn   *teach.*
        lose a winning Match   *lose a "match" (here both a competitive game and a triumphant pairing) in such a way as to win in reality. Juliet refers to a woman's submission to her lover.*

14   Hood . . . bating   *Juliet compares her wanton blood to an untrained ("unmann'd") falcon whose wings would flutter ("bate") unless the bird's head were hooded. In this image the hood would be the "black Mantle" (line 15) of matronly Night, who would turn "True-love acted" (line 16) from something unrestrained and socially unacceptable to something embodying "simple Modesty."*

23   fine   *refined, sparkling with tiny ("fine") spangles.*

25   garish Sun   *By contrast with the beauty of the Night, the Sun will be able to offer only a crudely glaring ("garish") light.*

26–28   O I have bought . . . enjoy'd.   *Juliet's imagery derives from the world of real estate transactions, and it foreshadows Romeo's use of similar phrasing in III.iii.106–7. Romeo has used a comparable metaphor in I.iv.106–11.*

Lovers can see to do their am'rous Rites
By their own Beauties; or, if Love be blind,
It best agrees with Night. Come, civil Night,   10
Thou sober-suited Matron all in black,
And learn me how to lose a winning Match
Play'd for a pair of stainless Maidenhoods.
Hood my unmann'd Blood, bating in my Cheeks,
With thy black Mantle till strange Love grow
    bold,   15
Think True-love acted simple Modesty.
Come, Night; come, Romeo; come, thou Day in
    Night:
For thou wilt lie upon the Wings of Night
Whiter than new Snow upon a Raven's Back.
Come, gentle Night; come loving, black-brow'd
    Night: 20
Give me my Romeo, and when he shall die,
Take him and cut him out in little Stars,
And he will make the Face of Heav'n so fine
That all the World will be in love with Night
And pay no Worship to the garish Sun.   25
O I have bought the Mansion of a Love
But not possess'd it; and though I am sold,
Not yet enjoy'd. So tedious is this Day
As is the Night before some Festival
To an impatient Child that hath new Robes   30
And may not wear them.

S.D. Cords   *the rope ladder by which Romeo will climb into Juliet's window.*

37 weraday   *welladay, roughly equivalent to "alas."*

40 envious   *both (a) jealous, and (b) malicious.*

45 Ay   *Here and elsewhere, the early texts print* I. *So Juliet's wordplay on* Ay *and* I *(and* Eye*) is even more emphatic there than in a modern edition such as this.*

47 Cockatrice   *a mythical serpent with the power to kill a victim by darting one glance from its eyes.*

49 Or those Eyes shot   *or those eyes darted. An eye hit by the "Death-darting Eye of Cockatrice" (line 47) could be described as "shot" or fatally wounded, as by a dart (arrow). The Nurse's following speech, emphasizing what she "saw . . . with [her] Eyes" and punctuated by "God save the Mark" (an expression to ward off evil when one has seen, heard, or spoken something of ill omen), reinforces this reading of Juliet's line.*

Enter Nurse with Cords.

O here comes my Nurse,
And she brings News; and ev'ry Tongue that
  speaks
But Romeo's Name speaks heav'nly Eloquence.
—Now, Nurse, what News? What hast thou there:
  the Cords
That Romeo bid thee fetch?

NURSE   [*Dropping Cords*] Ay, ay, the Cords.   35

JULIET   Ay me, what News? Why dost thou wring thy
  Hands?

NURSE   Ah weraday, he's dead, he's dead, he's dead!
We are undone, Lady, we are undone!
Alack the Day, he's gone, he's kill'd, he's dead!

JULIET   Can Heaven be so envious?

NURSE   Romeo can,   40
Though Heav'n cannot! O Romeo, Romeo:
Who ever would have thought it Romeo?

JULIET   What Dev'l art thou that dost torment me
  thus?
This Torture should be roar'd in dismal Hell!
Hath Romeo slain himself? Say thou but "Ay,"   45
And that bare Vowel "I" shall poison more
Than the Death-darting Eye of Cockatrice!
I am not I if there be such an "I"
Or those Eyes shot that makes thee answer "Ay."
If he be slain, say "Ay," or if not, "No":   50

54   **Corse**   *corpse.*

56   **s'ounded**   *swounded; that is, swooned.*

57   **Bankrout**   *bankrupt (with a pun on "break").*

59   **Earth**   *(a) Juliet's body, then (b) the ground.*

60   **press one heavy Bier**   *share one burial plinth.*

67   **Trumpet**   *Juliet refers to "the last trump" (1 Corinthians 15:52) signaling the Day of Judgment ("the gen'ral Doom").*

73   **O Serpent Heart . . . flow'ring Face**   *The Serpent was a primal image of Satan, owing to the manner of the Devil's first appearance in the Garden of Eden in Genesis 3, and some representations of the temptation of Eve showed the Serpent as a snake with a flower-like countenance. The images that follow (lines 74–85) all derive from the belief that the Devil had the power to transform himself into "an angel of light" (2 Corinthians 11:14).*

162

Brief Sounds determine of my Weal or Woe.

NURSE   I saw the Wound; I saw it with mine Eyes,
God save the Mark, here on his manly Breast!
A precious Corse, a bloody, piteous Corse:
Pale, pale as Ashes, all bedaub'd in Blood,   55
All in gore Blood! I s'ounded at the Sight!

JULIET   O break, my Heart: poor Bankrout, break at
once!
To Prison, Eyes: ne'er look on Liberty!
Vile Earth, to Earth resign: end Motion here,
And thou and Romeo press one heavy Bier.   60

NURSE   O Tybalt, Tybalt, the best Friend I had!
O courteous Tybalt, honest Gentleman:
That ever I should live to see thee dead!

JULIET   What Storm is this that blows so contrary?
Is Romeo slaught'red? And is Tybalt dead?   65
My dearest Cousin and my dearer Lord!
Then dreadful Trumpet, sound the gen'ral Doom:
For who is living if these two are gone?

NURSE   Tybalt is gone and Romeo banished:
Romeo that kill'd him, he is banished!   70

JULIET   O God, did Romeo's Hand shed Tybalt's Blood?

NURSE   It did, it did; alas the Day, it did!

JULIET   O Serpent Heart, hid with a flow'ring Face:
Did ever Dragon keep so fair a Cave?
Beautiful Tyrant! Fiend Angelical!   75
Dove-feather'd Raven! Wolvish, rav'ning Lamb!
Despised Substance of divinest Show!

163

81   **bow'r**   *bower; shelter with overhanging boughs.*

87   **naught**   *nothing, worthless; in this context, having undone themselves by proving their word of no value.*

88   **Aqua-vitae**   *a kind of brandy.*

Just Opposite to what thou justly seem'st:
A damned Saint, an honorable Villain!
—O Nature, what hadst thou to do in Hell   80
When thou didst bow'r the Spirit of a Fiend
In mortal Paradise of such sweet Flesh?
Was ever Book containing such vile Matter
So fairly bound? O that Deceit should dwell
In such a gorgeous Palace!

NURSE   There's no Trust,   85
No Faith, no Honesty in Men: all perjur'd,
All forsworn, all naught, all dissemblers.
Ah, where's my Man? Give me some Aqua-vitae!
These Griefs, these Woes, these Sorrows make me
     old!
Shame come to Romeo!

JULIET   Blister'd be thy Tongue   90
For such a Wish! He was not born to Shame!
Upon his Brow Shame is asham'd to sit:
For 'tis a Throne where Honor may be crown'd
Sole Monarch of the universal Earth.
O what a Beast was I to chide at him!   95

NURSE   Will you speak well of him that kill'd your
     Cousin?

JULIET   Shall I speak ill of him that is my
     Husband?
—Ah poor my Lord, what Tongue shall smooth thy
     Name
When I, thy three-hours' Wife, have mangled it?

102   native Spring   *natural source.*

103   tributary   *paying tribute, belonging to, with an analogy to
tributary streams and rivers.*

109   would forget it fain   *would like to forget it.*

117   needly will be   *needs or wishes to be.*
rank'd with   *in the company of.*

120   modern   *present.*

121   rearward   *bringing up the rear, coming last.*

But wherefore, Villain, didst thou kill my
   Cousin? 100
—That villain Cousin would have kill'd my
   Husband!
—Back, foolish Tears; back to your native
   Spring:
Your tributary Drops belong to Woe,
Which you, mistaking, offer up to Joy.
My Husband lives that Tybalt would have slain, 105
And Tybalt's dead that would have slain my
   Husband.
All this is Comfort. —Wherefore weep I then?
Some Word there was, worser than Tybalt's Death,
That murd'red me; I would forget it fain,
But O it presses to my Memory 110
Like damned guilty Deeds to Sinners' Minds:
"Tybalt is dead, and Romeo banished."
That "Banished," that one word "Banished,"
Hath slain ten thousand Tybalts. Tybalt's Death
Was Woe enough if it had ended there; 115
Or if sour Woe delights in Fellowship,
And needly will be rank'd with other Griefs,
Why follow'd not, when she said "Tybalt's dead,"
"Thy Father" or "thy Mother," nay, or both,
Which modern Lamentation might have mov'd? 120
But with a rearward following Tybalt's Death,
"Romeo is banished": to speak that Word
Is Father, Mother, Tybalt, Romeo, Juliet,

126   sound   *measure the depth of.*

132   beguil'd   *deceived, cheated.*

135   Widowed   *here pronounced with three syllables, to rhyme with*
      "to my Bed."

139   wot   *know.*

All slain, all dead. Romeo is "Banished":
There is no End, no Limit, Measure, Bound, 125
In that Word's Death; no Words can that Woe
 sound.
—Where is my Father and my Mother, Nurse?
NURSE Weeping and wailing over Tybalt's Corse.
Will you go to them? I will bring you thither.
JULIET Wash they his Wounds with Tears? Mine shall
 be spent, 130
When theirs are dry, for Romeo's Banishment.
Take up those Cords. —Poor Ropes, you are
 beguil'd,
Both you and I, for Romeo is exil'd:
He made you for a Highway to my Bed,
But I, a Maid, die Maiden Widowed. 135
Cords, Cords! —Come, Nurse, I'll to my Wedding
 Bed,
And Death, not Romeo, take my Maidenhead!
NURSE Hie to your Chamber! I'll find Romeo
To comfort you. I wot well where he is.
Hark ye, your Romeo will be here at Night. 140
I'll to him: he is hid at Lawrence' Cell.
JULIET O find him! Give this Ring to my true
 Knight,
And bid him come to take his last Farewell.

Exeunt.

III.iii   *The setting is the cell of Friar Lawrence.*

2   enamor'd of thy Parts   *in love with you.*

6   familiar   *here pronounced as a four-syllable word, with* -iar
            drawn out to ee-are.

8   Doom   *sentence.*

9   Doomsday   *the Last Judgment.*

Scene 3

Enter Friar Lawrence.

FRIAR LAWRENCE   Romeo, come forth, come forth,
    thou fearful Man:
    Affliction is enamor'd of thy Parts,
    And thou art wedded to Calamity.

Enter Romeo.

ROMEO   Father, what News? What is the Prince's
    Doom?
    What Sorrow craves acquaintance at my hand   5
    That I yet know not?
FRIAR LAWRENCE   Too familiar
    Is my dear Son with such sour Company!
    I bring thee Tidings of the Prince's Doom.
ROMEO   What less than Doomsday is the Prince's
    Doom?
FRIAR LAWRENCE   A gentler Judgment vanish'd from
    his Lips: 10
    Not Body's Death, but Body's Banishment.
ROMEO   Ha, "Banishment"? Be merciful: say "Death."
    For Exile hath more Terror in his Look,
    Much more than Death. Do not say "Banishment"!

17   without Verona Walls   *outside Verona's walls.*

21   misterm'd   *misnamed.*

22   Golden Axe   *an apt euphemism, as if a victim of execution would feel better knowing that his head will be going first class when it falls.*

24   rude   *ignorant, unsophisticated.*

26   rush'd aside   *a reference to the fact that the law was not only brushed aside but done so hastily.*

33   Validity   *legitimacy, fidelity to their natural state.*

41   fly   *flee. Romeo puns on* flies.

FRIAR LAWRENCE Hence from Verona art thou banished: 15
　　Be patient, for the World is broad and wide.
ROMEO There is no World without Verona Walls
　　But Purgatory, Torture, Hell itself:
　　Hence "Banished" is banish'd from the World,
　　And World's Exile is Death. Then "Banished" 20
　　Is Death misterm'd: calling Death "Banished,"
　　Thou cut'st my Head off with a Golden Axe
　　And smil'st upon the Stroke that murders me.
FRIAR LAWRENCE O deadly Sin, O rude
　　Unthankfulness!
　　Thy fault our Law calls Death, but the kind Prince, 25
　　Taking thy part, hath rush'd aside the Law
　　And turn'd that black word "Death" to Banishment.
　　This is dear Mercy, and thou seest it not!
ROMEO 'Tis Torture and not Mercy! Heav'n is here
　　Where Juliet lives; and ev'ry Cat and Dog 30
　　And little Mouse, ev'ry unworthy thing,
　　Live here in Heaven and may look on her,
　　But Romeo may not. More Validity,
　　More honorable State, more Courtship lives
　　In carrion Flies than Romeo: they may seize 35
　　On the white Wonder of dear Juliet's Hand
　　And steal immortal Blessing from her Lips,
　　Who ev'n in pure and vestal Modesty
　　Still blush, as thinking their own Kisses sin.
　　But Romeo may not, he's Banished. 40
　　Flies may do this, but I from this must fly:

173

45   mean   *base, lowly.*

52   fond   *foolish.*

55–56 Adversity's sweet Milk, Philosophy . . . banished.   *The Friar's remarks would have reminded Elizabethans of Bo- ethius' classic* Consolation of Philosophy, *a work written while the author was in prison awaiting execution in the year 524. Boethius had been translated into English by the Queen herself, and his work was a standard treatment of how "right reason" could rise above the worst that fickle Fortune could do to a person. According to Lady Philosophy, who visits Bo- ethius in his adversity, a man should view suffering as a blessing: a reminder of how fleeting all temporal happiness can be, and God's way of telling him to turn his thoughts to eternity in Heaven, beyond the ups and downs of life on Earth.*

59   Displant   *transplant, relocate.*

63   dispute   *reason. Philosophical arguments were often referred to as disputations, and it is characteristic of the Friar to insist on fitting Romeo's emotional problems into the abstract cate- gories of scholastic philosophy. Romeo, on the other hand, is so preoccupied with what he feels that he is unwilling to consider the possibility that there might be some value in attempting to think objectively about his situation.*

They are Freemen, but I am Banished.
And say'st thou yet that Exile is not Death?
Hadst thou no Poison mix'd, no sharp-ground
    Knife,
No sudden means of Death, though ne'er so mean,   45
But "Banished" to kill me? "Banished"?
O Friar, the Damned use that Word in Hell:
Howling attends it! How hast thou the Heart,
Being a Divine, a ghostly Confessor,
A Sin-absolver, and my Friend profess'd,   50
To mangle me with that word "Banished"?

FRIAR LAWRENCE   Thou fond, mad Man, hear me a
    little speak.

ROMEO   O thou wilt speak again of Banishment.

FRIAR LAWRENCE   I'll give thee Armor to keep off
    that Word:
Adversity's sweet Milk, Philosophy,   55
To comfort thee though thou art banished.

ROMEO   Yet "Banished"? Hang up Philosophy!
Unless Philosophy can make a Juliet,
Displant a Town, reverse a Prince's Doom,
It helps not, it prevails not. Talk no more!   60

FRIAR LAWRENCE   O then I see that Mad Men have no
    Ears!

ROMEO   How should they when that Wise Men have no
    Eyes!

FRIAR LAWRENCE   Let me dispute with thee of thy
    Estate.

70 **Taking the . . . Grave** *As Romeo prostrates himself on the floor of Friar Lawrence's cell, he suggests that he is determining the length of the grave he will need. Whether he is "taking the Measure" of the grave in another sense (getting the better of it) is another question.*

73 **enfold me** *hide me away.*

77 **Simpleness** *folly, simplemindedness.*

79 **Errant** *the Nurse's pronounciation of* errand, *probably intended by the playwright as a comic malapropism.*

ROMEO   Thou canst not speak of that thou dost not
feel.
Wert thou as young as I, Juliet thy Love,   65
An hour but marri'd, Tybalt murdered,
Doting like me, and like me banished,
Then might'st thou speak, then might'st thou
tear thy Hair
And fall upon the Ground as I do now,
Taking the Measure of an unmade Grave.   70

A series of knocks at the Door.

FRIAR LAWRENCE   Arise, one knocks! Good Romeo,
hide thy self!
ROMEO   Not I, unless the breath of Heartsick Groans,
Mist-like, enfold me from the search of Eyes.
FRIAR LAWRENCE   Hark, how they knock! —Who's
there —Romeo, arise:
Thou wilt be taken! —Stay awhile! —Stand up,   75
Run to my Study! —By and by! —God's will,
What Simpleness is this? —I come, I come!
Who knocks so hard? Whence come you? What's
your will?
NURSE   [*Within*] Let me come in, and you shall
know my Errant:
I come from Lady Juliet!
FRIAR LAWRENCE   [*Opening the Door*] Welcome then!   80

84   Case   *condition. But the Nurse's phrasing unintentionally
        suggests another meaning of* Case *as well (see the note to
        II.iv.51), an implication reinforced by the command to
        "Stand up" in line 88 and the reference to "so deep an O" in
        line 90.*

88   and   *if*

90   an O   *The Nurse refers to the despairing cry of Romeo in his
        misery. But the shape of the letter* O *was itself suggestive of a
        hole or pit such as the depression into which Romeo has fallen.*

91   Ah Sir, ah Sir!   *The meter in this line (which begins with
        Romeo's greeting to the Nurse) calls for the Nurse to stress
        "ah" rather than "Sir."*

97   conceal'd   *Both the meter and the parallelism with* cancel'd
        dictate a stress on the first syllable.

102   deadly Level   *dead aim.*

NURSE   O holy Friar, O tell me, holy Friar,
    Where is my Lady's Lord? Where's Romeo?
FRIAR LAWRENCE   There on the Ground, with his own
      Tears made drunk.
NURSE   O he is even in my Mistress' Case,
    Just in her Case. O woeful Sympathy,   85
    Piteous Predicament! Ev'n so lies she,
    Blubb'ring and weeping, weeping and blubb'ring.
    —Stand up, stand up! Stand and you be a Man!
    For Juliet's sake, for her sake, rise and stand:
    Why should you fall into so deep an O?   90
ROMEO   Nurse!
NURSE   Ah Sir, ah Sir! Death's the end of all!
ROMEO   Spak'st thou of Juliet? How is't with her?
    Doth not she think me an old Murderer
    Now I have stain'd the Childhood of our Joy
    With Blood remov'd but little from her own?   95
    Where is she? And how doth she? And what says
    My conceal'd Lady to our cancel'd Love?
NURSE   O she says nothing, Sir, but weeps and weeps,
    And now falls on her Bed, and then starts up,
    And "Tybalt!" calls, and then on Romeo cries,   100
    And then down falls again.
ROMEO   As if that Name,
    Shot from the deadly Level of a Gun,
    Did murder her as that Name's cursed Hand

105–6   In what vile part . . . lodge?   *This speech echoes in an excruciatingly ironic way Juliet's meditation on Romeo's name in II.ii.38–49.*
sack   *loot, pillage.*

107   Hold thy desp'rate Hand!   *In the First Quarto, a stage direction indicates that after Romeo "offers to stab himself" the Nurse "snatches the dagger away." But the dialogue suggests that it is the Friar who intervenes to stop him from self-slaughter.*

110   unreasonable   *unreasoning. Because reason was considered to be a faculty unique to man, the Friar compares Romeo's "Fury" to that of a "Beast."*

112   ill-beseeming Beast   *The Friar says that Romeo's behavior is so "unseemly" that it would ill become even a beast.*

117   doing . . . Self   *a reminder that suicide was regarded as a mortal sin, resulting from despair and leading to damnation.*

118   rail'st thou on   *complain about.*

122   Usurer   *one who hoards his bounty. The Friar's moral derives from such texts as Matthew 25:14–30.*

124   bedeck   *adorn.*

125   a form of Wax   *a lifeless figure, resembling a man only in appearance. In I.iii.76, the Nurse commended Paris to Juliet as a "Man of Wax."*

126   Digressing   *deviating.*

Murder'd her Kinsman. O tell me, Friar, tell me,
In what vile part of this Anatomy   105
Doth my Name lodge? Tell me that I may sack
The hateful Mansion.   *He prepares to stab himself.*
FRIAR LAWRENCE   Hold thy desp'rate Hand!
Art thou a Man? Thy Form cries out thou art!
Thy Tears are Womanish; thy wild Acts
Denote th' unreasonable Fury of a Beast!   110
Unseemly Woman in a seeming Man,
And ill-beseeming Beast in seeming both:
Thou hast amaz'd me! By my Holy Order,
I thought thy Disposition better temper'd.
Hast thou slain Tybalt? Wilt thou slay thy Self?   115
And slay thy Lady that in thy Life lives
By doing damned Hate upon thy Self?
Why rail'st thou on thy Birth, the Heav'n, and
    Earth,
Since Birth and Heav'n and Earth all three do
    meet
In thee at once, which thou at once wouldst lose?   120
Fie, fie, thou sham'st thy Shape, thy Love, thy
    Wit,
Which like a Usurer abound'st in all,
And usest none in that true Use indeed
Which should bedeck thy Shape, thy Love, thy Wit.
Thy noble Shape is but a form of Wax   125
Digressing from the Valor of a Man;
Thy dear Love sworn but hollow Perjury,

181

131   Flask   *container.*

141   Array   *raiment, dress.*

145   decreed   *planned, decided.*

147   look thou   *see that you.*
      Watch   *the volunteer citizens' guard.*

150   blaze   *proclaim.*

Killing that Love which thou hast vow'd to
    cherish;
Thy Wit, that Ornament to Shape and Love,
Misshapen in the Conduct of them both,   130
Like Powder in a skill-less Soldier's Flask,
Is set afire by thine own Ignorance,
And thou dismemb'red with thine own Defense.
What, rouse thee, Man: thy Juliet is alive,
For whose dear sake thou wast but lately dead!   135
There art thou happy. Tybalt would kill thee,
But thou slew'st Tybalt. There art thou happy.
The Law that threat'ned Death becomes thy Friend
And turns it to Exile. There art thou happy.
A pack of Blessings light upon thy Back;   140
Happiness courts thee in her best Array;
But like a misbehav'd and sullen Wench,
Thou pout'st upon thy Fortune and thy Love.
Take heed, take heed, for such die miserable.
Go get thee to thy Love as was decreed;   145
Ascend her Chamber; hence and comfort her.
But look thou stay not till the Watch be set,
For then thou canst not pass to Mantua,
Where thou shalt live till we can find a Time
To blaze your Marriage, reconcile your Friends,   150
Beg Pardon of the Prince, and call thee back
With twenty hundred thousand times more Joy
Than thou went'st forth in Lamentation.
—Go before, Nurse; commend me to thy Lady,

161   chide   *scold, probably meant playfully.*

165   your State   *your situation.*

170   good Hap   *good happening, happy occurrence.*

172   Joy past Joy   *an earthly joy that surpasses the Joy (bliss) of Heaven.*

173   brief   *briefly.*

And bid her hasten all the House to Bed, 155
Which heavy Sorrow makes them apt unto.
Romeo is coming.

NURSE O Lord, I could have stay'd here all the
Night
To hear good Counsel! O what Learning is!
—My Lord, I'll tell my Lady you will come. 160

ROMEO Do so, and bid my Sweet prepare to chide.

Nurse offers to go and turns again.

NURSE Here, Sir, a Ring she bid me give you, Sir.
Hie you, make haste, for it grows very late. *Exit.*

ROMEO How well my Comfort is reviv'd by this!

FRIAR LAWRENCE Go hence, goodnight. And here
stands all your State: 165
Either be gone before the Watch be set
Or by the break of Day disguise from hence.
Sojourn in Mantua; I'll find out your Man,
And he shall signify from time to time
Ev'ry good Hap to you that chances here. 170
Give me thy Hand. 'Tis late: farewell, goodnight.

ROMEO But that a Joy past Joy calls out on me,
It were a Grief so brief to part with thee.
Farewell. *Exeunt separately.*

III.iv   *The setting is a room in Capulet's house.*

2   move   *persuade.*

11   mew'd up to   *enclosed in.*
         Heaviness   *despondency, mourning.*

12   Tender   *offer.*

17   mark you me?   *This and other gestures make it clear that
         Capulet treats his wife in much the same way that he manages
         his servants.*

18   soft   *hush for a moment, hold it.*

Scene 4

Enter old Capulet, his Wife, and Paris.

CAPULET   Things have fall'n out, Sir, so unluckily
That we have had no time to move our Daughter.
Look you, she lov'd her kinsman Tybalt dearly,
And so did I. Well, we were born to die.
'Tis very late: she'll not come down tonight.   5
I promise you, but for your Company,
I would have been abed an hour ago.
PARIS   These times of Woe afford no times to woo:
—Madam, goodnight; commend me to your
Daughter.
LADY CAPULET   I will, and know her Mind early
tomorrow;   10
Tonight she's mew'd up to her Heaviness.
                    Paris offers to go, and Capulet calls him again.
CAPULET   Sir Paris, I will make a desp'rate Tender
Of my Child's Love: I think she will be rul'd
In all respects by me; nay more, I doubt it not.
—Wife, go you to her ere you go to Bed;   15
Acquaint her here of my Son Paris' Love,
And bid her (mark you me?) on Wednesday next—
—But soft, what Day is this?
PARIS   Monday, my Lord.

---

20   A' Thursday   *on Thursday.*

24   so late   *so recently.*

25   held him carelessly   *had no feelings for him or for his loved
        ones.*

32   against   *in preparation for.*

CAPULET   Monday, ha, ha! Well, Wednesday is too
      soon;
      A' Thursday let it be. —A' Thursday, tell her,   20
      She shall be married to this Noble Earl.
      —Will you be ready? Do you like this Haste?
      We'll keep no great ado, a friend or two,
      For hark you, Tybalt being slain so late,
      It may be thought we held him carelessly,   25
      Being our Kinsman, if we revel much.
      Therefore we'll have some half a dozen Friends,
      And there an end. But what say you to Thursday?
PARIS   My Lord, I would that Thursday were tomorrow.
CAPULET   Well, get you gone. A' Thursday be it then.   30
      —Go you to Juliet ere you go to Bed;
      Prepare her, Wife, against this Wedding Day.
      —Farewell, my Lord.   *Exit Paris.*
            —Light to my Chamber, ho!
      Afore me, it's so very late that we
      May call it early by and by. Goodnight.   *Exeunt.*   35

III.v *The setting is Juliet's bedroom, represented by a window above the main stage.*

7–8 what envious Streaks . . . East *It is typical of Romeo's tendency to allegorize experience that he sees the streaks of pre-dawn light on the clouds as "envious" of the lovers' happiness.*

8 sev'ring Clouds *The clouds Romeo sees are "sev'ring" in three senses: they are (a) dispersing, separating from one another, (b) separating night from day, and (c) most importantly, separating Romeo from Juliet.*

9 Night's Candles *the stars and planets.*
   jocund Day *cheerful, jocular Day; here personified as standing on tiptoe as if prepared to peer in on the lovers and expose their secret.*

13 Meteor *possibly a reference to a meteor in the modern sense (a "shooting star"), but more likely an allusion to the "will o' th' wisp," a luminous gas thought to be "exhaled" or drawn by the Sun from low-lying marshes.*

20 pale Reflex of Cynthia's Brow *dim light reflected from the face of the Moon (here identified with Cynthia, the Goddess of the Moon).*

Scene 5

Enter Romeo and Juliet aloft.

JULIET   Wilt thou be gone? It is not yet near Day.
It was the Nightingale and not the Lark
That pierc'd the fearful hollow of thine Ear:
Nightly she sings on yond Pomegranate Tree.
Believe me, Love, it was the Nightingale.   5
ROMEO   It was the Lark, the Herald of the Morn,
No Nightingale. Look, Love, what envious Streaks
Do lace the sev'ring Clouds in yonder East.
Night's Candles are burnt out, and jocund Day
Stands tiptoe on the misty Mountaintops.   10
I must be gone and live, or stay and die.
JULIET   Yond Light is not Daylight, I know it, I:
It is some Meteor that the Sun exhales
To be to thee this Night a Torchbearer
And light thee on thy way to Mantua.   15
Therefore stay yet; thou needst not to be gone.
ROMEO   Let me be ta'en; let me be put to death;
I am content, so thou wilt have it so.
I'll say yon gray is not the Morning's Eye;
'Tis but the pale Reflex of Cynthia's Brow.   20
Nor that is not the Lark whose Notes do beat

22   vaulty Heav'n   *the vaulted sky; specifically, the crystalline spheres believed to enclose the Globe in concentric circles.*

27   Lark . . . out of Tune   *The Lark now sings out of tune because his notes are a breach of the harmony the lovers have enjoyed during the night.*

29   Division   *a musical term referring to a melodic phrase, and sometimes to melody in general. Juliet puns on the more common sense of the word, alluded to in line 30.*

31   change   *exchange.*

33   affray   *make afraid, frighten.*

34   Hunting thee   *pursuing you.*
         Hunt's-up   *a morning song to wake up huntsmen.*

The vaulty Heav'n so high above our Heads.
I have more care to stay than will to go:
Come, Death, and welcome; Juliet wills it so.
How is't, my Soul? Let's talk; it is not Day.   25
JULIET   It is, it is! Hie hence; be gone away!
It is the Lark that sings so out of Tune,
Straining harsh Discords and unpleasing Sharps.
Some say the Lark makes sweet Division;
This doth not so, for she divideth us.   30
Some say the Lark and loathed Toad change Eyes;
O now I would they had chang'd Voices too,
Since Arm from Arm that Voice doth us affray,
Hunting thee hence with Hunt's-up to the Day.
O now be gone: more light and light it grows!   35
ROMEO   More light and light; more dark and dark our
        Woes!

Enter Nurse, hastily.

NURSE   Madam!
JULIET   Nurse?
NURSE   Your Lady Mother is coming to your Chamber;
        The Day is broke; be wary, look about.   *Exit.*   40
JULIET   Then Window, let Day in and let Life out.
ROMEO   Farewell, farewell; one Kiss and I'll
        descend.   *He goes down, using the Cord Ladder.*
JULIET   Art thou gone so, Love? Lord? Ay, Husband,
        Friend?

44   ev'ry Day in th' Hour   *a hyperbolic variation on the phrase "every hour in the day," indicating how slowly time will pass for Juliet while she is severed from Romeo.*

55   Methinks . . . low   *The Second Quarto and the First Folio set off "thou art so low" in parenthetical commas. Modern editions normally place the initial comma before* now. *This edition follows the First Quarto, which provides no commas.*

56   bottom of a Tomb   *The position of the lovers at this point mirrors that of the initial Balcony Scene (II.ii), with Romeo below and Juliet above. Subsequent events will prove Juliet's "ill-divining Soul" (line 54) to be prophetic.*

59   Dry Sorrow drinks our Blood.   *It was thought that the sighs of love drew blood away from the heart, an idea also echoed in* A Midsummer Night's Dream, *III.ii.97 ("Sighs of Love, that costs the fresh Blood dear"). Here those sighs are attributed to a thirsty figure of Sorrow personified.*

67   so   *The word here carries the weight of an intensifier meaning "extraordinarily."*

68   unaccustom'd   *unusual, departing from the customary norm.* procures   *draws.*

I must hear from thee ev'ry Day in th' Hour,
For in a Minute there are many Days.   45
O by this count I shall be much in Years
Ere I again behold my Romeo.
ROMEO   Farewell;
I will omit no opportunity
That may convey my greetings, Love, to thee.   50
JULIET   O think'st thou we shall ever meet again?
ROMEO   I doubt it not, and all these Woes shall
    serve
For sweet Discourses in our Times to come.
JULIET   O God, I have an ill-divining Soul:
Methinks I see thee now thou art so low   55
As one dead in the bottom of a Tomb!
Either my Eyesight fails or thou look'st pale.
ROMEO   And trust me, Love, in my Eye so do you:
Dry Sorrow drinks our Blood. Adieu, adieu!   *Exit.*
JULIET   O Fortune, Fortune, all Men call thee
    Fickle.   60
If thou art Fickle, what dost thou with him
That is renown'd for Faith? Be fickle, Fortune:
For then I hope thou wilt not keep him long,
But send him back.
CAPULET'S WIFE   [*Within*] Ho, Daughter, are you up?   65
JULIET   Who is't that calls? It is my Lady Mother!
Is she not down so late or up so early?
What unaccustom'd Cause procures her hither?
            She goes down from the Window and enters below.

195

69   how now   *how are you?*

74   still   *always.*
      want of Wit   *lack of judgment.*

82   Villain . . . asunder!   *This line, almost certainly to be spo-*
      ken as an aside, is most likely to be intended as a statement that
      the concepts of "Villain" and "Romeo" are miles apart
      ("asunder").

83   God pardon him   *This was a formulaic phrase usually ut-*
      tered as a pious expression, with the speaker giving little or no
      thought to its content. Juliet probably speaks it in the conven-
      tional manner while meaning it sincerely.

196

Enter Juliet's Mother.

CAPULET'S WIFE   Why how now, Juliet?

JULIET   Madam, I am not well.

CAPULET'S WIFE   Evermore weeping for your Cousin's
    Death?   70
    What, wilt thou wash him from his Grave with
        Tears?
    And if thou couldst, thou couldst not make him
        live.
    Therefore have done: some Grief shows much of
        Love,
    But much of Grief shows still some want of Wit.

JULIET   Yet let me weep for such a feeling Loss.   75

CAPULET'S WIFE   So shall you feel the Loss, but not
    the Friend
    Which you weep for.

JULIET   Feeling so the Loss,
    I cannot choose but ever weep the Friend.

CAPULET'S WIFE   Well, Girl, thou weep'st not so
    much for his Death
    As that the Villain lives which slaughter'd him.   80

JULIET   What Villain, Madam?

CAPULET'S WIFE   That same villain Romeo.

JULIET   [*Aside*] Villain and he be many Miles
        asunder!
    [*To her Mother*] God pardon him, I do with all
        my Heart;

87   Would . . . Death!   *Again, Juliet says one thing to please her Mother, but privately means something quite different.*

90   Runagate   *both (a) renegade (traitor), and (b) runaway (a person banished or fled).*

91   unaccustom'd Dram   *a potion that will be both unexpected and unprecedented in its potency.*

95–98   With Romeo . . . temper it   *Most modern editions change the period to a dash in line 95, to yield a reading in which Juliet tells her Mother she will never be satisfied till she sees "Romeo—dead." This edition retains the punctuation in the Second Quarto and First Folio texts, based on the interpretation that "dead" is an adjective Juliet applies to her grieving heart. At the end of line 96 both early texts supply a colon. Here that punctuation is lightened to a comma, on the assumption that there is an implied "that" following "Madam" in line 97.*

98   temper   *mix in further ingredients. While saying this to her Mother, Juliet is thinking that she would in fact dilute the potion so that its sole effect would be to help Romeo sleep contentedly.*

And yet no Man like he doth grieve my Heart!

CAPULET'S WIFE   That is because the Traitor
    Murderer lives.   85

JULIET   Ay Madam, from the reach of these my Hands;
    Would none but I might venge my Cousin's death!

CAPULET'S WIFE   We will have Vengeance for it, fear
    thou not.
    Then weep no more; I'll send to one in Mantua
    (Where that same banish'd Runagate doth live)   90
    Shall give him such an unaccustom'd Dram
    That he shall soon keep Tybalt company;
    And then I hope thou wilt be satisfied.

JULIET   Indeed I never shall be satisfied
    With Romeo till I behold him. Dead   95
    Is my poor Heart, so for a Kinsman vex'd,
    Madam, if you could find out but a Man
    To bear a Poison, I would temper it
    That Romeo should upon receipt thereof
    Soon sleep in quiet. O how my Heart abhors   100
    To hear him nam'd and cannot come to him
    To wreak the Love I bore my Cousin
    Upon his Body that hath slaughter'd him!

CAPULET'S WIFE   Find thou the Means, and I'll find
    such a Man.
    But now I'll tell thee joyful Tidings, Girl.   105

JULIET   And Joy comes well in such a needy Time.
    What are they, I beseech your Ladyship?

110   sorted out   *picked out, fixed upon.*

116   happ'ly   *The word used here is* happily. *But its metrical position, calling for it to be pronounced as a two-syllable word, merges it with* haply, *a word whose ironic connotations (by chance, by accident) are even more appropriate to the context.*

119   I wonder   *I am astonished.*

127   drizzle Dew   *It is not certain whether Capulet is thinking of* dew *in the normal sense (in which case* drizzle *would mean "shed") or of* drizzle *in the normal sense (in which case* dew *refers to its residue of fine, spray-like drops). The contrast with "rains downright" (line 129) is clear in either case.*

CAPULET'S WIFE   Well, well, thou hast a careful
    Father, Child,
    One who, to put thee from thy Heaviness,
    Hath sorted out a sudden Day of Joy,   110
    That thou expects not, nor I look'd not for.
JULIET   Madam, in happy time, what Day is that?
CAPULET'S WIFE   Marry, my Child, early next
    Thursday morn
    The gallant, young, and noble Gentleman,
    The County Paris, at Saint Peter's Church,   115
    Shall happ'ly make thee there a joyful Bride.
JULIET   Now, by Saint Peter's Church and Peter too,
    He shall not make me there a joyful Bride!
    I wonder at this Haste, that I must wed
    Ere he that should be Husband comes to woo!   120
    I pray you tell my Lord and Father, Madam,
    I will not marry yet; and when I do I swear
    It shall be Romeo, whom you know I hate,
    Rather than Paris! These are News indeed!
CAPULET'S WIFE   Here comes your Father; tell him so
    your self,   125
    And see how he will take it at your hands!

Enter Capulet and Nurse.

CAPULET   When the Sun sets, the Earth doth drizzle
    Dew;
    But for the Sunset of my Brother's Son,

201

130   Conduit   *probably a reference to an elaborately carved foun-
      tain in which the water spouts from a human form in the
      center.*

132   counterfeits   *resembles.*
      Bark   *a small sailing vessel. Romeo will compare himself to a
      bark in V.iii.118.*

139   Decree   *Capulet probably means "decision," but "decree"
      conveys the nature of the situation with absolute precision.*

140   will none   *will have none of it.*

142   Soft, take me with you   *Slow down, let me be sure I follow
      you.*

144   Is she not proud?   *Capulet means "Is she not proud of the
      match we have arranged for her?"*

148   what I hate   *The next line suggests that Juliet refers not to
      Paris but to the way her parents have arranged the marriage
      without consulting her or considering her wishes.*

152   Minion   *here, a spoiled favorite.*

It rains downright.
How now, a Conduit, Girl! What, still in Tears?   130
Evermore show'ring? In one little Body
Thou counterfeits a Bark, a Sea, a Wind:
For still thy Eyes, which I may call the Sea,
Do ebb and flow with Tears; the Bark thy Body is,
Sailing in this salt Flood; the Wind's thy Sighs,   135
Who, raging with thy Tears and they with them,
Without a sudden Calm will overset
Thy Tempest-tossed Body. —How now, Wife,
Have you deliver'd to her our Decree?

CAPULET'S WIFE   Ay Sir, but she will none, she
    gives you thanks!   140
I would the Fool were married to her Grave!

CAPULET   Soft, take me with you, take me with you,
    Wife:
How will she none? Doth she not give us thanks?
Is she not proud? Doth she not count her blest,
Unworthy as she is, that we have wrought   145
So worthy a Gentleman to be her Bridegroom?

JULIET   Not proud you have, but thankful, that you
    have:
Proud can I never be of what I hate,
But thankful ev'n for Hate that is meant Love.

CAPULET   How, how? How, how? Chopp'd Logic! What
    is this?   150
"Proud" and "I thank you"? And "I thank you not"
And yet "not proud"? Mistress Minion, you

154   fettle your fine Joints   *prepare your refined limbs. Capulet uses alliteration here (fettle, fine) to give his words maximum emphasis. In this context,* fettle *suggests* fetters *(shackles).*

156   Hurdle   *a wooden sled on which criminals were conveyed to execution, an image that proves prophetically apt.*

157   green-sickness Carrion   *the corpse of a girl who died of "green sickness," a form of anemia.*

158   Tallow Face   *Tallow, from which candles were made, was pale in color; Capulet is probably referring to Juliet's bloodless complexion.*

        Fie . . . mad?   *Though these words would apply more aptly to Capulet, they are probably to be addressed to Juliet. Only later (line 176) does Lady Capulet offer a mild word of protest to her husband.*

165   My Fingers itch.   *Capulet means that he is having difficulty resisting the urge to strike Juliet.*

169   Hilding   *base wretch.*

170   too blame   *too blameworthy.*

        rate   *berate.*

172   smatter   *prattle.*

        Gossips   *garrulous old ladies.*

173   Treason   *insubordination.*

        O God'i'god-den!   *O God give you good evening! Here used as a mild oath.*

Thank me no Thankings, nor proud me no Prouds,
But fettle your fine Joints 'gainst Thursday next
To go with Paris to Saint Peter's Church,   155
Or I will drag thee on a Hurdle thither!
Out, you green-sickness Carrion! Out, you
    Baggage!
You Tallow Face!
CAPULET'S WIFE   Fie, fie! What, are you mad?
JULIET   Good Father, I beseech you on my Knees,
Hear me with patience but to speak a Word—   160
CAPULET   Hang thee, young Baggage! Disobedient
    Wretch!
I tell thee what: get thee to Church a' Thursday,
Or never after look me in the Face!
Speak not, reply not, do not answer me!
My Fingers itch. —Wife, we scarce thought us
    blest   165
That God had lent us but this only Child;
But now I see this one is one too much
And that we have a Curse in having her:
Out on her! Hilding!
NURSE   God in Heaven bless her!
You are too blame, my Lord, to rate her so!   170
CAPULET   And why, my Lady Wisdom? Hold your
    Tongue!
Good Prudence, smatter with your Gossips! Go!
NURSE   I speak no Treason.
CAPULET   O God'i'god-den!

205

175   Utter . . . Bowl   *mumble your grave wisdom over a cup of hot punch with your fellow gossips.*

177   God's Bread   *an oath referring to the wafer representing the body of Christ in the Communion service.*

178   Tide   *Capulet may mean the interval determined by the tides, but it is more likely that he is using the word generically to refer to any indefinite period or season of time.*

182   Demesnes   *land holdings, domains.*
        Lin'd   *descended. The word in the Second Quarto is "liand"; in the First Quarto, "traind"; and in the First Folio, "allied."*

183   Parts   *aspects, qualities.*

185   puling   *whimpering.*

186   Mammet   *puppet doll. Capulet is accustomed to treating Juliet as a mammet, but not to having her respond to him like a real human being with a mind and will of her own.*
        tender   *fragile, not yet mature.*

190   Graze   *Capulet's use of this verb has the effect of reducing Juliet to the status of a farm animal.*

191   I do not use to jest   *I am not in the habit of speaking in jest.*

192   Lay Hand on Heart, advise   *Speak to your heart.*

195   I'll ne'er acknowledge thee   *Capulet is threatening to disclaim any relationship to Juliet, to disinherit her.*

NURSE May not one speak?

CAPULET   Peace, you mumbling Fool!
　　Utter your gravity o'er a Gossips' Bowl,   175
　　For here we need it not.

CAPULET'S WIFE   You are too hot.

CAPULET God's Bread, it makes me mad!
　　Day, Night; Hour, Tide, Time; Work, Play;
　　Alone, in Company: still my Care hath been
　　To have her match'd. And, having now provided   180
　　A Gentleman of Noble Parentage,
　　Of fair Demesnes, Youthful and Nobly Lin'd,
　　Stuff'd, as they say, with Honorable Parts,
　　Proportion'd as one's thought would wish a Man,
　　And then to have a wretched, puling Fool,   185
　　A whining Mammet, in her Fortunes tender,
　　To answer "I'll not wed, I cannot love,
　　I am too young, I pray you pardon me"!
　　—But and you will not wed, I'll pardon you:
　　Graze where you will, you shall not house with
　　　me!   190
　　Look to't, think on't; I do not use to jest.
　　Thursday is near. Lay Hand on Heart, advise:
　　And you be mine, I'll give you to my Friend;
　　And you be not, hang, beg, starve, die i' th'
　　　Streets,
　　For by my Soul, I'll ne'er acknowledge thee,   195
　　Nor what is mine shall never do thee good.

207

203   dim Monument   *dark tomb.*

211   practice Stratagems   *play tricks.*

212   soft   *weak, fragile.*

215   and all the World to Nothing   *The Nurse seems to be saying that the odds ("all the World" as opposed to "Nothing") are overwhelmingly against Romeo's ever coming back to claim Juliet as his wife. Another possible reading is that, for all practical purposes, Romeo has ceased to exist, both in the eyes of the world and (if she is pragmatic in her thinking) in the eyes of Juliet. The second reading would call for a comma after* Nothing. *Either interpretation is consistent with the Nurse's point of view.*

216–   That . . . by Stealth.   *The Nurse is assuming that Juliet*
17   *will take the practical course and marry Paris. If so, she says, Romeo will be unable to "challenge" the marriage publicly, only privately ("by Stealth") if at all.*

218   Case   *matter, situation.*

Trust to 't, bethink you: I'll not be forsworn!

Exit.

JULIET   Is there no Pity sitting in the Clouds
That sees into the Bottom of my Grief?
—O sweet my Mother, cast me not away!   200
Delay this Marriage for a Month, a Week;
Or if you do not, make the Bridal Bed
In that dim Monument where Tybalt lies.

LADY CAPULET   Talk not to me, for I'll not speak a
word.
Do as thou wilt, for I have done with thee!   *Exit.*   205

JULIET   O God! —O Nurse, how shall this be
prevented?
My Husband is on Earth, my Faith in Heaven:
How shall that Faith return again to Earth
Unless that Husband send it me from Heaven
By leaving Earth? Comfort me! Counsel me!   210
Alack, alack, that Heav'n should practice
Stratagems
Upon so soft a Subject as my self!
What say'st thou? Hast thou not a word of Joy?
Some Comfort, Nurse!

NURSE   Faith, here it is: Romeo
Is banished, and all the World to Nothing   215
That he dares ne'er come back to challenge you,
Or if he do, it needs must be by Stealth.
Then, since the Case so stands as now it doth,
I think it best you married with the County.

221   Dishclout   *dishcloth.*

223   Beshrow   *beshrew, curse. This spelling reflects the way the word was frequently pronounced, by analogy with* sew, shew, *and* Shrewsbury.

229   Amen.   *Juliet probably speaks this under her breath, or at least in such a way that the Nurse fails to understand that Juliet is commending the Nurse's willingness to "beshrow" both her heart and her soul if she is not speaking with sincerity.*

230   Well . . . much.   *Juliet means this ironically, but she delivers it in such a way that the Nurse takes it at face value.*

235   Ancient . . . Fiend!   *Juliet is applying these names to the Nurse, but implicit in her remarks is the idea that it is Satan ("the Fiend" and the original source of the Fall that led to damnation) who speaks through her with the advice to forswear her marriage vows. When Juliet dismisses the Nurse with the words "Go, Counselor" (line 239), she is echoing "Get thee behind me, Satan" (Matthew 16:23).*

240   Twain   *two, divided.*

O he's a lovely Gentleman; 220
Romeo's a Dishclout to him! An Eagle, Madam,
Hath not so green, so quick, so fair an Eye
As Paris hath! Beshrew my very Heart,
I think you're happy in this second Match,
For it excels your first; or if it did not, 225
Your first is dead, or 'twere as good he were,
As living here and you no use to him.

JULIET   Speak'st thou this from thy Heart?

NURSE   And from my Soul,
Too, else beshrew them both.

JULIET   Amen.

NURSE   What?

JULIET   Well, thou hast comforted me marv'lous much. 230
Go in and tell my Lady I am gone,
Having displeas'd my Father, to Lawrence' Cell,
To make Confession and to be absolv'd.

NURSE   Marry, I will, and this is wisely done.   *Exit.*

JULIET   Ancient Damnation! O most wicked Fiend! 235
Is it more Sin to wish me thus forsworn
Or to dispraise my Lord with that same Tongue
Which she hath prais'd him with above compare
So many thousand times? Go, Counselor:
Thou and my Bosom henceforth shall be Twain. 240
I'll to the Friar to know his Remedy;
If all else fail, my self have pow'r to die.

                                        Exit.

IV.i   *The setting is the cell of Friar Lawrence.*

3   **And . . . Haste**   *and I am nothing to impede his haste. Although this line can be interpreted to mean that Paris is not reluctant to retard Capulet's haste, the context suggests that what Paris is telling the Friar is that he is powerless or reluctant to do anything to cross the will of his future father-in-law. The phrase* nothing slow *probably means "no impediment."*

8   **Venus . . . House of Tears**   *Paris means that the Goddess of Love cannot be expected to be effectual in a household in the throes of mourning. His phrasing also carries an astrological play on words, based on the idea that the planet Venus does not have a beneficent influence ("smiles not") when she is in one of the "houses" of the Zodiac associated with water (Aquarius or Pisces).*

Act Four

Scene 1

Enter Friar Lawrence and County Paris.

FRIAR LAWRENCE   On Thursday, Sir? The Time is very
    short.
PARIS   My Father Capulet will have it so,
    And I am nothing slow to slack his Haste.
FRIAR LAWRENCE   You say you do not know the Lady's
    Mind?
    Uneven is the Course: I like it not. 5
PARIS   Immod'rately she weeps for Tybalt's Death,
    And therefore have I little talk'd of Love:
    For Venus smiles not in a House of Tears.
    Now Sir, her Father counts it dangerous
    That she do give her Sorrow so much Sway, 10

13   minded   *attended.*
      alone   *in solitude. Both adjectives refer to Juliet's tears rather than to Juliet herself.*

14   Society   *association with other people.*

15   of   *for.*

20   must be   *Like Juliet's parents, Paris assumes that Juliet has nothing to say about the matter.*

21   certain Text   *sure saying (because it is tautological, asserting that something is identical with itself).*

27   Price   *value, worth.*

And in his Wisdom hastes our Marriage
To stop the inundation of her Tears,
Which, too much minded by her self alone,
May be put from her by Society.
Now do you know the Reason of this Haste.   15
FRIAR LAWRENCE   [*Aside*] I would I knew not why it
　　should be slow'd!

Enter Juliet.

Look, Sir! here comes the Lady toward my Cell.
PARIS   Happily met, my Lady and my Wife!
JULIET   That may be, Sir, when I may be a Wife.
PARIS   That "may be" must be, Love, on Thursday
　　next.   20
JULIET   What must be shall be.
FRIAR LAWRENCE   That's a certain Text.
PARIS   Come you to make Confession to this Father?
JULIET   To answer that I should confess to you.
PARIS   Do not deny to him that you love me.
JULIET   I will confess to you that I love him.   25
PARIS   So will ye, I am sure, that you love me.
JULIET   If I do so, it will be of more Price
　　Being spoke behind your Back than to your Face.
PARIS   Poor Soul, thy Face is much abus'd with
　　Tears!
JULIET   The Tears have got small Victory by that,   30
　　For it was bad enough before their Spite.

215

34   **to my Face**   *both (a) to my own face, and (b) openly (not behind my back).*

35   **Thy Face is mine**   *Paris is attempting to be gracious, but he succeeds only in sounding tedious and overbearing.*

39   **pensive**   *reflective, sad.*

40   **entreat**   *request.*

41   **shield**   *forbid, prevent.*

47   **strains**   *both (a) constrains or forces, and (b) taxes.*
        compass   *reach, limit.*

48   **prorogue**   *defer, postpone.*

53   **Resolution**   *resolve, intention. By saying "call my Resolution wise," Juliet is asking the Friar to bestow his blessing on her determination to commit suicide.*

54   **presently**   *immediately, at this present moment.*

216

PARIS   Thou wrong'st it more than Tears with that
      Report.
JULIET   That is no Slander, Sir, which is a Truth,
      And what I spake, I spake it to my Face.
PARIS   Thy Face is mine, and thou hast sland'red it.   35
JULIET   It may be so, for it is not mine own.
      —Are you at Leisure, holy Father, now,
      Or shall I come to you at evening Mass?
FRIAR LAWRENCE   My Leisure serves me, pensive
      Daughter, now.
      —My Lord, we must entreat the Time alone.   40
PARIS   God shield I should disturb Devotion.
      —Juliet, on Thursday early will I rouse ye;
      Till then adieu, and keep this holy Kiss.   *Exit.*
JULIET   O shut the Door, and when thou hast done so,
      Come weep with me: past Hope, past Cure, past
      Help!   45
FRIAR LAWRENCE   O Juliet, I already know thy Grief:
      It strains me past the compass of my Wits!
      I hear thou must, and nothing may prorogue it,
      On Thursday next be married to this County.
JULIET   Tell me not, Friar, that thou hear'st of this   50
      Unless thou tell me how I may prevent it!
      If in thy Wisdom thou canst give no Help,
      Do thou but call my Resolution wise,
      And with this Knife I'll help it presently.
      God join'd my Heart and Romeo's, thou our Hands,   55
      And ere this Hand, by thee to Romeo seal'd,

57   **Label to another Deed**   *Juliet probably means this phrase in a legal sense. Picking up on "seal'd" in the preceding line, she appears to be using "Label" to refer to a strip of parchment, bearing the official seal, that was attached to a deed (such as a marriage license).*

58   **treacherous Revolt**   *traitorous insubordination. To break her vow to Romeo would be to violate her sworn obedience to both her earthly lord and her Lord in Heaven.*

61   **present Counsel**   *instant guidance.*

63   **Umpeer**   *umpire, judge.*

64   **Commission**   *authority vested in the Friar.*

65   **Issue**   *outcome; here, the conclusion of a legal proceeding.*

69   **desperate**   *done only in extreme, apparently hopeless situations.* **Desperate** *is derived from* **despair**, *the absence of hope in theological terms, and that is probably why the Friar calls his remedy "a kind of Hope."*

75   **cop'st**   *contends with, rivals. The Friar's meaning is that the shame Juliet seeks to escape is as terrible as death itself would be.*

81   **Charnel-house**   *originally a tomb (with* **charnel** *derived from the Latin word for flesh), but by Shakespeare's time a building next to a graveyard for the housing of unearthed skulls and bones.*

Shall be the Label to another Deed,
Or my true Heart with treacherous Revolt
Turn to another, this shall slay them both!
Therefore, out of thy long-experienc'd Time,   60
Give me some present Counsel, or behold,
'Twixt my Extremes and Me this bloody Knife
Shall play the Umpeer, arbitrating that
Which the Commission of thy Years and Art
Could to no Issue of true Honor bring.   65
Be not so long to speak: I long to die
If what thou speak'st speak not of Remedy.

FRIAR LAWRENCE   Hold, Daughter, I do spy a kind of
  Hope,
Which craves as desperate an Execution
As that is desp'rate which we would prevent.   70
If, rather than to marry County Paris,
Thou hast the strength of will to slay thy self,
Then it is likely thou wilt undertake
A thing like Death to chide away this Shame,
That cop'st with Death himself, to 'scape from
  it.   75
And if thou dar'st, I'll give thee Remedy.

JULIET   O bid me leap, rath'r than marry Paris,
From off the Battlements of any Tower,
Or walk in Thievish Ways; or bid me lurk
Where Serpents are; chain me with roaring Bears,   80
Or hide me nightly in a Charnel-house,
O'ercover'd quite with Dead-men's rattling Bones,

83   reeky Shanks   *foul-smelling limbs.*
       chapless   *jawless.*

91   look   *see.*

93   Vial   *small bottle.*

94   distilling   *trickling down and flowing through the body.*
       Liquor   *medicinal solution.*

95   presently   *instantly.*

96   drowsy Humour   *sleep-inducing fluid.*

97   native Progress   *natural movement.*
       surcease   *suspend operation.*

102   supple Government   *resiliency, flexibility.*

103   stark   *barren of life.*

104   shrunk   *shrunken.*

With reeky Shanks and yellow chapless Skulls;
Or bid me go into a new-made Grave,
And hide me with a Dead-man in his Shroud   85
(Things that, to hear them told, have made me
    tremble),
And I will do it without Fear or Doubt,
To live an unstain'd Wife to my sweet Love.
FRIAR LAWRENCE   Hold then, go home, be merry, give
    consent
To marry Paris. Wednesday is tomorrow;   90
Tomorrow night look that thou lie alone
(Let not the Nurse lie with thee in thy Chamber).
Take thou this Vial, being then in Bed,
And this distilling Liquor drink thou off,
When presently through all thy Veins shall run   95
A cold and drowsy Humour: for no Pulse
Shall keep his native Progress, but surcease;
No Warmth, no Breath shall testify thou livest;
The Roses in thy Lips and Cheeks shall fade
To many Ashes, thy Eyes' Windows fall,   100
Like Death when he shuts up the Day of Life;
Each Part, depriv'd of supple Government,
Shall stiff and stark and cold appear like Death.
And in this borrow'd likeness of shrunk Death
Thou shalt continue two and forty hours,   105
And then awake as from a pleasant Sleep.
Now when the Bridegroom in the Morning comes
To rouse thee from thy Bed, there art thou dead;

109   Manner   *custom.*

113   against thou shalt awake   *in preparation for your waking.*

114   our Drift   *our intentions, the direction of our plans.*

116   watch   *wait for vigilantly.*

119   inconstant Toy   *trifle or doubt that interferes with one's "constancy" or resolve.*

120   Abate   *diminish (literally, beat down).*

125   afford   *carry forward.*

Then, as the Manner of our Country is,
In thy best Robes uncover'd on the Bier,   110
Thou shalt be borne to that same ancient Vault
Where all the Kindred of the Cap'lets lie.
In the mean time, against thou shalt awake,
Shall Romeo by my Letters know our Drift,
And hither shall he come, and he and I   115
Will watch thy Waking, and that very Night
Shall Romeo bear thee hence to Mantua.
And this shall free thee from this present Shame
If no inconstant Toy nor womanish Fear
Abate thy Valor in the acting it.   120
JULIET   Give me, give me! O tell me not of Fear!
FRIAR LAWRENCE   Hold, get you gone, be strong and
    Prosperous in this Resolve. I'll send a Friar with
    Speed to Mantua with my Letters to thy Lord.
JULIET   Love give me Strength, and Strength shall
    help afford.   125
    Farewell, dear Father.   *Exeunt.*

IV.ii   *The setting for this scene is a room in Capulet's house.*

2   cunning   *skilled (literally, knowing).*

6   ill Cook   *here* ill *probably means both "bad" and "unwell."*

8   lick his Fingers   *It was proverbial that one who would not lick his fingers had no faith in his own work. With a cook, it might mean that he lacked confidence in the ingredients. With an "ill Cook" (line 6), it might also mean that he was unwilling to eat food his own hands had contaminated.*

10   unfurnish'd   *unprepared.*

12   forsooth   *in truth.*

14   Harlotry   *worthlessness, disobedience.*

Scene 2

Enter Father Capulet, Mother, Nurse, and Servingmen,
two or three.

CAPULET So many Guests invite as here are writ.

                                   Exit one Servant.

  —Sirrah, go hire me twenty cunning Cooks.

SERVANT You shall have none ill, Sir: for I'll
  try if they can lick their Fingers.

CAPULET How canst thou try them so?   5

SERVANT Marry Sir, 'tis an ill Cook that cannot
  lick his own Fingers; therefore he that cannot
  lick his Fingers goes not with me.

CAPULET Go, be gone.   *Exit second Servant.*

  —We shall be much unfurnish'd for this Time.   10

  —What, is my Daughter gone to Friar Lawrence?

NURSE Ay forsooth.

CAPULET Well, he may chance to do some good on
  her:
  A peevish, self-willed Harlotry it is.

Enter Juliet.

NURSE See where she comes from Shrift with merry
  Look.   15

16   gadding   *going idly about.*

19   Behests   *commands.*

23–24   Send for the County . . . morning.   *Before Capulet addresses a word to Juliet, he commands that Paris be notified of her change of mind; he also moves up the wedding date by a day.*

26   becomed   *becoming, seemly, maidenly.*

33   Closet   *private chamber.*

34   sort   *select.*

38   short in our Provision   *deficient in our preparations. Having been overruled by her husband a moment earlier, Lady Capulet objects again. Significantly, however, her concerns center on "Provision" for the wedding guests rather than on preparing her daughter for an event to which Juliet herself seems all but incidental. In this line* provision *would be pronounced as a full four-syllable word (pro-víz-ee-on).*

226

CAPULET How now, my Headstrong: where have you
    been gadding?
JULIET Where I have learnt me to repent the Sin
    Of disobedient Opposition
    To you and your Behests, and am enjoin'd
    By holy Lawrence to fall prostrate here   20
    To beg your Pardon.   *She kneels down.*
              Pardon, I beseech you;
    Henceforward I am ever rul'd by you.
CAPULET Send for the County: go tell him of this!
    I'll have this Knot knit up tomorrow morning.
JULIET I met the youthful Lord at Lawrence' Cell   25
    And gave him what becomed Love I might,
    Not stepping o'er the bounds of Modesty.
CAPULET Why I am glad on 't; this is well; stand
      up;
    This is as 't should be. —Let me see the County:
    Ay marry, go, I say, and fetch him hither.   30
    Now, afore God, this reverend holy Friar,
    All our whole City is much bound to him.
JULIET Nurse, will you go with me into my Closet
    To help me sort such needful Ornaments
    As you think fit to furnish me tomorrow?   35
CAPULET'S WIFE No, not till Thursday; there is
      time enough.
CAPULET Go, Nurse, go with her; we'll to Church
      tomorrow.   *Exeunt Juliet and Nurse.*
CAPULET'S WIFE We shall be short in our Provision:

41   deck up her   *Capulet emphasizes the word* her, *which is placed in a stressed position both syntactically and metrically. His point is that he, being the "Huswife for this once" (line 43), will deck up the house while his wife helps the Nurse deck up Juliet.*

45   prepare up him   *Capulet stresses the word* him, *which parallels the emphasis in the similar phrasing of line 41.*

46   wondrous light   *wondrously cheerful.*

47   reclaim'd.   *Having been prepared to disclaim his daughter, Capulet is now rejoicing over her suitability for reclamation. What had seemed lost, he reflects, is now found.*

IV.iii   *The setting now shifts to Juliet's private chamber.*

3   Orisons   *prayers.*

5   cross   *at cross purposes with Heaven's will.*

'Tis now near Night.

CAPULET   Tush, I will stir about,
And all things shall be well, I warr'nt thee,
    Wife.   40
Go thou to Juliet, help to deck up her.
I'll not to Bed tonight; let me alone:
I'll play the Huswife for this once. —What ho!
—They are all forth. Well, I will walk my self
To County Paris, to prepare up him   45
Against tomorrow. My Heart is wondrous light,
Since this same wayward Girl is so reclaim'd.

                                              Exeunt.

Scene 3

Enter Juliet and Nurse.

JULIET   Ay, those Attires are best. But gentle
    Nurse,
I pray thee leave me to my self tonight:
For I have need of many Orisons
To move the Heav'ns to smile upon my State,
Which, well thou know'st, is cross and full of
    Sin.   5

7 cull'd *picked out.*

8 behooveful *appropriate, required for the occasion.*
   State *ceremony.*

11 full all *completely full.*

15 cold *chilling.*
   thrills *a wonderfully apt verb, combining a sense of intense*
    apprehension with the sensation of shivering.

Enter Juliet's Mother.

CAPULET'S WIFE   What, are you busy, ho? Need you my
    help?
JULIET   No, Madam, we have cull'd such Necessaries
    As are behooveful for our State tomorrow.
    So please you, let me now be left alone,
    And let the Nurse this night sit up with you: 10
    For I am sure you have your hands full all
    In this so sudden Business.
CAPULET'S WIFE   Goodnight.
    Get thee to Bed and rest, for thou hast need.
JULIET   Farewell.   *Exeunt Juliet's Mother and Nurse.*
          God knows when we shall meet again.
    I have a faint, cold Fear thrills through my
      Veins,   15
    That almost freezes up the Heat of Life.
    I'll call them back again to comfort me.
    —Nurse! —What should she do here?
    My dismal Scene I needs must act alone.
    —Come, Vial.   20
    What if this Mixture do not work at all?
    Shall I be married then tomorrow morning?
    No, no, this shall forbid it. —Lie thou there.
            She places a Knife where she can reach it.
    —What if it be a Poison which the Friar
    Subtly hath minist'red to have me dead,   25
    Lest in this Marriage he should be dishonor'd

29   still   *always.*
         tried   *proven to be.*

33   stifled   *suffocated.*

36   like   *likely; also the meaning in line 45.*

37   Conceit   *thought, concept.*

42   green   *newly placed. The word* green *suggests both the color of rotting flesh and the color of fresh sprouts.*

43   fest'ring   *decomposing.*

44   resort   *come, spend time.*

47   Shrikes   *shrieks. The original spelling preserves a more strident-sounding word than the one conveyed by modern spelling.*
         Mandrakes' . . . Earth   *It was widely believed that the mandrake plant shrieked when pulled from the earth, and there were some who thought that madness or death, or both, came to anyone who heard that shriek. It is fitting that Juliet should think about mandrakes at this moment, because it is likely that the sleeping potion she is about to drink was extracted from a type of mandrake plant.*

49   distraught   *distracted, crazed (a stronger term in Shakespeare's time than in our own).*

50   Environed   *surrounded.*

Because he married me before to Romeo?
I fear it is, and yet methinks it should not:
For he hath still been tried a Holy Man.
How if when I am laid into the Tomb,   30
I wake before the time that Romeo
Come to redeem me? There's a fearful Point!
Shall I not then be stifled in the Vault,
To whose foul Mouth no healthsome Air breathes
    in,
And there die strangled ere my Romeo comes?   35
Or if I live, is it not very like
The horrible Conceit of Death and Night,
Together with the Terror of the Place,
As in a Vault, an ancient Receptacle
Where for this many hundred years the Bones   40
Of all my buried Ancestors are pack'd,
Where bloody Tybalt, yet but green in Earth,
Lies fest'ring in his Shroud, where, as they say,
At some hours in the Night Spirits resort—
Alack, alack, is it not like that I,   45
So early waking (what with loathsome Smells,
And Shrikes like Mandrakes' torn out of the
    Earth,
That living Mortals, hearing them, run mad)—
O if I wake, shall I not be distraught,
Environed with all these hideous Fears,   50
And madly play with my Forefathers' Joints,
And pluck the mangled Tybalt from his Shroud,

233

53   **Rage**   *mad frenzy.*

56   spit   *impale, run through.*

IV.iv   *The setting shifts to one of the larger rooms of the house, but with Juliet still lying behind the drawn curtain at the back of the stage.*

2   **Pastry**   *the chamber where pastry was baked.*

3   **second Cock**   *A sixteenth-century book on* **Husbandry** *notes that cocks crowed "at midnight, at three, and an hour before day."*

4   **Curfew bell . . . o'clock**   *Just as a bell was rung in the evening to alert people that it was time to cover their fires (the original meaning of the word* curfew*) and retire, another bell was rung in the morning to signal that it was time to arise.*

5   **Bak'd-meats**   *meat pies.*
       Angelica   *evidently the name of the Nurse.*

6   **Cot-quean**   *a man who does household chores as if he were a wife.*

And in this Rage, with some great Kinsman's Bone,
As with a Club, dash out my desp'rate Brains?
—O look! Methinks I see my Cousin's Ghost   55
Seeking out Romeo, that did spit his Body
Upon a Rapier's Point. —Stay, Tybalt, stay!
—Romeo, I come: this do I drink to thee.

> *She falls upon her Bed within the Curtains.*

Scene 4

Enter Lady of the House and Nurse, with Herbs.

CAPULET'S WIFE Hold: take these Keys and fetch more
    Spices, Nurse.
NURSE They call for Dates and Quinces in the Pastry.

Enter old Capulet.

CAPULET Come, stir, stir, stir! The second Cock hath
    crow'd,
    The Curfew Bell hath rung, 'tis three o'clock:
    Look to the Bak'd-meats, good Angelica;   5
    Spare not for Cost.
NURSE   Go, you Cot-quean, go!

8   watching   *staying up rather than going to bed.*

11   Mouse-hunt   *one who hunts mice (specifically, a cat or a weasel); an allusion to Capulet's earlier days as a woman-chaser.*

13   Jealous Hood   *a jealous person. Capulet's response is probably meant to be a good-humored reply to his wife's teasing dig, and is no doubt spoken while she is still within earshot.*

20   Mass   *by the Mass, a mild oath.*

21   Loggerhead   *blockhead, stupid person. Whether the servant's comment about a "Head . . . that will find out Logs" (line 18) is meant to suggest that he is calling himself a loggerhead is unclear. He may simply be saying that he knows how to find logs without Peter's help. Or he may be making another joke, perhaps one that has to do with a hangover. In any case, it is obvious that Capulet enjoys both the servant's comment and his own jest in reply to it.*

       'tis Day   *When it suits his purposes, Shakespeare contrives to make time move very rapidly in his dramatic scenes.*

236

Get you to Bed: faith, you'll be sick tomorrow
For this Night's watching.

CAPULET   No, not a whit. What, I have watch'd ere
now
All night for lesser cause, and ne'er been sick.   10

CAPULET'S WIFE   Ay, you have been a Mouse-hunt in
your Time,
But I will watch you from such Watching now!

                              Exeunt Lady Capulet and Nurse.

CAPULET   A Jealous Hood, a Jealous Hood!

Enter Servants with Spits and Logs and Baskets.

Now, Fellow, what is there?

FIRST SERVANT   Things for the Cook, Sir, but I know
not what.   15

CAPULET   Make haste, make haste.   *Exit First Servant.*
                              —Sirrah, fetch drier Logs.
Call Peter: he will show thee where they are.

SECOND SERVANT   I have a Head, Sir, that will find
out Logs,
And never trouble Peter for the matter.

CAPULET   Mass, and well said! A merry Whoreson, ha!   20
Thou shalt be Loggerhead.   *Exit Second Servant.*
                              Good faith, 'tis Day;
The County will be here with Music straight,
For so he said he would.   *Music plays within.*
                              I hear him near.

IV.v   *The setting remains essentially unchanged, except that by going to the curtains on the stage the Nurse brings the rest of the household into Juliet's bedroom. There would be no break in the action between this scene and the one immediately preceding.*

2   Sluggabed   *a person who habitually oversleeps.*

6   set up his Rest   *set his hopes, resolved to himself. The phrase has associations (a) from primero, a card game in which one who "sets up his Rest" wagers all on one hand; (b) from military life, where one used a "rest" to support the heavy barrel of a musket before firing; and (c) from tilting, where one held a lance aloft for the charge. And of course the Nurse engages in sexual wordplay when she puns on* Rest *in line 7.*

10   take you   *greet you. The Nurse also jests on the sexual meaning of the phrase.*

—Nurse! —Wife! What, ho! —What, Nurse, I say!

Enter Nurse.

Go waken Juliet; go and trim her up.   25
I'll go and chat with Paris. Hie, make haste,
Make haste: the Bridegroom he is come already!
Make haste, I say!   *Exit.*

Scene 5

Nurse goes to Curtains.

NURSE   Mistress! What, Mistress! Juliet! —Fast, I
        warr'nt her, she—
     Why, Lamb! Why, Lady! Fie, you Sluggabed!
     Why, Love, I say! Madam! Sweetheart! Why, Bride!
     What, not a Word? You take your Pennyworth's now;
     Sleep for a week; for the next night, I warrant,   5
     The County Paris hath set up his Rest
     That you shall rest but little, God forgive me!
     Marry and amen! —How sound is she asleep!
     I must needs wake her. —Madam, Madam, Madam!
     Ay, let the County take you in your Bed!   10

12   down   *back in bed.*

19   my only Life!   *The disparity between what Juliet's mother*
      says here and what we have seen in earlier scenes should not
      lead us to assume that her grief is necessarily to be regarded as
      insincere. It is more likely that Shakespeare is simply portray-
      ing the Capulets as parents who are unaware of what their
      past treatment of their daughter reveals about their values. As
      the scene progresses, however, it becomes clear that Shake-
      speare expects the audience to see the family's lamentations as
      ludicrously excessive.

25   Out   *here, roughly equivalent to O.*

He'll fright you up, i'faith, will it not be?

She draws back the Curtains.

What, dress'd and in your Clothes, and down
   again?
I must needs wake you. Lady, Lady, Lady!
—Alas, alas! —Help, help! My Lady's dead!
—O weraday, that ever I was born!   15
—Some Aqua-vitae, ho! —My Lord! My Lady!

Enter Juliet's Mother.

CAPULET'S WIFE   What Noise is here?
NURSE   O lamentable Day!
CAPULET'S WIFE   What is the matter?
NURSE   Look, look! O heavy Day!
CAPULET'S WIFE   O me, O me, my Child, my only
   Life!
Revive! Look up, or I will die with thee!   20
Help, help! Call help!

Enter Juliet's Father.

CAPULET   For shame, bring Juliet forth: her Lord is
   come.
NURSE   She's dead, deceas'd; she's dead, alack the Day!
CAPULET'S WIFE   Alack the Day, she's dead, she's
   dead, she's dead!
CAPULET   Ha, let me see her! Out, alas, she's cold!   25

36   Death . . . thy Wife   *Capulet's personification of Death as a grim bridegroom is in keeping with his basic tendency to abstract from experience only what relates to his own concerns. Its effect is to divert attention from Juliet and focus it on Paris, who has been denied a bride, and on Capulet himself, who has been denied an heir and an opportunity to advance socially by means of his alliance with a Count.*

41   thought long   *long anticipated.*

Her Blood is settled, and her Joints are stiff;
Life and these Lips have long been separated.
Death lies on her like an untimely Frost
Upon the sweetest Flow'r of all the Field.

NURSE O lamentable Day!

CAPULET'S WIFE   O woeful Time!   30

CAPULET Death, that hath ta'en her hence to make
    me wail,
    Ties up my Tongue and will not let me speak.

Enter Friar Lawrence and the County Paris
with the Musicians.

FRIAR LAWRENCE Come, is the Bride ready to go to
    Church?

CAPULET Ready to go, but never to return.
    O Son, the Night before thy Wedding Day   35
    Hath Death lain with thy Wife. There she lies,
    Flower as she was, deflow'r'd by him.
    Death is my Son-in-Law, Death is my Heir:
    My Daughter he hath wedded. I will die
    And leave him all: Life, Living, all is Death's.   40

PARIS Have I thought long to see this Morning's
    Face,
    And doth it give me such a Sight as this?

CAPULET'S WIFE Accurs'd, unhappy, wretched,
    hateful Day!
    Most miserable Hour that e'er Time saw

243

45   In lasting labor   *in the lengthy toil.*

47   solace   *take comfort.*

48   catch'd   *snatched.*

55   Beguil'd   *cheated.*

59   martyr'd   *Capulet is probably using the term in its broad sense, to refer to murder and mutilation. But the word would also have had its usual modern sense, derived from the Greek word for "witness." In that sense ("sacrificed") it foreshadows Capulet's concluding speech in the play (V.iii.303–4).*

60   Uncomfortable   *bringing no comfort. By contrast, in V.iii.148 Friar Lawrence is described as "comfortable."*

65   Confusion's Cure   *The Latin root of the word* confusio *allows for meanings that range from a mild mixup to total devastation.*

66   Confusions   *The Friar here refers to the chaotic medley of outcries.*

67   Had part   *shared equally. Similarly, in line 69* part *means "half interest."*

70   part   *Here, while retaining the implications of its previous uses, the word shades into a different meaning, more or less equivalent to "commitment." The Friar is now presenting Heaven as Juliet's advocate, taking her part and keeping its part of the bargain in a way her earthly friends could not.*

244

In lasting labor of his Pilgrimage!　　　　　45
But one, poor one, one poor and loving Child;
But one thing to rejoice and solace in;
And cruel Death hath catch'd it from my Sight!
NURSE　O woe! O woeful, woeful, woeful Day!
Most lamentable Day, most woeful Day　　　50
That ever, ever I did yet behold!
O Day, O Day, O Day, O hateful Day!
Never was seen so black a Day as this.
O woeful Day, O woeful Day!
PARIS　Beguil'd, divorced, wronged, spited, slain!　55
Most detestable Death, by thee beguil'd,
By cruel, cruel Thee quite overthrown!
O Love, O Life! Not Life, but Love in Death!
CAPULET　Despis'd, distressed, hated, martyr'd,
　　　kill'd!
　　—Uncomfortable Time, why cam'st thou now　60
To murder, murder our Solemnity?
　　—O Child, O Child! My Soul, and not my Child!
Dead art thou! —Alack, my Child is dead,
And with my Child my Joys are buried.
FRIAR LAWRENCE　Peace ho, for shame! Confusion's
　　　Cure lives not　　　　　65
In these Confusions. Heaven and your self
Had part in this fair Maid; now Heav'n hath all,
And all the better is it for the Maid.
Your part in her you could not keep from Death,
But Heaven keeps his part in eternal Life.　　70

245

72   **advanc'd** *The word here means both "advantaged" (bene-fited) and "elevated" in social rank. In the next line, the Friar plays on both meanings with his observation that Juliet, in death, has now been granted the ultimate "promotion" (line 71).*

76   **well** *It was customary to speak of the dead as "well" (in a beatific afterlife).*

82   **fond Nature** *The Friar seems to be referring to Nature pri-marily in the sense of "human nature" (the feelings that are a part of being human), which is "fond" (foolish) in its inabil-ity to see what Reason perceives—that life in the sublunary world is only a pilgrimage to eternal life "above the Clouds" (line 74).*

84   **ordained** *planned, ordered. Here pronounced as a three-syl-lable word.*

85   **Office** *intended or proper function.*

86   **Instruments** *the musical instruments represented in the con-sort of minstrels commissioned for the wedding celebration.*

87   **Cheer** *the food to be provided for the wedding guests.*

88   **Sullen Dirges** *mournful funeral marches.*

94   **low'r** *frown.*
        Ill *sin, failing.*

The most you sought was her Promotion,
For 'twas your Heaven she should be advanc'd;
And weep ye now, seeing she is advanc'd
Above the Clouds as high as Heav'n itself?
O in this Love you love your Child so ill   75
That you run mad, seeing that she is well.
She's not well marri'd that lives marri'd long,
But she's best marri'd that dies marri'd young.
Dry up your Tears, and stick your Rosemary
On this fair Corse and, as the Custom is,   80
In all her best Array, bear her to Church;
For though fond Nature bids us all lament,
Yet Nature's Tears are Reason's Merriment.

CAPULET   All things that we ordained Festival
Turn from their Office to black Funeral: 85
Our Instruments to Melancholy Bells,
Our Wedding Cheer to a sad Burial Feast,
Our Solemn Hymns to Sullen Dirges change,
Our Bridal Flow'rs serve for a Buried Corse,
And all things change them to the contrary.   90

FRIAR LAWRENCE   Sir, go you in; and Madam, go with
     him;
And go, Sir Paris; every one prepare
To follow this fair Corse unto her Grave.
The Heav'ns do low'r upon you for some Ill;
Move them no more by crossing their high Will.   95

100   the Case may be amended   *The Fiddler takes the Nurse's use of "Case" in the preceding line (where it means "instance" or "situation") and applies it to his instrument case, pretending that the Nurse is telling him it is "pitiful" and in need of repair. His phrase also alludes to a proverbial saying, "the case is altered," another variation on "all things change them to the contrary" (line 90).*

101   "Heart's Ease"   *like "My Heart is Full" in line 106, a popular song.*

106   merry Dump   *A "dump" was a mournful or plaintive melody, written from the point of view of someone "down in the dumps." In effect, Peter is requesting the Musicians to play a merry sad song.*

111   give it you soundly   *Peter alludes to the practice of giving a tip to musicians in appreciation of their "sounds." But what he means is that he will "let them have it," and resoundingly.*

113   the Gleek   *here, an insulting gibe at the Minstrel's expense.*

114   the Minstral   *In all likelihood, Peter's words are accompanied by a rude gesture, to which the musician replies in kind with one to signify the "Serving-creature" (line 116).*

248

*Exeunt all but the Nurse and the Musicians, casting
Rosemary on Juliet's body and shutting the Curtains.*

FIRST MINSTREL   Faith, we may put up our Pipes and
   be gone.
NURSE   Honest good fellows, ah, put up, put up;
   For well you know this is a pitiful Case.
FIDDLER   Ay, by my troth, the Case may be amended.   100
                                             Exit Nurse.

Enter Peter.

PETER   Musicians, O Musicians: "Heart's Ease,"
   "Heart's Ease"! O and you will have me live,
   play "Heart's Ease."
FIDDLER   Why "Heart's Ease"?
PETER   O Musicians, because my Heart itself plays   105
   "My Heart is Full." O play me some merry Dump to
   comfort me.
MINSTRELS   Not a Dump we; 'tis no time to play now.
PETER   You will not then?
MINSTRELS   No.   110
PETER   I will then give it you soundly.
FIRST MINSTREL   What will you give us?
PETER   No Money, on my faith, but the Gleek; I will
   give you the Minstrel.
FIRST MINSTREL   Then will I give you the   115
   Serving-creature!

249

119   carry no Crotchets   *A crotchet was, among other things, a quarter note in music. Here Peter is reducing the Minstrel to a crotchet, just as the Minstrel in the preceding line has reduced Peter from a servingman to a serving-creature. Peter is saying that he will bear or put up with no crotchety musicians, and he probably emphasizes his words with a gesture resembling the hook-like shape of a quarter note. The phrase "carry no Crotchets" is here equivalent to "not carry Coals" (I.i.1).*

119–   re you . . . note me   *As Peter names the two notes,* re *and*
20   fa, *he probably points his dagger at the two Minstrels.*

124   put out your Wit   *The Second Minstrel is telling Peter to put away his dagger and display ("put out") his "Wit" (common sense) instead.*

128   griping   *clutching, distressing.*

135   Prates!   *(He) speaks idle nonsense.*
        Hugh Rebeck   *Peter is naming the Minstrels after their instruments. A* Catling *(line 132) was a lute string made of catgut; a* Rebeck *(line 135) was a forerunner of the violin; and a* Soundpost *(line 138) was a peg under the bridge of a stringed instrument.*

142–   no Gold for Sounding   *Peter says that he will give the*
43   *Musicians no payment for playing ("Sounding"). The only "Redress" (line 145) or compensation they can expect, in other words, is the "speedy Help" that Music's own "silver Sound" provides. In other words, like Virtue, Music is its own reward.*

PETER [*Drawing*] Then will I lay the
    Serving-creature's Dagger on your Pate! I will
    carry no Crotchets; I'll *re* you, I'll *fa* you, do
    you note me? 120
FIRST MINSTREL And you *re* us and *fa* us, you note
    us!
SECOND MINSTREL Pray you put up your Dagger, and
    put out your Wit.
PETER Then have at you with my Wit! I will 125
    dry-beat you with an iron Wit, and put up my
    iron Dagger. Answer me like Men:
        When griping Griefs the Heart doth wound
        And doleful Dumps the Mind oppress,
        Then Music with her silver Sound— 130
    Why "silver Sound"? Why "Music with her silver
    Sound"? —What say you, Simon Catling?
FIRST MINSTREL Marry Sir, because Silver hath a
    sweet Sound.
PETER Prates! —What say you, Hugh Rebeck? 135
SECOND MINSTREL I say "silver Sound" because
    Musicians sound for Silver.
PETER Prates too! —What say you, James Soundpost?
THIRD MINSTREL Faith, I know not what to say.
PETER O I cry you mercy, you are the Singer! I 140
    will say for you: it is "Music with her silver
    Sound" because Musicians have no Gold for
    Sounding.

251

148   **Jack**   *a coarse, unrefined fellow.*

149   stay   *wait for.*
       Dinner   *It is now approaching noon.*

Then Music with her silver Sound
With speedy Help doth lend Redress.   *Exit.*   145
FIRST MINSTREL   What a pestilent Knave is this
   same!
SECOND MINSTREL   Hang him, Jack! Come, we'll in
   here, tarry for the Mourners, and stay Dinner.

Exeunt.

V.i   *The scene shifts to Mantua, where the banished Romeo awaits some word from Juliet.*

1–2   **If I . . . hand.**   *Romeo is saying that dreams sometimes deceive us by making us think that things are better than they are in reality. Ironically, the dream he describes proves to be a "flatt'ring" version of the play's final scene.*

2   presage   *foreshadow.*

3   Bosom's Lord   *heart.*

5   **Lifts me above the Ground**   *Romeo's phrasing echoes what he said in I.iv.19–22, just before he entered the Capulet party where he met Juliet.*

10–11   **Ah me . . . Joy.**   *If "Love's Shadows" (Love's dreams and imaginings) are so "rich in Joy," how much more sweetness does "Love itself" possess?*

Act Five

Scene 1

Enter Romeo.

ROMEO If I may trust the flatt'ring truth of Sleep,
My Dreams presage some joyful News at hand.
My Bosom's Lord sits lightly in his Throne,
And all this Day an unaccustom'd Spirit
Lifts me above the Ground with cheerful Thoughts.   5
I dreamt my Lady came and found me dead
(Strange Dream that gives a Dead-man leave to
    think)
And breath'd such Life with Kisses in my Lips
That I reviv'd and was an Emperor.
Ah me, how sweet is Love itself possess'd   10
When but Love's Shadows are so rich in Joy.

S.D. booted *wearing riding boots, probably with spurs.*

17 she is well *Balthasar's words echo the Friar's in IV.v.73, and carry the implication that, being in Heaven, Juliet is in bliss.*

18 Her Body sleeps *What the audience knows is that these words are true literally rather than metaphorically.*

21 presently *instantly.*

23 Office *responsibility.*

24 deny you, Stars *This is the reading in both the Second Quarto and the First Folio. The First Quarto reads "defy my Stars." Both phrases mean much the same: Romeo is declaring himself a cosmic rebel, and he says that henceforth he will take his destiny into his own hands.*

26 Post-horses *horses kept at a post-house for hire by travelers in need of getting somewhere "post-haste."*

28–29 import / Some Misadventure *foretell some mishap.*

29 Tush *a mild expression of dismissal.*

32 No matter *never mind, it doesn't matter.*

Enter Romeo's man Balthasar, booted.

News from Verona! —How now, Balthasar?
Dost thou not bring me Letters from the Friar?
How doth my Lady? Is my Father well?
How fares my Lady Juliet? That I ask again,   15
For nothing can be ill if she be well.
BALTHASAR   Then she is well and nothing can be ill:
Her Body sleeps in Capel's Monument,
And her Immortal Part with Angels lives.
I saw her laid low in her Kindred's Vault   20
And presently took post to tell it you.
O pardon me for bringing these Ill News
Since you did leave it for my Office, Sir.
ROMEO   Is it e'en so? —Then I deny you, Stars!
—Thou know'st my Lodging; get me Ink and Paper   25
And hire Post-horses: I will hence tonight.
BALTHASAR   I do beseech you, Sir, have Patience:
Your Looks are pale and wild, and do import
Some Misadventure.
ROMEO   Tush, thou art deceiv'd.
Leave me, and do the thing I bid thee do.   30
Hast thou no Letters to me from the Friar?
BALTHASAR   No, my good Lord.
ROMEO   No matter; get thee gone,
And hire those Horses. I'll be with thee
   straight.   *Exit Balthasar.*
—Well, Juliet, I will lie with thee tonight.

38   'a   *he.*

39   Weeds   *clothes.*
      overwhelming   *overhanging.*

40   Culling of Simples   *sorting out herbs.*

45   beggarly account   *wretched assortment.*

47   Packthread   *twine for parcels.*
      Cakes of Roses · *rose petals compressed and used for perfume.*

48   Show   *display of wares.*

52   caitiff   *literally, captive; trapped in misery.*

—Let's see for Means. —O Mischief, thou art
   swift   35
To enter in the Thoughts of desp'rate Men:
I do remember an Apothecary
(And hereabouts 'a dwells), which late I noted
In tatt'red Weeds, with overwhelming Brows,
Culling of Simples. Meager were his Looks;   40
Sharp Misery had worn him to the Bones;
And in his needy Shop a Tortoise hung,
An Alligator stuff'd, and other Skins
Of ill-shap'd Fishes; and about his Shelves
A beggarly account of empty Boxes,   45
Green earthen Pots, Bladders and musty Seeds,
Remnants of Packthread, and old Cakes of Roses
Were thinly scatter'd to make up a Show.
Noting this Penury, to my self I said
"An' if a Man did need a Poison now,   50
Whose sale is present Death in Mantua,
Here lives a caitiff Wretch would sell it him."
O this same Thought did but forerun my Need,
And this same needy Man must sell it me.
As I remember, this should be the House.   55
Being Holiday, the Beggar's Shop is shut.
What ho, Apothecary!
APOTHECARY   [*Within*] Who calls so loud?
ROMEO   Come hither, Man.

Enter Apothecary.

---

59   **forty Ducats**   *A ducat was a gold coin, and forty ducats would have been enough for a very expensive ring or its equivalent.*

60   **soon-speeding Gear**   *quick-working compound.*

63   **Trunk**   *body.*

64–65   **hasty Powder . . . Womb**   *This image recalls what the Friar said in II.vi.10–11 and in III.iii.131–33.*

67   **any he**   *any one.*
       utters   *gives out.*

68–75   **Art thou . . . Will**   *By depicting the Apothecary's situation in abstract terms, Romeo endeavors to obtain the poison he needs without seeming to implicate the poor Apothecary in a crime for which either must feel responsible.*

82   **Compounds**   *mixed drugs.*

ROMEO   I see that thou art Poor.
    Hold, there is forty Ducats: let me have
    A dram of Poison, such soon-speeding Gear   60
    As will disperse itself through all the Veins,
    That the Life-weary Taker may fall dead,
    And that the Trunk may be discharg'd of Breath
    As violently as hasty Powder fir'd
    Doth hurry from the fatal Cannon's Womb.   65
APOTHECARY   Such mortal Drugs I have, but Mantua's
    Law
    Is Death to any he that utters them.
ROMEO   Art thou so bare and full of Wretchedness
    And fear'st to die? Famine is in thy Cheeks,
    Need and Oppression starveth in thy Eyes,   70
    Contempt and Begg'ry hangs upon thy Back:
    The World is not thy Friend, nor the World's Law.
    The World affords no Law to make thee Rich:
    Then be not Poor, but break it and take this.
APOTHECARY   My Poverty, but not my Will, consents.   75
ROMEO   I pray thy Poverty and not thy Will.
APOTHECARY   Put this in any Liquid Thing you will
    And drink it off; and if you had the Strength
    Of twenty Men, it would dispatch you straight.
ROMEO   There is thy Gold: worse Poison to Men's
    Souls,   80
    Doing more Murder in this loathsome World,
    Than these poor Compounds that thou may'st not
    sell.

261

84   get thy self in Flesh   *This phrase suggests that the Apothe-
      cary is so emaciated as to be almost naked of flesh. His cadav-
      erous appearance is no doubt intended to remind the audience
      of traditional images of such allegorical types as Despair and
      Death, both of which are pertinent to Romeo's spiritual state
      at this point in the play.*

85   Cordial   *a health-giving liquid, a drink or medicine to stimu-
      late the heart.*

V.ii *The setting for this scene is the cell of Friar Lawrence. The stage
      direction suggests that Friar John and Friar Lawrence enter
      from different doors. Possibly Friar John's voice is to be heard
      within (that is, from behind the door he enters) before he
      emerges into view of Friar Lawrence and the audience.*

5   barefoot Brother   *a reminder that Franciscan Friars were to
      take vows of poverty and live simply.*

6   to associate me   *to accompany me, be my associate.*

8   Searchers of the Town   *volunteers whose duty was to search
      out possible carriers of the plague and quarantine them to
      avoid spread of the infection. The London theatres had been
      closed for much of 1592–93 because of the plague; the situa-
      tion described here would therefore have been familiar to
      Shakespeare's original theatregoers.*

12   stay'd   *suspended, delayed.*

I sell thee Poison; thou hast sold me none.
Farewell; buy Food and get thy self in Flesh.

Exit Apothecary.

—Come, Cordial and not Poison: go with me   85
To Juliet's Grave, for there must I use thee.

Exit.

Scene 2

Enter Friar John to Friar Lawrence.

FRIAR JOHN   Holy Franciscan Friar! Brother, ho!
FRIAR LAWRENCE   This same should be the Voice of
    Friar John.
    Welcome from Mantua! What says Romeo?
    Or if his Mind be writ, give me his Letter.
FRIAR JOHN   Going to find a barefoot Brother out,   5
    One of our Order to associate me
    Here in this City visiting the Sick,
    And finding him, the Searchers of the Town,
    Suspecting that we both were in a House
    Where the infectious Pestilence did reign,   10
    Seal'd up the Doors and would not let us forth,
    So that my speed to Mantua there was stay'd.

263

---

18   nice   *small, inconsequential, innocent.*
        Charge   *weight, command, importance.*

21   Crow   *crowbar, a tool for prying things open.*
        straight   *directly, immediately.*

23   Monument   *the Capulet's burial monument, mausoleum.*

24   hours   *here pronounced as a two-syllable word.*

25   beshrew   *blame, upbraid.*

26   Accidents   *occurrences (specifically, the circumstances surrounding Juliet's "death").*

FRIAR LAWRENCE   Who bare my Letter then to
    Romeo?

FRIAR JOHN   I could not send it—here it is again—
    Nor get a Messenger to bring it thee,   15
    So fearful were they of Infection.

FRIAR LAWRENCE   Unhappy Fortune! By my
    Brotherhood,
    The Letter was not nice but full of Charge,
    Of dear Import, and the neglecting it
    May do much Danger. Friar John, go hence,   20
    Get me an Iron Crow, and bring it straight
    Unto my Cell!

FRIAR JOHN   Brother, I'll go and bring it thee.

                                       Exit.

FRIAR LAWRENCE   Now must I to the Monument
    alone.
    Within three hours will fair Juliet wake;
    She will beshrew me much that Romeo   25
    Hath had no Notice of these Accidents;
    But I will write again to Mantua,
    And keep her at my Cell till Romeo come.
    Poor living Corse, clos'd in a Dead-man's Tomb!

                                       Exit.

V.iii.   *The setting for this final scene is the Churchyard, with the Capulets' Monument represented in a prominent position on the stage.*

S.D.   Sweet-water   *perfumed water.*

1   aloof   *at a distance.*

3   lay thee all along   *lie at full length on the ground.*

6   loose, unfirm   *These adjectives refer to the Churchyard, whose ground is "unfirm" from gravedigging.*

8   some thing   *spelled as a single word in line 18 below; evidently spelled as two words at this point in the Second Quarto to signal that the metrical stress is to fall on* thing.

11   adventure   *take my chances.*

12   Flow'r   *Paris addresses Juliet.*

14   dew   *sprinkle.*

15   wanting   *lacking.*
        distill'd by   *either (a) discharged by, or (b) mixed with, diluted by.*

16   Obsequies   *rites for the dead.*

266

Scene 3

Enter Paris and his Page, with Flowers and
Sweet-water and a Torch.

PARIS   Give me thy Torch, Boy. Hence and stand
    aloof.
  Yet put it out, for I would not be seen.
  Under yond Yew-trees lay thee all along,
  Holding thy Ear close to the hollow Ground,
  So shall no Foot upon the Churchyard tread,   5
  Being loose, unfirm with digging up of Graves,
  But thou shalt hear it. Whistle then to me
  As Signal that thou hear'st some thing approach.
  Give me those Flow'rs. Do as I bid thee: go!
PAGE   [*Aside*] I am almost afraid to stand alone   10
  Here in the Churchyard, yet I will adventure.
                              He retires.
PARIS   Sweet Flow'r, with Flow'rs thy Bridal Bed I
    strew.
  O Woe, thy Canopy is Dust and Stones,
  Which with Sweet-water nightly I will dew,
  Or, wanting that, with Tears distill'd by Moans.   15
  The Obsequies that I for thee will keep
  Nightly shall be to strew thy Grave and weep.

267

21   Muffle   *wrap or cloak.*

22   Mattock   *a type of pickaxe, designed both to dig and to cut.*
wrenching Iron   *crowbar.*

25   charge   *command.*

30–31   take thence . . . Ring   *Since Romeo does not in fact take a ring from Juliet's finger, it seems most likely that this explanation is offered merely to keep Balthasar from interfering. Paris, who is presumably too far away to hear Romeo, has no way of knowing Romeo's true intent; nor, of course, is he aware of Romeo's relationship with Juliet.*

38   inexorable   *unrelenting, implacable.*

39   empty   *famished, ravenously hungry.*

The Boy gives Warning: something doth approach.
What cursed Foot wanders this way tonight
To cross my Obsequies and True-love's Rite?   20
What, with a Torch? —Muffle me, Night, a while.

He retires.

Enter Romeo and his man Balthasar, with a Torch,
a Mattock, and a Crow of Iron.

ROMEO   Give me that Mattock and the wrenching Iron.
Hold, take this Letter: early in the Morning
See thou deliver't to my Lord and Father.
Give me the Light. Upon thy Life I charge thee,   25
Whate'er thou hear'st or see'st, stand all aloof,
And do not interrupt me in my Course.
Why I descend into this Bed of Death
Is partly to behold my Lady's Face,
But chiefly to take thence from her dead Finger   30
A precious Ring, a Ring that I must use
In dear Employment. Therefore hence be gone.
But if thou jealous dost return to pry
In what I farther shall intend to do,
By Heaven I will tear thee Joint by Joint   35
And strew this hungry Churchyard with thy Limbs!
The Time and my Intents are savage wild,
More fierce and more inexorable far
Than empty Tigers or the roaring Sea.

43   For all this same   *for all that he and I have said. Balthasar shows true loyalty to and concern for Romeo when he decides to stand watch despite Romeo's stern warnings.*

45   Maw   *mouth and throat of a voracious animal.*

47   enforce   *force.*

48   in despite   *in defiance, spite.*

54   unhallow'd Toil   *unholy labors.*

60   Fly   *flee.*
       these gone   *these who have died.*

BALTHASAR   I will be gone, Sir, and not trouble ye.   40
ROMEO   So shalt thou show me Friendship. Take thou
    that: *He hands him Money.*
  Live and be prosp'rous; and farewell, good
  Fellow.
BALTHASAR   [*Aside*] For all this same, I'll hide me
    here about:
  His Looks I fear, and his Intents I doubt.
                                 He retires.
ROMEO   Thou detestable Maw, thou Womb of Death,   45
  Gorg'd with the dearest Morsel of the Earth,
  Thus I enforce thy rotten Jaws to open
  And in despite I'll cram thee with more Food.
                           He opens the Tomb.
PARIS   [*Aside*] This is that banish'd, haughty
    Mountague
  That murd'red my Love's Cousin, with which Grief   50
  It is supposed the Fair Creature died,
  And here is come to do some vill'nous Shame
  To the dead Bodies. I will apprehend him.
                      He draws and steps forth.
  —Stop thy unhallow'd Toil, vile Mountague!
  Can Vengeance be pursu'd further than Death?   55
  Condemned Villain, I do apprehend thee:
  Obey and go with me, for thou must die!
ROMEO   I must indeed, and therefore came I hither.
  Good, gentle Youth, tempt not a desp'rate Man;
  Fly hence and leave me. Think upon these gone: 60

68 Conjurations *entreaties. Paris may also be thinking of the "unhallow'd" nature of Romeo's mission, in which case he is probably assuming that anyone who seeks to pursue vengeance "further than death" is in league with evil spirits. This reading derives from the First Quarto; the Second Quarto reads* commiration; *later Quartos and the First Folio read* commiseration.

76 betossed *unsettled, tormented.*

78 should have *was to have.*

84 Lanthorn *lantern. The old spelling is retained here partly as a guide to pronunciation, and partly as a reminder that windows (whether in lanterns or in buildings) were made of thin sheets of horn in Shakespeare's time. Here the word probably refers to the lantern dome designed to admit sunlight to a church or cathedral. Romeo's lantern image provides yet another link between this play and the "Pyramus and Thisby" playlet in* A Midsummer Night's Dream.

Let that affright thee. I beseech thee, Youth,
Put not another Sin upon my Head
By urging me to Fury. O be gone!
By Heav'n I love thee better than my self,
For I come hither arm'd against my self. 65
Stay not: begone, live, and hereafter say
A Madman's Mercy bid thee run away.

PARIS   I do defy thy Conjurations
And apprehend thee for a Felon here.

ROMEO   Wilt thou provoke me? Then have at thee,
   Boy!   *They fight.*   70

PAGE   O Lord, they fight! I will go call the
   Watch.   *Exit.*

PARIS   O I am slain! If thou be merciful,
Open the Tomb, lay me with Juliet.

ROMEO   In faith I will.   *Paris dies.*
            —Let me peruse this Face.
Mercutio's Kinsman, noble County Paris!   75
What said my Man when my betossed Soul
Did not attend him as we rode? I think
He told me Paris should have married Juliet.
Said he not so? Or did I dream it so?
Or am I mad, hearing him talk of Juliet,   80
To think it was so? —O give me thy Hand:
One writ with me in sour Misfortune's Book.
I'll bury thee in a triumphant Grave.
            He opens the Tomb to reveal Juliet.
A Grave? O no, a Lanthorn, slaught'red Youth:

273

86   **Feasting Presence**   *probably a reference to the celebration of Holy Communion, a feast in which the Divine presence is made manifest.*

89   **Keepers**   *prison guards.*

90   **Light'ning**   *The "lightening" Romeo refers to is a sense of exhilaration similar to the state he described in V.i.1–5.*

94   **Ensign**   *standard-bearer, officer who carried the royal insignia.*

95   **crimson**   *Romeo assumes that the color in Juliet's features is still lingering despite her death. He has no way of knowing that the crimson is only now returning to her lips and cheeks as the effect of the Friar's potion wears off.*

103   **unsubstantial**   *without substance or body.*

105   **Paramour**   *royal mistress.*

110   **set up . . . Rest**   *establish my eternal resting place. This phrase echoes the Nurse's words about Paris (IV.v.6–7).*

111   **shake the Yoke**   *throw off the harness. Romeo's image suggests that he thinks of himself as an ox or other beast of burden. By taking his own life, he hopes to rid his "Flesh" (line 112) of all the cares the World and the Stars have placed on his back.*

       inauspicious Stars   *unlucky conjunction of the planets. An Elizabethan familiar with astrology would have observed that suicide normally indicated, not liberation from, but enslavement to and defeat by "the Stars."*

274

For here lies Juliet, and her Beauty makes 85
This Vault a Feasting Presence full of Light.
Death, lie thou there by a Dead-man interr'd.

He lays Paris in the Tomb.

—How oft when Men are at the point of Death
Have they been Merry? Which their Keepers call
A Light'ning before Death. O how may I 90
Call this a Light'ning? —O my Love, my Wife:
Death, that hath suck'd the Honey of thy Breath,
Hath had no power yet upon thy Beauty!
Thou art not conquer'd: Beauty's Ensign yet
Is crimson in thy Lips and in thy Cheeks, 95
And Death's pale Flag is not advanced there.
—Tybalt, liest thou there in thy bloody Sheet?
O what more Favor can I do to thee
Than with that Hand that cut thy Youth in twain
To sunder his that was thine Enemy? 100
Forgive me, Cousin. —Ah dear Juliet,
Why art thou yet so Fair? Shall I believe
That unsubstantial Death is amorous,
And that the lean, abhorred Monster keeps
Thee here in dark to be his Paramour? 105
For fear of that I still will stay with thee,
And never from this Pallet of dim Night
Depart again; here, here will I remain,
With Worms that are thy Chambermaids; O here
Will I set up my everlasting Rest 110
And shake the Yoke of inauspicious Stars

114–   seal . . . Death   *Romeo's imagery derives from the realm of*
15   *legal contracts. He is, in effect, completing a purchase and*
        thus closing a deal (as one who is in a "righteous" or legally
        entitled position to "seal" a "Bargain"). Death is "engross-
        ing" both in its role as purchaser (buying a "gross" or large
        quantity of goods) and in its role as the one who writes
        ("engrosses") the contract. The bargain is "dateless" because
        it will be for eternity.

116–   Conduct . . . Pilot   *Romeo addresses the poison.*
17

118   Bark   *Romeo's body. (Compare Capulet's use of the term in*
        III.v.134–35.)

120   quick   *rapid. Ironically,* quick *also meant "alive," "living."*

S.D.   Crow   *crowbar.*

122   stumbled   *The Friar's use of this verb is an ironic echo of his*
        earlier counsel to Romeo: "Wisely and slow: they stumble that
        run fast" (II.iii.94).

126   Grubs   *grubworms.*

276

From this World-wearied Flesh. —Eyes, look your
    last;
Arms take your last Embrace; and Lips, O you
The Doors of Breath, seal with a righteous Kiss
A dateless Bargain to engrossing Death!   115

He kisses Juliet.

—Come, bitter Conduct; come unsavory Guide.
Thou desp'rate Pilot, now at once run on
The dashing Rocks thy seasick, weary Bark.
[*Drinking*] Here's to my Love. —O true Apothecary:
Thy Drugs are quick. Thus with a Kiss I die.   120

He falls.

Enter Friar Lawrence with Lantern, Crow, and Spade.

FRIAR LAWRENCE   Saint Francis be my speed: how oft
    tonight
    Have my old Feet stumbled at Graves! Who's there?
BALTHASAR   Here's one a Friend, and one that knows
    you well.
FRIAR LAWRENCE   Bliss be upon you! Tell me, good
    my Friend,
    What Torch is yond that vainly lends his Light   125
    To Grubs and eyeless Skulls? As I discern,
    It burneth in the Capels' Monument.
BALTHASAR   It doth so, Holy Sir, and there's my
    Master,
    One that you love.

133   fearfully   *threateningly.*

135–   Fear . . . thing!   *The Friar probably speaks these lines to*
36   *himself as he rushes toward the tomb.*

136   unthrifty   *unfortunate (literally, unthriving).*

142   Master-less   *separated from their masters or owners.*

148   comfortable   *comforting, bearing comfort.*

FRIAR LAWRENCE   Who is it?

BALTHASAR   Romeo.

FRIAR LAWRENCE   How long hath he been there?

BALTHASAR   Full half an hour.   130

FRIAR LAWRENCE   Go with me to the Vault.

BALTHASAR   I dare not, Sir:
 My Master knows not but I am gone hence,
 And fearfully did menace me with Death
 If I did stay to look on his Intents.

FRIAR LAWRENCE   Stay then, I'll go alone. —Fear comes
 upon me;   135
 O much I fear some ill, unthrifty thing!

BALTHASAR   As I did sleep under this Yew-tree here,
 I dreamt my Master and another fought
 And that my Master slew him.

FRIAR LAWRENCE   [*Calling*] Romeo!
   Friar stoops and looks on the Blood and Weapons.
 —Alack, alack, what Blood is this which stains   140
 The stony Entrance of this Sepulcher?
 What mean these Master-less and gory Swords
 To lie discolor'd by this place of Peace?
      He enters the Tomb.
 Romeo! O pale! Who else? What, Paris too?
 And steep'd in Blood? Ah what an unkind Hour   145
 Is guilty of this lamentable Chance?
 The Lady stirs.   *Juliet rises.*

JULIET   O comfortable Friar, where is my Lord?
 I do remember well where I should be,

155   Bosom   *lap.*

163   Churl   *lowborn servant. Normally a term of contempt,* churl *is here used chidingly but with the deepest love.*

165   Haply   *perhaps; but "happily" may be implied as well.*

166   die with a Restorative   *A restorative was a cordial or medicine to stimulate the heart. Juliet's words echo Romeo's description of the poison as "Cordial and not Poison" in V.i.85.*

167   warm   *another exquisitely painful reminder of how crucial a role timing plays in the tragic outcome of this play.*

And there I am. Where is my Romeo? *Noise within.* 150
FRIAR LAWRENCE   I hear some Noise, Lady: come
    from that nest
Of Death, Contagion, and unnatural Sleep.
A greater Pow'r than we can contradict
Hath thwarted our Intents. Come, come away.
Thy Husband in thy Bosom there lies dead,   155
And Paris too. Come, I'll dispose of thee
Among a Sisterhood of holy Nuns.
Stay not to question, for the Watch is coming.
Come, go, good Juliet! I dare no longer stay!
JULIET   Go get thee hence: for I will not away.   160

                                Exit Friar Lawrence.

—What's here? A Cup clos'd in my True-love's
    Hand?
Poison I see hath been his timeless End!
—O Churl! Drink all, and left no friendly Drop
To help me after? I will kiss thy Lips:
Haply some Poison yet doth hang on them   165
To make me die with a Restorative.

                                   She kisses Romeo.

Thy Lips are warm!

         Enter Paris' Boy and the Watch.

CHIEF WATCHMAN   Lead, Boy: which way?
JULIET   Yea, Noise? Then I'll be brief. O happy
    Dagger,

170   **Sheath** *Juliet refers to her breast, where she plunges the dagger. In a play in which there have been so many references to knives and sheathes (both literal and metaphorical), this final gesture is surely intended by the playwright as a way of linking the imagery of sexuality and violence—the two manifestations of "hot blood" at the core of the tragedy.*

173   **attach** *detain, arrest.*

179–   **Ground . . . Ground** *both (a) the earth of the Church-*
80   *yard, and (b) the basis or reason for what has happened.*

181   **Circumstance** *evidence, detail, information.*
       descry *perceive.*

This is thy Sheath; there rust and let me die. 170

She stabs herself and falls.

PAGE   This is the Place: there where the Torch doth burn.

CHIEF WATCHMAN   The Ground is bloody; search about the Churchyard.

Go, some of you: whoe'er you find, attach.

Exeunt some Watchmen.

Pitiful Sight! Here lies the County slain,
And Juliet bleeding, warm, and newly dead, 175
Who here hath lain this two days buried.
Go tell the Prince; run to the Capulets;
Raise up the Mountagues! Some others search:

Exeunt others.

We see the Ground whereon these Woes do lie,
But the true Ground of all these piteous Woes 180
We cannot without Circumstance descry.

*Enter some of the Watch with Romeo's man
Balthasar.*

SECOND WATCHMAN   Here's Romeo's Man; we found him in the Churchyard.

CHIEF WATCHMAN   Hold him in safety till the Prince come hither.

Enter another Watchman with Friar Lawrence.

283

188   Misadventure   *terrible occurrence.*

189   our Person   *The Prince employs the royal* we. *In the Renais-*
       sance a ruler was assumed to gather into his own person all his
       subjects (a tradition whose echoes still reverberate in the
       phrase "the body politic").

190   shrike   *shrieked.*

THIRD WATCHMAN   Here is a Friar, that trembles,
    sighs, and weeps.
    We took this Mattock and this Spade from him   185
    As he was coming from this Churchyard's side.
CHIEF WATCHMAN   A great Suspicion: stay the Friar
    too.

Enter the Prince and Attendants.

PRINCE   What Misadventure is so early up
    That calls our Person from our morning Rest?

Enter old Capulet and his Wife, with Others.

CAPULET   What should it be that is so shrike abroad?   190
CAPULET'S WIFE   O the People in the Street cry
    "Romeo,"
    Some "Juliet," and some "Paris," and all run
    With open Outcry toward our Monument.
PRINCE   What Fear is this which startles in your
    Ears?
CHIEF WATCHMAN   Sovereign, here lies the County
    Paris slain,   195
    And Romeo dead, and Juliet, dead before,
    Warm and new-kill'd.
PRINCE   Search, seek, and know how this foul Murder
    comes.

285

203   House   *sheath, scabbard.*

214   Untaught   *Mountague's phrase alludes both to Romeo's youth and to the lack of experience and wisdom his act exemplifies.*

215   press   *shove ahead.*

216   Seal up the Mouth of Outrage   *The Prince fears yet another outbreak of feuding.*

218   Spring   *source.*

219   General   *commanding officer.*

CHIEF WATCHMAN   Here is a Friar, and slaughter'd
        Romeo's Man,
    With Instruments upon them fit to open   200
    These Dead-men's Tombs.
CAPULET   O Heav'ns! O Wife, look how our Daughter
        bleeds!
    This Dagger hath mista'en, for lo his House
    Is empty on the Back of Mountague
    And it mis-sheathed in my Daughter's Bosom!   205
CAPULET'S WIFE   O me, this sight of Death is as a
        Bell
    That warns my Old Age to a Sepulcher.

Enter Mountague.

PRINCE   Come, Mountague, for thou art early up,
    To see thy Son and Heir, now early down.
MOUNTAGUE   Alas, my Liege, my Wife is dead tonight;   210
    Grief of my Son's Exile hath stopp'd her Breath.
    What further Woe conspires against mine Age?
PRINCE   Look and thou shalt see.
MOUNTAGUE   O thou Untaught, what Manners is in this,
    To press before thy Father to a Grave?   215
PRINCE   Seal up the Mouth of Outrage for a while,
    Till we can clear these Ambiguities
    And know their Spring, their Head, their true
        Descent;
    And then will I be Gen'ral of your Woes

287

225   make against me   *testify against me, make me look suspect.*

226   impeach and purge   *accuse and exonerate.*

229   Date of Breath   *remaining lifetime.*

237   Siege   *seizure.*

238   perforce   *by force.*

And lead you ev'n to Death. Mean time forbear,   220
And let Mischance be slave to Patience.
Bring forth the Parties of Suspicion.

FRIAR LAWRENCE   I am the greatest, able to do least,
Yet most suspected, as the Time and Place
Doth make against me, of this direful Murder: 225
And here I stand, both to impeach and purge
My self condemned and my self excus'd.

PRINCE   Then say at once what thou dost know in
   this.

FRIAR LAWRENCE   I will be brief, for my short Date
   of Breath
Is not so long as is a tedious Tale.   230
Romeo there dead was Husband to that Juliet,
And she there dead, that's Romeo's faithful Wife:
I marri'd them, and their stol'n Marriage Day
Was Tybalt's Doomsday, whose untimely Death
Banish'd the new-made Bridegroom from this City,   235
For whom, and not for Tybalt, Juliet pin'd.
You, to remove that Siege of Grief from her,
Betroth'd and would have marri'd her perforce
To County Paris. Then comes she to me,
And with Wild Looks bid me devise some Mean   240
To rid her from this second Marriage,
Or in my Cell there would she kill her self.
Then gave I her (so tutor'd by my Art)
A Sleeping Potion, which so took effect
As I intended, for it wrought on her   245

289

247   as this dire Night   *as he did on this terrible night.*

255   closely   *in hiding.*

264   Violence   *here pronounced glidingly so as to constitute two syllables metrically.*

266   ought   *anything.*

The Form of Death. Mean time I writ to Romeo
That he should hither come, as this dire Night,
To help to take her from her borrow'd Grave,
Being the time the Potion's Force should cease.
But he which bore my Letter, Friar John,   250
Was stay'd by Accident, and yesternight
Return'd my Letter back. Then all alone
At the pre-fixed Hour of her Waking
Came I to take her from her Kindred's Vault,
Meaning to keep her closely at my Cell   255
Till I conveniently could send to Romeo.
But when I came, some minute ere the Time
Of her Awak'ning, here untimely lay
The noble Paris and true Romeo dead.
She wakes, and I entreated her come forth   260
And bear this Work of Heav'n with Patience;
But then a Noise did scare me from the Tomb,
And she, too desp'rate, would not go with me,
But as it seems did Violence on her Self.
All this I know, and to the Marriage   265
Her Nurse is privy. And if ought in this
Miscarried by my Fault, let my old Life
Be sacrific'd some Hour before his Time
Unto the rigor of severest Law.
PRINCE   We still have known thee for a Holy Man.   270
      Where's Romeo's Man? What can he say to this?
BALTHASAR   I brought my Master News of Juliet's
      Death,

273   in post   *in haste.*

276   going   *here treated as a single syllable metrically.*

280   what made . . . place?   *What made your Master come to this place?*

283   Anon   *shortly.*

286   make good   *verify, corroborate.*

292   Scourge   *punishment; literally, a whip.*

294   Winking at   *closing my eyes to, failing to attend to.*

295   Brace   *pair (Mercutio and Paris).*

And then in post he came from Mantua
To this same Place, to this same Monument.
This Lett'r he early bid me give his Father,   275
And threat'ned me with Death, going in the Vault,
If I departed not and left him there.
PRINCE   Give me the Letter; I will look on it.
Where is the County's Page that rais'd the
   Watch?
Sirrah, what made your Master in this Place?   280
PAGE   He came with Flow'rs to strew his Lady's
   Grave,
And bid me stand aloof, and so I did.
Anon comes one with Light to ope the Tomb,
And by and by my Master drew on him,
And then I ran away to call the Watch.   285
PRINCE   This Letter doth make good the Friar's
   Words:
Their course of Love, the Tidings of her Death;
And here he writes that he did buy a Poison
Of a poor 'Pothecary and therewithal
Came to this Vault to die and lie with Juliet.   290
Where be these Enemies? —Capulet, Mountague,
See what a Scourge is laid upon your Hate,
That Heav'n finds means to kill your Joys with
   Love!
And I for Winking at your Discords too
Have lost a Brace of Kinsmen. All are punish'd.   295
CAPULET   O brother Mountague, give me thy Hand.

293

297   Jointure   *the sum reserved for the wife in the event that her husband should die first and leave her widowed.*

299   raise her Statue   *erect a statue in her image.*

S.D.   Exeunt omnes.   *The stage direction probably indicates a processional exit for everyone (omnes) remaining on stage.*

This is my Daughter's Jointure, for no more
Can I demand.

MOUNTAGUE   But I can give thee more:
For I will raise her Statue in pure Gold,
That whiles Verona by that Name is known   300
There shall no Figure at such rate be set
As that of True and Faithful Juliet.

CAPULET   As rich shall Romeo's by his Lady's lie,
Poor Sacrifices of our Enmity.

PRINCE   A glooming Peace this Morning with it
    brings;   305
The Sun for Sorrow will not show his Head.
Go hence to have more talk of these Sad Things.
Some shall be pardon'd and some punished:
For never was a Story of more Woe
Than this of Juliet and her Romeo.   *Exeunt omnes.*   310

FINIS

TITUS ANDRONICUS

NAMES OF THE ACTORS

SATURNINUS, Son to the late Emperor of Rome; later
    Emperor
BASSIANUS, Younger Brother to Saturninus; rival for the
    Empery, and betrothed of Lavinia

TITUS ANDRONICUS, Roman General; conqueror of the
    Goths
MARCUS ANDRONICUS, Tribune of the People; Titus'
    Brother

LUCIUS
QUINTUS
MARTIUS   SONS TO TITUS ANDRONICUS
MUTIUS

LAVINIA, Daughter to Titus Andronicus
YOUNG LUCIUS, Son to Lucius
PUBLIUS, Son to Marcus Andronicus

SEMPRONIUS
CAIUS   KINSMEN TO TITUS ANDRONICUS
VALENTINE

TAMORA, former Queen of the Goths; later Empress of Rome

ALARBUS
DEMETRIUS   SONS TO TAMORA
CHIRON

AARON, a Moor beloved by Tamora

AEMILIUS, a noble Roman and Nuntius (Messenger)
CLOWN who carries Titus' message to Saturninus
NURSE who brings Blackamoor Child from Tamora
CHILD begotten by Aaron and born to Tamora

SENATORS, TRIBUNES, FOLLOWERS, SOLDIERS, ATTEN-
   DANTS

I.i.   *The first scene takes place before the Senate House in Rome, with one part of the stage designated as the burial monument of the Andronici.*

1   Noble . . . Right   *As the eldest son of the deceased Emperor, Saturninus calls for the support of the Patricians, Rome's aristocracy. In the Elizabethan period,* Patrons *meant both "patterns" and "sponsors," and Saturninus invokes the first meaning of the word when he suggests that his patrons are also "patterns" of his claim to the crown. After all, they hold their own positions by "Successive Title" (line 4), the laws of primogeniture whereby the eldest son automatically inherits his father's estate. They thus have a direct interest in his succession.*

5   first-born Son, that was the last   *first-born son of him who was the last. This interpretation of the phrase assumes that Shakespeare is using an elliptical construction (with some words omitted but implied). Another possibility is that as the oldest son Saturninus has been serving as acting Emperor (and thus wearing the Diadem) for an interim period since his father's death.*

6   ware   *wore.*
        imperial Diadem   *crown of the Emperor.*

8   wrong . . . Indignity   *dishonor a first-born son with the indignity of being passed over for a younger brother.*

Act One

Scene 1

Flourish. Enter the Tribunes (among them Marcus Andronicus)
and Senators aloft. Then enter Saturninus and his Followers
at one Door, and Bassianus and his Followers
at the other, with Drums and Trumpets.

SATURNINUS   Noble Patricians, Patrons of my Right,
Defend the justice of my Cause with Arms;
And Countrymen, my loving Followers,
Plead my Successive Title with your Swords.
I am the first-born Son, that was the last   5
That ware th' imperial Diadem of Rome:
Then let my Father's Honors live in me,
Nor wrong mine Age with this Indignity.

301

9   Romanes   *Romans. In the Quarto and Folio texts the word is normally spelled either* Romanes *or* Romaines. *Here the original spelling is retained in lines where the word's metrical position might have called for a stress on the second syllable.*

10   Caesar's Son   *After Octavius Caesar (Augustus), all Roman Emperors were referred to as Caesar.*

12   Keep . . . Capitol   *preserve then this means of access to rule. Bassianus refers to a system of election based on merit rather than on birthright.*

20   People of Rome   *the Roman citizenry as a whole. As a Tribune, Marcus Andronicus represents the Plebeians, but his reference to the Senate in line 27 shows that his ad hoc "special Party" (line 21) speaks for the Patricians as well.*

22   'lection   *election; here contracted for metrical purposes.*

23   Pius   *pious. This was a potent word in Roman civilization, evoking such patriotic virtues as fidelity, courage, and self-sacrifice.*

27   accited   *cited, summoned.*

28   barb'rous Goths   *Germanic tribes that invaded and eventually took over the Roman Empire in the third, fourth, and fifth centuries A.D.*

30   yok'd   *harnessed, brought under control. The term was normally used in reference to domesticated animals (such as oxen) or bondmen (slaves).*

BASSIANUS   Romanes, Friends, Foll'wers, Fav'rers of
     my Right,
   If ever Bassianus, Caesar's Son,   10
   Were gracious in the Eyes of royal Rome,
   Keep then this Passage to the Capitol
   And suffer not Dishonor to approach
   Th' Imperial Seat (to Virtue consecrate,
   To Justice, Cont'nence, and Nobility),   15
   But let Desert in pure Election shine,
   And, Romans, fight for Freedom in your Choice.

     Enter Marcus Andronicus aloft with the Crown.

MARCUS ANDRONICUS   Princes, that strive by Factions
     and by Friends
   Ambitiously for Rule and Empery,
   Know that the People of Rome, for whom we stand   20
   A special Party, have by common Voice,
   In 'lection for the Roman Empery,
   Chos'n Andronicus, surnamed Pius
   For many good and great Deserts to Rome.
   A nobler Man, a braver Warrior,   25
   Lives not this day within the City Walls.
   He by the Senate is accited home
   From weary Wars against the barb'rous Goths,
   That with his Sons, a Terror to our Foes,
   Hath yok'd a Nation strong, train'd up in Arms.   30
   Ten years are spent since first he undertook

35-38   and . . . Goths   *Editions subsequent to the First Quarto omit this passage, evidently on the assumption that it is incompatible with the events to follow in lines 99–150. But* At this Day *(line 35) probably means "at this time," the day of Titus' return on the five previous occasions (line 33). If so, it indicates that the sacrifice of the noblest prisoner of Rome's enemies was an established ritual, not an act of capricious cruelty.*

43   Whom . . . succeed   *whom you would now like to see worthily succeeded.*

44   in . . . Right   *in the right of the Capitol and the Senate.*

45   pretend   *profess, claim (probably not meant as pejoratively as the phrasing would imply in modern usage).*

48   Plead your Deserts   *make the case for your merits.*

49   How fair . . . Thoughts!   Fair *probably combines such meanings as "reasonably," "justly," and "reassuringly." It is difficult to determine how sincerely Saturninus speaks these words. Subsequent events would suggest that he intends them ironically, whether or not he shows it.*

50   affy   *trust, have faith in.*

54   humbled all   *completely dedicated.*

58   in . . . weigh'd   *Bassianus alludes to the traditional image of Justice as a blindfolded (and therefore impartial) woman who "weighed" the two sides of a case on balance scales.*

This Cause of Rome and chastised with Arms
Our En'mies' Pride; five times he hath return'd
Bleeding to Rome, bearing his valiant Sons
In Coffins from the Field, and at this Day 35
To th' Monument of that Andronici
Done Sacrifice of Expiation
And slain the noblest Pris'ner of the Goths.
And now at last, lad'n with Honor's spoils,
Returns the good Andronicus to Rome, 40
Renowned Titus, flourishing in Arms.
Let us entreat, by Honor of his Name
Whom worthily you would have now succeed,
And in the Capitol and Senate's Right,
Whom you pretend to honor and adore, 45
That you withdraw you and abate your Strength,
Dismiss your Foll'wers, and, as Suitors should,
Plead your Deserts in Peace and Humbleness.
SATURNINUS   How fair the Tribune speaks to calm my
    Thoughts!
BASSIANUS   Marcus Andronicus, so I do affy 50
    In thy Uprightness and Integrity,
    And so I love and honor thee and thine,
    Thy noble Brother Titus and his Sons,
    And her to whom my Thoughts are humbled all,
    Gracious Lavinia, Rome's rich Ornament, 55
    That I will here dismiss my loving Friends
    And to my Fortunes and the People's Favor
    Commit my Cause in balance to be weigh'd.

62   the Cause   *both (a) his quest for the empery, and (b) the judicial case to be decided.*

64   confident and kind   *trusting and well-disposed.*

66   Competitor   *here both (a) cohort (the usual meaning in Shakespeare's time), and (b) contestant.*

S.D.   Flourish   *a musical fanfare, probably featuring trumpets. The stage directions in the First Folio call for numerous flourishes not indicated in the First Quarto printing. These flourishes probably reflect actual stage practice.*
        They . . . Senate House.   *In all likelihood, the original staging called for Marcus, Saturninus, and Bassianus to enter the door at the rear of the stage, ascend through the tiring house (the backstage room where actors attired themselves) behind the facade to the gallery above, and then reappear on the upper level with the Senators and Tribunes.*

68   Patron   *both (a) pattern, and (b) supporter and defender.*

71   circumscribed   *brought within the confines of order.*

Exeunt the Soldiers of Bassianus.

SATURNINUS   Friends, that have been thus forward in
    my Right,

I thank you all and here dismiss you all,   60

And to the love and favor of my Country

Commit my Self, my Person, and the Cause.

                    Exeunt the Soldiers of Saturninus.

Rome, be as just and gracious unto me

As I am confident and kind to thee.

Open the Gates and let me in.

BASSIANUS   Tribunes,   65

And me, a poor Competitor.

          Flourish. They go up into the Senate-house.

        Enter a Captain.

CAPTAIN   Romanes make way: the good Andronicus,

Patron of Virtue, Rome's best Champion,

Successful in the Battles that he fights,

With Honor and with Fortune is return'd   70

From where he circumscribed with his Sword

And brought to yoke the Enemies of Rome.

    Sound Drums and Trumpets. Then enter two of Titus' Sons
    (Martius and Mutius). After them two Men bearing a Coffin
    covered with black. Then two other Sons (Lucius and Quin-
    tus). After them, Titus Andronicus. Then Tamora, the Queen
    of Goths, and two of her Sons (Chiron and Demetrius), with

73   **Weeds**   *clothes.*

74   **Bark**   *small sailing vessel.*
Fraught   *freight.*

75   **Lading**   *load, cargo.*

76   **weigh'd her Anchorage**   *anchored.*

77   **Laurel boughs**   *Victors were traditionally garlanded with boughs of laurel.*

80   **Thou great Defender of this Capitol**   *Jupiter (Jove), often named "Jupiter Capitolinus," ruler of the Roman Gods.*

83   **King Priam**   *the King of Troy and father of fifty sons, among them Paris (whose seduction of Helen started the Trojan War) and Hector (Troy's chief defender).*

84   **poor Remains**   *small remainder (namely, four sons).*

86   **latest Home**   *final resting place.*

89–91   **Titus . . . Styx?**   *These lines are spoken as if they represented a reproach from the Goths to their conqueror, who has been so zealous that he has neglected his own family.*

89   **unkind**   *unnatural (specifically, "unlike a father").*

91   **Styx**   *the river that encircled Hades. Souls could not cross Styx until their bodies were properly buried on Earth.*

93   **wont**   *accustomed to do. The souls of the dead communicated without speech.*

308

Aaron the Moor, and others as many as can be, including
Tamora's son Alarbus and other Goths held prisoner. The two
Men set down the Coffins, and Titus speaks.

TITUS   Hail, Rome, Victorious in thy Mourning Weeds!
Lo, as the Bark that hath discharg'd his Fraught
Returns with precious Lading to the Bay   75
From whence at first she weigh'd her Anchorage,
Cometh Andronicus, bound with Laurel boughs,
To re-salute his Country with his Tears:
Tears of true Joy for his return to Rome.
—Thou great Defender of this Capitol,   80
Stand gracious to the Rites that we intend.
—Romanes, of five and twenty valiant Sons,
Half of the number that King Priam had,
Behold the poor Remains, alive and dead.
These that survive, let Rome reward with love;   85
These that I bring unto their latest Home,
With Burial amongst their Ancestors.
Here Goths have giv'n me leave to sheathe my
    Sword:
Titus, unkind and careless of thine own,
Why suffer'st thou thy Sons, unburi'd yet,   90
To hover on the dreadful Shore of Styx?
Make way to lay them by their Bretheren.
                                    They open the Tomb.
—There greet in silence as the Dead are wont,
And sleep in peace, slain in your Country's Wars.

309

---

99   Goths   *This name is normally spelled* Gothes *in the play, and it was probably pronounced with a long o that made the word sound like* goats *(see the pun at II.iii.110). The Gothic tribes were often called "barb'rous" (see line 28 above); this adjective (derived from Greek) was meant to echo the strange-sounding, sheep-like "babble" of peoples the Greeks and Romans considered uncivilized.*

101   Ad manes fratrum   *Latin for "to the souls of our brothers."*

104   Prodigies   *here, disastrous events in punishment for unperformed rites.*

108   rue   *show ruth (pity) for.*

112   Sufficeth not   *Is it not enough?*

113   beautify thy Triumphs   *adorn your celebrations as tokens of victory.*

115   slaughter'd . . . Streets   *Tamora refuses to allow for any distinction between wanton slaughter and a ritual sacrifice to appease the spirits of the Underworld.*

310

  —O sacred Receptacle of my Joys,   95
  Sweet cell of Virtue and Nobility,
  How many Sons hast thou of mine in store,
  That thou wilt never render to me more!
LUCIUS Give us the proudest Pris'ner of the Goths,
  That we may hew his Limbs and on a Pile,   100
  Ad manes fratrum, sacrifice his Flesh
  Before this earthy Prison of their Bones,
  That so the Shadows be not unappeas'd,
  Nor we disturb'd with Prodigies on Earth.
TITUS I give him you, the Noblest that survives,   105
  The eldest Son of this distressed Queen.
TAMORA Stay, Roman Brethren! Gracious Conqueror,
  Victorious Titus, rue the Tears I shed,
  A Mother's Tears in passion for her Son:
  And if thy Sons were ever dear to thee,   110
  O think my Son to be as dear to me.
  Sufficeth not that we are brought to Rome
  To beautify thy Triumphs, and return
  Captive to thee and to thy Roman Yoke,
  But must my Sons be slaughter'd in the Streets   115
  For valiant doings in their Country's Cause?
  O if to fight for King and Commonweal
  Were piety in thine, it is in these.
  Andronicus, stain not thy Tomb with Blood.
  Wilt thou draw near the nature of the Gods?   120
  Draw near them then in being merciful:
  Sweet Mercy is Nobility's true Badge.

124 **pardon me** *Titus probably means this sincerely. He is carrying out what he believes to be a mandatory religious ceremony, not a judicial execution or an act of malice; considerations of justice and mercy are thus irrelevant to him.*

130 **Fire** *here pronounced disyllabically (fý-er).*

131 **pile of Wood** *wood piled to make a funeral pyre.*

132 **hew** *chop.*
   clean *completely. The word is probably also meant to convey the idea of that which is cleansed by a purifying fire.*

133 **irreligious Piety!** *For Tamora and her two remaining sons, Titus' act of "piety" is anything but religious. In their eyes, the Romans, not the Goths, are the true barbarians.*

135 **Oppose . . . Rome!** *Don't compare the Scythians (a people proverbial for their cruelty) to the "ambitious" (overweening) Romans.*

138 **stand resolv'd** *remain resolute.*
   withal *as well, at the same time.*

139 **Queen of Troy** *Hecuba, wife of King Priam. After the fall of Troy, she was taken to Greece as a slave. King Polymnestor of Thrace was one of her captors.*

141 **Thracian Tyrant** *King Polymnestor, who killed Hecuba's son Polydoros; Hecuba took revenge by plucking out his eyeballs.*

144 **quit** *requite, pay back.*

Thrice-noble Titus, spare my first-born Son!

TITUS   Patient your self, Madam, and pardon me.
These are their Brethren whom your Goths beheld   125
Alive and dead, and for their Brethren slain
Religiously they ask a Sacrifice:
To this your Son is mark'd, and die he must
T' appease their groaning Shadows that are gone.

LUCIUS   Away with him, and make a Fire straight,   130
And with our Swords upon a pile of Wood
Let's hew his Limbs till they be clean consum'd.

Exit Titus' Sons with Alarbus.

TAMORA   O cruel, irreligious Piety!

CHIRON   Was ever Scythia half so barbarous?

DEMETRIUS   Oppose not Scythia to ambitious Rome!   135
Alarbus goes to rest, and we survive
To tremble under Titus' threat'ning Look.
Then Madam, stand resolv'd; but hope withal
The self-same Gods that arm'd the Queen of Troy
With opportunity of sharp Revenge   140
Upon the Thracian Tyrant in his Tent
May favor Tamora, the Queen of Goths
(When Goths were Goths, and Tamora was Queen),
To quit the bloody Wrongs upon her Foes.

Re-enter the Sons of Andronicus.

LUCIUS   See, Lord and Father, how we have perform'd   145
Our Roman Rites: Alarbus' Limbs are lopp'd,

147 Entrails *Alarbus' internal organs.*

148 Smoke like Incense *Lucius' use of this analogy reinforces the notion that the slaying and burning of Alarbus should be viewed as an act of propitiation (an atoning sacrifice) to the Gods—not as an act of justice, revenge, or wanton malice.*

149 Remaineth nought *nothing remains to be done.*

150 'larums *alarums, trumpet calls.*

152 latest *last.*

154 readiest *best-prepared and most dedicated.*

156 Envy *malice.*
     swells *grows, puffs up (as with pride).*

157 damned Drugs *poisonous plants.*
     Storms *here used metaphorically to refer to warfare.*

158 Noise *metaphorical for strife and conflict.*

162 Lo *behold, see.*
     tributary *both (a) paid in tribute, and (b) flowing down like a stream, contributing to the flow of a larger river that will eventually empty into the sea.*

163 Obsequies *rites for the dead.*

168 reserv'd *preserved.*

And Entrails feed the sacrificing Fire,
Whose Smoke like Incense doth perfume the Sky.
Remaineth nought but to inter our Brethren,
And with loud 'larums welcome them to Rome.   150

TITUS   Let it be so; and let Andronicus
Make this his latest Farewell to their Souls.

Trumpets sound; they lay the Coffin in the Tomb.

—In Peace and Honor rest you here, my Sons;
Rome's readiest Champions, repose you here in
    rest,
Secure from worldly Chances and Mishaps.   155
Here lurks no Treason, here no Envy swells,
Here grow no damned Drugs, here are no Storms,
No Noise, but Silence and eternal Sleep.
In Peace and Honor rest you here, my Sons.

Enter Lavinia.

LAVINIA   In Peace and Honor live Lord Titus long;   160
My noble Lord and Father, live in Fame.
Lo at this Tomb my tributary Tears
I render for my Brethren's Obsequies;
And at thy Feet I kneel, with Tears of Joy   *She kneels.*
Shed on this Earth, for thy return to Rome.   165
O bless me here with thy victorious Hand,
Whose fortunes Rome's best Citizens applaud.

TITUS   Kind Rome, that hast thus lovingly reserv'd

315

169   **Cordial of mine Age** *comfort of my declining years.* Cordial *stems from the Latin word for "heart" (cor, cordis); the word was used to refer to a restorative to stimulate or "glad" the heart.*

171   **eternal Date** *eternity.*

173   **Gracious** *both (a) well-favored, and (b) magnanimous in victory, not vaunting his glories or demeaning his defeated foes.*

177   **alike in all** *all equal (in honor).*

180   **aspir'd to** *both (a) aimed for, and (b) risen to, attained.*
    Solon's Happiness *According to Herodotus, the Greek philosopher, Solon responded to Croesus' boast about his happiness by saying "Call no man happy until he is dead." Solon's statement was proverbial as a warning against complacency and pride. Here Marcus cites the proverb as part of a conventional message of comfort to those who survive the deceased; soon his words will prove unwittingly prophetic.*

185   **Palliament** *here, a robe to be worn by a candidate for office.*

188   **Candidatus** *a Latin word meaning "white-robed."*

189   **Headless Rome** *leaderless Rome. It was conventional to speak of the state as a body (whence our term "body politic").*

192   **What** *why.*

195   **set abroad** *set afoot.*

316

The Cordial of mine Age to glad my Heart!
—Lavinia, live; outlive thy Father's Days,   170
And Fame's eternal Date, for Virtue's Praise.
MARCUS   Long live Lord Titus, my beloved Brother,
Gracious Triumpher in the Eyes of Rome!
TITUS   Thanks, gentle Tribune, noble Brother Marcus.
MARCUS   And welcome, Nephews, from successful Wars,   175
You that survive, and you that sleep in Fame.
Fair Lords, your Fortunes are alike in all
That in your Country's Service drew your Swords;
But safer Triumph is this Fun'ral Pomp
That hath aspir'd to Solon's Happiness   180
And triumphs over Chance in Honor's Bed.
—Titus Andronicus, the People of Rome,
Whose Friend in Justice thou hast ever been,
Send thee by me, their Tribune and their Trust,
This Palliament of white and spotless Hue,   185
And name thee in Election for the Empire
With these our late-deceased Emp'ror's Sons:
Be *Candidatus* then, and put it on,
And help to set a Head on Headless Rome.
TITUS   A better Head her glorious Body fits   190
Than his that shakes for Age and Feebleness.
What should I don this Robe and trouble you?
Be chos'n with Proclamations today,
Tomorrow yield up Rule, resign my Life,
And set abroad new Bus'ness for you all?   195
Rome, I have been thy Soldier forty years,

317

199   Knighted in Field   *acknowledged for valor on the field of battle.*

203   Upright   *both (a) aloft, erect, and (b) righteously, justly. In lines 201–3 Titus is playing on the notion that he is now too old and feeble to hold up the Emperor's scepter (ornamental staff to indicate authority); what he needs instead, he implies, is a walking staff to hold himself erect.*

204   obtain and ask   *obtain merely by asking.*

205   canst thou tell?   *Can you presume to speak with such authority?*

215   from themselves   *from their present disposition.*

218   My Faction . . . Friends   *if you will strengthen my group of political followers by adding the support of your friends.*

220   Meed   *reward, payment.*

And led my Country's Strength successfully,
And buri'd one and twenty valiant Sons,
Knighted in Field, slain manfully in Arms,
In Right and Service of their noble Country.   200
Give me a Staff of Honor for mine Age,
But not a Scepter to control the World:
Upright he held it, Lords, that held it last.

MARCUS   Titus, thou shalt obtain and ask the Empery.

SATURNINUS   Proud and ambitious Tribune, canst thou
     tell?   205

TITUS   Patience, Prince Saturninus.

SATURNINUS   Romans, do me right:
     Patricians, draw your Swords, and sheathe them
        not
     Till Saturninus be Rome's Emperor.
     —Andronicus, would thou were shipp'd to Hell   210
     Rather than rob me of the People's Hearts!

LUCIUS   Proud Saturnine, int'rrupter of the good
     That noble-minded Titus means to thee!

TITUS   Content thee, Prince: I will restore to thee
     The People's Hearts, and wean them from
        themselves.   215

BASSIANUS   Andronicus, I do not flatter thee,
     But honor thee, and will do till I die.
     My Faction if thou strengthen with thy Friends,
     I will most thankful be; and Thanks to Men
     Of noble Minds is honorable Meed.   220

TITUS   People of Rome, and People's Tribunes here,

319

222   Suffrages   *votes (in this case, votes of confidence, proxies).*

225   gratulate   *give thanks for, rejoice in, salute.*

226   admits   *sends to them, approves.*

228   create   *make Emperor.*

230   Titan's Rays   *the Sun's rays. The Sun God, usually called either Helios or Hyperion, was a descendant of the Titans and was often referred to as Titan.*

231   ripen Justice   *allow justice to flourish like a Sun-ripened fruit.*

232   elect by my Advice   *select on the basis of my judgment.*

234   of ev'ry sort   *representing every class of Roman society.*

239   Election   *here pronounced as a four-syllable word.*

240   thanks in part of thy Deserts   *partial thanks for the fuller thanks you actually deserve (with more thanks to be expressed in "deeds" to follow).*

241   Gentleness   *generosity of spirit bespeaking a true gentleman.*

242   for an onset   *as a beginning.*
       advance   *both (a) elevate in rank, and (b) make prosper.*

246   Pantheon   *temple honoring all the Roman deities. The word is spelled* Panthan *in the Quarto and Folio texts and is to be pronounced disyllabically.*
       espouse   *marry.*

247   Motion   *move, proposed action.*

I ask your Voices and your Suffrages:
Will ye bestow them friendly on Andronicus?

TRIBUNES   To gratify the good Andronicus,
And gratulate his safe return to Rome,   225
The People will accept whom he admits.

TITUS   Tribunes, I thank you, and this Suit I make:
That you create our Emp'ror's eldest Son,
Lord Saturnine, whose Virtues will, I hope,
Reflect on Rome as Titan's Rays on Earth   230
And ripen Justice in this Commonweal.
Then if you will elect by my Advice,
Crown him, and say "Long live our Emperor!"

MARCUS   With Voices and Applause of ev'ry sort,
Patricians and Plebeians, we create   235
Lord Saturninus Rome's great Emperor,
And say "Long live our Emp'ror Saturnine!"

Flourish, while those aloft descend and enter below.

SATURNINUS   Titus Andron'cus, for thy Favors done
To us in our Election this day,
I give thee thanks in part of thy Deserts,   240
And will with Deeds requite thy Gentleness:
And for an onset, Titus, to advance
Thy Name and honorable Family,
Lavinia will I make my Emperess,
Rome's Royal Mistress, Mistress of my Heart,   245
And in the sacred Pantheon her espouse.
Tell me, Andron'cus, doth this Motion please
    thee?

321

250 in sight of Rome *with all of Rome to witness it.*

254 Presents *the gifts Titus has just presented.*
    imperious *imperial (referring to Saturninus' dominion over
    the Empire).*

255 Tribute *payment to indicate loyalty and obedience.*

256 Ensigns *insignia, visible signs or tokens.*

259 record *take note of.*

260 unspeakable Deserts *deservings beyond description.*

262 Now . . . Emp'ror *Titus addresses this to Tamora to make
    it clear that he has now surrendered her to the new Emperor.
    He also implies that Saturninus can be expected to treat her
    with the same noble spirit he has just shown to Titus.*

263 for . . . State *because of your honor and your position.*

265 Hue *color. Saturninus probably means this both literally (as a
    reference to a complexion darker than that of the Romans,
    though less swarthy than that of a Moor) and figuratively (as
    a reference to Tamora's fiery spirit, her "complexion" in the
    older sense relating to the complex of humours in her psycho-
    logical makeup).*

266 a new *Most modern editions emend to* anew. *The Quarto and
    Folio texts suggest that Saturninus means "a new Lady."*

270 Usage *treatment.*

272 he comforts you *he who comforts you.*

TITUS   It doth, my worthy Lord, and in this Match
        I hold me highly honor'd of your Grace.
        And here in sight of Rome, to Saturnine,   250
        King and Commander of our Commonweal,
        The wide World's Emp'ror, do I consecrate
        My Sword, my Chariot, and my Prisoners,
        Presents well worthy Rome's imperious Lord.
        Receive them, then, the Tribute that I owe,   255
        Mine Honor's Ensigns humbled at thy Feet.
SATURNINUS   Thanks, noble Titus, Father of my Life.
        How proud I am of thee and of thy Gifts
        Rome shall record; and when I do forget
        The least of these unspeakable Deserts,   260
        Romanes, forget your Fealty to me.
TITUS   [To Tamora] Now, Madam, are you pris'ner to
            an Emp'ror,
        To him that, for your Honor and your State,
        Will use you nobly, and your Followers.
SATURNINUS   A goodly Lady, trust me, of the Hue   265
        That I would choose were I to choose a new.
        —Clear up, fair Queen, that cloudy Countenance.
        Though chance of War hath wrought this change of
            Cheer,
        Thou com'st not to be made a Scorn in Rome:
        Princely shall be thy Usage ev'ry way.   270
        Rest on my Word, and let not Discontent
        Daunt all your Hopes. Madam, he comforts you
        Can make you greater than the Queen of Goths.

323

274   **this**   *Saturninus appears to be referring to the "princely Courtesy" (line 276) he has just shown to Tamora. Significantly, these are the first words he has addressed to Lavinia directly; it seems to have occurred neither to him nor to Titus to consult her wishes about the wedding plans that have just been completed.*

275   **sith**   *since.*

283   **this . . . Right**   *this thing which is both reasonable and right.*

284   **Suum cuique**   *"to each his own," a motto epitomizing the Roman understanding of property rights. When he says "his own" (line 285), Marcus refers to Bassianus' betrothal to Lavinia (alluded to in lines 54–55). In his view, Lavinia is already promised to Bassianus.*

286   **if Lucius live!**   *a vow of resolve roughly equivalent to "on my life!" or "or I'll die trying!"*

287   **avaunt!**   *away from me, out of my sight!*

288   **surpris'd**   *taken by surprise.*

—Lavinia, you are not displeas'd with this?

LAVINIA　Not I, my Lord, sith true Nobility　　　　　　275
　　Warrants these Words in princely Courtesy.

SATURNINUS　Thanks, sweet Lavinia. —Romans, let us
　　go:
　　Ransomless here we set our Pris'ners free.
　　Proclaim our Honors, Lords, with Trump and Drum.

> *Flourish. Exeunt Saturninus, Tamora, Demetrius,*
> *Chiron, and Aaron.*

BASSIANUS　Lord Titus, by your leave, this Maid is
　　mine.　　　　　　　　　　　　　　　　　　　　　280

TITUS　How, Sir?　　　　　　*Bassianus seizes Lavinia.*
　　Are you in earnest then, my Lord?

BASSIANUS　Ay, noble Titus, and resolv'd withal
　　To do my self this Reason and this Right.

MARCUS　*Suum cuique* is our Roman Justice:
　　This Prince in justice seizeth but his own.　　　　285

LUCIUS　And that he will and shall, if Lucius live!

TITUS　Traitors, avaunt! —Where is the Emp'ror's
　　Guard?
　　—Treason, my Lord! Lavinia is surpris'd!

> *Re-enter Saturninus and his Followers.*

SATURNINUS　Surpris'd? By whom?

BASSIANUS　　　　　　　　　By him that justly may
　　Bear his Betroth'd from all the World away!　　　290

> *Exeunt Bassianus and Marcus, with Lavinia.*

292   Door   *here pronounced disyllabically (dó-or).*

299   My Sons . . . dishonor me! *Titus feels dishonored because his sons have defied not only his own authority but that of the Emperor to whom he has just vowed loyalty. If he felt any qualms about giving his daughter to the Emperor despite her prior commitment to Bassianus, he has set those qualms aside in keeping with the higher loyalty he has pledged to Rome and her duly elected ruler.*

MUTIUS   Brothers, help to convey her hence away,
    And with my Sword I'll keep this Door safe!
                    Exeunt Lucius, Quintus, and Martius.
TITUS   Follow, my Lord, and I'll soon bring her back!
MUTIUS   My Lord, you pass not here!
TITUS   What, Villain Boy,
    Barr'st me my way in Rome?
MUTIUS   Help, Lucius, help!   295
                    Titus kills Mutius.

        During the Fray, exeunt Saturninus, Tamora,
            Demetrius, Chiron, and Aaron.

        Re-enter Lucius.

LUCIUS   My Lord, you are unjust, and more than so:
    In wrongful Quarrel you have slain your Son!
TITUS   Nor thou nor he are any Sons of mine:
    My Sons would never so dishonor me!
    Traitor, restore Lavinia to the Emperor!   300
LUCIUS   Dead, if you will, but not to be his Wife
    That is another's lawful promis'd Love!

        Enter aloft the Emperor, with Tamora and her
            two Sons and Aaron the Moor.

SATURNINUS   No, Titus, no; the Emp'ror needs her
    not,

        327

305   **I'll trust by leisure**   *I'll trust in my own good time (that is, not soon).*

308   **Was . . . Stale**   *Was there no one else to make an object of contempt or ridicule? The word* **Stale** *carries a number of negative connotations here, including (a) a decoy or stalking horse used for purposes of alluring another, (b) soiled goods, and (c) a person whose expressions of love are held up to scorn.*

310–   **proud . . . Hands**   *Saturninus' charge is incompatible*
11   *with what we have just witnessed, and it calls into question the sincerity of his earlier motive in "honoring" Titus with a request to marry the woman he knew to be the betrothed of his younger brother and chief political rival.*

313   **Changing Piece**   *promiscuous woman; this term picks up on two senses of the word* **change** *(a) shift in loyalty, and (b) exchange for money or other favors. The term probably also refers to a "piece of change," a coin passed from one hand to another.*

316   **bandy**   *exchange blows.*

317   **ruffle**   *swagger.*

327   **Sith**   *since.*

328

Nor her, nor thee, nor any of thy Stock.
I'll trust by leisure him that mocks me once,   305
Thee never, nor thy trait'rous, haughty Sons,
Confed'rates all thus to dishonor me.
Was none in Rome to make a Stale
But Saturnine? Full well, Andronicus,
Agree these Deeds with that proud Brag of thine   310
That said'st I begg'd the Empire at thy Hands.
TITUS   O monstrous! What reproachful Words are
    these?
SATURNINUS   But go thy ways; go give that Changing
    Piece
To him that flourish'd for her with his Sword.
A Valiant Son-in-Law thou shalt enjoy: 315
One fit to bandy with thy Lawless Sons,
To ruffle in the Commonwealth of Rome!
TITUS   These words are Razors to my wounded Heart.
SATURNINUS   And therefore, lovely Tam'ra, Queen of
    Goths,
That like the stately Phoebe 'mongst her Nymphs   320
Dost overshine the gallant'st Dames of Rome,
If thou be pleas'd with this my sudden Choice,
Behold, I choose thee, Tam'ra, for my Bride,
And will create thee Emperess of Rome.
Speak, Queen of Goths, dost thou applaud my
    Choice?   325
—And here I swear by all the Roman Gods,
Sith Priest and Holy Water are so near

329

328   Tapers   *candles, used in Roman wedding ceremonies.*

329   for Hymeneus' Stand   *Hymen was the God of Marriage, and Hymeneus' stand may refer to the place designated for the performance of wedding ceremonies (an altar, dais, or ceremonial table). Another possibility is that* stand *is a verb here and the phrase means "everything stands in readiness for Hymeneus." The early texts do not use apostrophes to indicate possession.*

331   climb   *ascend into.*

337   Panthean Lords   *Here, by analogy with the Pantheon (literally, the temple of all the Gods), Saturninus coins an adjective to dignify "all the Lords" of Rome. Modern editions normally emend this line to read "Ascend, fair Queen, Pantheon. Lords, accompany . . . ."*

342   bid to wait upon   *invited to pay honor to.*

343   walk alone   *walk in isolation from either attendants (the soldiers whose command he has just surrendered) or the trappings of ceremony (such as the procession from which he has just been excluded). Titus is suddenly cut off from all the associations that have given his life definition.*

344   challenged   *accused and thus forced to defend one's honor (here pronounced trisyllabically).*

346   a bad Quarrel   *an unjust quarrel, a quarrel in which Titus took the wrong side.*

348   Confed'rates in   *parties to.*

And Tapers burn so bright and every thing
In readiness for Hymeneus' Stand,
I will not re-salute the Streets of Rome   330
Or climb my Palace till from forth this Place
I lead espous'd my Bride along with me.
TAMORA   And here in sight of Heav'n to Rome I swear,
If Saturnine advance the Queen of Goths,
She will a Handmaid be to his Desires,   335
A loving Nurse, a Mother to his Youth.
SATURNINUS   Ascend, fair Queen. —Panthean Lords,
    accompany
Your noble Emp'ror and his lovely Bride,
Sent by the Heavens for Prince Saturnine,
Whose Wisdom hath her Fortune conquered.   340
There shall we consummate our Spousal Rites.
                              Exeunt all but Titus.
TITUS   I am not bid to wait upon this Bride.
Titus, when wert thou wont to walk alone,
Dishonor'd thus and challenged of Wrongs?

Re-enter Marcus, Lucius, Quintus, and Martius.

MARCUS   O Titus, see, O see what thou hast done: 345
In a bad Quarrel slain a virtuous Son!
TITUS   No, foolish Tribune, no; no Son of mine,
Nor thou, nor these, Confed'rates in the Deed
That hath dishonor'd all our Family:
Unworthy Brother and unworthy Sons!   350

351 as becomes *as is fitting; as becomes Mutius' life as a soldier and as Titus' son.*

352 Bretheren *brethren. Here trisyllabic for metrical reasons.*

354 hundreth *hundred. An older spelling still in active use in Shakespeare's time; in this passage the word was not modernized until the 1663 Third Folio printing of* Titus Andronicus.

355 sumptuously re-edified *rebuilt at great expense.*

356 Servitors *servants. Titus feels that Mutius' act has been treasonous.*

357 Brawls *base quarrels, conflicts with no nobility of purpose to justify them.*

364 vouch 't *maintain it in combat.*

365 in my despite *despite my objections.*

368 stroke *struck.*
   Crest *the coronet above a coat of arms on an escutcheon or shield; by association, a symbol of the honor of its owner.*

370 repute *consider.*

372 not with himself *not himself, beside himself.*

LUCIUS But let us give him Burial, as becomes;
　　Give Mutius Burial with our Bretheren.
TITUS Traitors, away! He rests not in this Tomb:
　　This Monument five hundreth years hath stood,
　　Which I have sumptuously re-edified.　　　　　　　　355
　　Here none but Soldiers and Rome's Servitors
　　Repose in Fame, none basely slain in Brawls.
　　Bury him where you can; he comes not here.
MARCUS My Lord, this is Impiety in you.
　　My Nephew Mutius' deeds do plead for him;　　　360
　　He must be buri'd with his Bretheren.
QUINTUS, MARTIUS And shall, or him we will
　　accompany!
TITUS "And shall"! What Villain was it spake that
　　word?
MARTIUS He that would vouch 't in any place but
　　here.
TITUS What, would you bury him in my despite?　　365
MARCUS No, noble Titus, but entreat of thee
　　To pardon Mutius and to bury him.
TITUS Marcus, ev'n thou hast stroke upon my Crest,
　　And with these Boys mine Honor thou hast
　　wounded.
　　My Foes I do repute you ev'ry one,　　　　　　　370
　　So trouble me no more, but get you gone.
QUINTUS He is not with himself: let us withdraw.
MARTIUS Not I, till Mutius' Bones be buried.
　　　　　　　　　　　The Brother and the Sons kneel.

333

376   **Speak . . . speed.** *Speak no more if all the rest of you want to prosper (avoiding the fate of Mutius).*

379   **Suffer** *permit.*

382   **Thou . . . barbarous.** *Marcus appeals to Titus' sense of what defines a Roman: an absence of the barbarity characteristic of such peoples as the Goths and the Scythians.*

383   **upon advice** *after due consideration.*
      Ajax *One of the Greek warriors who fought against the Trojans, Ajax was so furious when the slain Achilles' armor was awarded to Odysseus that he went mad and slaughtered a flock of sheep whom he mistook for Agamemnon and the other Greek generals. Upon awakening to the baseness of his actions, he felt so humiliated that he stabbed himself.*

384   **wise Laertes' Son** *crafty Odysseus (Ulysses in Roman mythology), who persuaded Agamemnon to set aside his objections and give Ajax an honorable burial.*

385   **for 's** *for his. Here the meter calls for the speaker to glide over his.*

392   **Trophies** *memorial tokens, such as armor worn or won in battle.*

393–
94   **No . . . Cause.** *These lines have the sound of a formulaic rite, and one whose lofty sentiments Titus probably finds difficult to apply to the circumstances of Mutius' demise.*

MARCUS   Brother, for in that Name doth Nature
        plead—
MARTIUS   Father, and in that Name doth Nature
        speak—   375
TITUS   Speak thou no more if all the rest will
        speed.
MARCUS   Renowned Titus, more than half my Soul—
LUCIUS   Dear Father, Soul and Substance of us all—
MARCUS   Suffer thy Brother Marcus to inter
        His noble Nephew here in Virtue's Nest,   380
        That died in Honor and Lavinia's Cause.
        Thou art a Roman: be not barbarous.
        The Greeks upon advice did bury Ajax,
        That slew himself, and wise Laertes' Son
        Did graciously plead for 's Funerals.   385
        Let not young Mutius then, that was thy Joy,
        Be barr'd his Entrance here.
TITUS   Rise, Marcus, rise;
        The dismall'st Day is this that e'er I saw,
        To be dishonor'd by my Sons in Rome!   *All rise.*
        Well, bury him, and bury me the next.   390
                            They put him in the Tomb.
LUCIUS   There lie thy Bones, sweet Mutius, with thy
        Friends,
        Till we with Trophies do adorn thy Tomb.
ALL   [*Kneeling*] No man shed Tears for noble Mutius;
        He lives in Fame that died in Virtue's Cause.
                All rise. Exeunt all but Marcus and Titus.

335

395   Dumps   *doldrums, moods of despondency.*

400–1   Is . . . far?   *The Quarto and Folio texts give these, as well as the three surrounding lines, to Titus. But it would seem to make more sense to assign to Marcus a question that follows so naturally from his query in lines 396–97.*

402   Yes . . . remunerate.   *This is probably meant by the playwright to come across as wishful thinking. In line 399, Titus expressed his first doubts about the sequence of events that led to his present plight. There it seems to have entered his mind that Saturninus' selection of Lavinia may have been no more than a "device" to incite familial and civil strife and provide the Emperor a pretext for the elevation of Tamora. Now Titus makes a valiant effort to set those doubts aside.*

403   play'd your Prize   *won your contest. This was a term from fencing, and it referred to a competition in which victory qualified one for membership in the fencing fraternity.*

409–   Rape . . . Wife   *Most modern editions follow the First Folio*
10   *and place a question mark at the end of this clause. But Saturninus' response ("you are very short with us," line 413) would suggest that the First Quarto pronunciation, followed here, is a more reliable indication of how the lines should be spoken. Rather than take a posture that would seem to be either challenging or defensive, Bassianus is endeavoring to defuse the quarrel between himself and Saturninus by being as matter-of-fact as he can.*

412   that   *that which.*

336

MARCUS   My Lord, to step out of these dreary Dumps,   395
    How comes it that the subtle Queen of Goths
    Is of a sudden thus advanc'd in Rome?
TITUS   I know not, Marcus, but I know it is,
    Wheth'r by Device or no the Heav'ns can tell.
MARCUS   Is she not then beholding to the Man   400
    That brought her for this high Good Turn so far?
TITUS   Yes, and will nobly him remunerate.

Flourish. Enter the Emperor, Tamora, and her two Sons,
with the Moor, at one Door. Enter at the other Door
Bassianus and Lavinia, with others.

SATURNINUS   So, Bassianus, you have play'd your
    Prize;
    God give you joy, Sir, of your gallant Bride!
BASSIANUS   And you of yours, my Lord. I say no
    more,   405
    Nor wish no less, and so I take my leave.
SATURNINUS   Traitor, if Rome have Law or we have
    Power,
    Thou and thy Faction shall repent this Rape.
BASSIANUS   Rape call you it, my Lord, to seize my
    own,
    My true-betrothed Love, and now my Wife;   410
    But let the Laws of Rome determine all;
    Meanwhile am I possess'd of that is mine.
SATURNINUS   'Tis good, Sir: you are very short with us.

337

414   **if we live**   *if we live to do so. Here Saturninus uses the royal we, based on the convention that a monarch incorporated his people in his person.*

420   **Opinion**   *reputation.*

424   **controll'd**   *kept under control; countered, opposed.*
    that   *that which.*
    frankly   *freely, without restraint.*

428   **leave**   *cease.*

429   **those**   *Titus refers to his brother and his sons.*

434   **indiff'rently**   *impartially, as one who is not a member of either faction and is thus able to be indifferent to matters that would bias my judgment.*

437   **put it up**   *put up with it, set it aside.*

438   **forfend**   *forbid.*

439   **author to dishonor you**   *an agent to anything that would dishonor you.*

440   **undertake**   *vouch, stand surety.*

But if we live, we'll be as sharp with you.

BASSIANUS   My Lord, what I have done, as best I may   415
Answer I must, and shall do with my Life.
Only thus much I give your Grace to know:
By all the Duties that I owe to Rome,
This noble Gentleman, Lord Titus here,
Is in Opinion and in Honor wrong'd,   420
That in the rescue of Lavinia
With his own Hand did slay his youngest Son,
In zeal to you, and highly mov'd to wrath
To be controll'd in that he frankly gave.
Receive him then to favor, Saturnine,   425
That hath express'd himself in all his Deeds
A Father and a Friend to thee and Rome.

TITUS   Prince Bassianus, leave to plead my Deeds:
'Tis thou, and those, that have dishonor'd me.
Rome and the righteous Heavens be my Judge   430
How I have lov'd and honor'd Saturnine.

TAMORA   My worthy Lord, if ever Tamora
Were gracious in those Princely Eyes of thine,
Then hear me speak indiff'rently for all,
And at my Suit, Sweet, pardon what is past.   435

SATURNINUS   What, Madam, be dishonor'd openly,
And basely put it up without Revenge?

TAMORA   Not so, my Lord; the Gods of Rome forfend
I should be author to dishonor you!
But on mine Honor dare I undertake   440
For good Lord Titus' Innocence in all,

339

442   Fury not dissembled   *unfeigned anger.*
      speaks his Griefs   *bespeaks (testifies to) the sincerity of his sense of being aggrieved (treated wrongly) by his sons and brother.*

444   noble a   *spoken as two syllables here (nó-bl'a). There were various types of metrical elision in common use in Shakespeare's time. This one, where the final syllable of one word is dropped in order to glide into the first syllable of the next, was known as* ecthlipsis. *When the first syllable of the second word was dropped (as in* be 't), *it was* synaloepha.
      on vain Suppose   *on empty suppositions, unfounded suspicions.*

447   Dissemble   *conceal.*

453   at entreats   *in response to entreaties.*
      let me alone   *leave it to me to handle.*

455   race   *raze, erase, root out.*

456   trait'rous   *traitorous, treasonous. The omitted vowel is an instance of the practice known as* syncope, *the artificial shortening of a word for metrical purposes.*

457   sued   *here pronounced disyllabically (sué-ed). When a word was artificially lengthened for metrical purposes, the technique was known as* diaeresis.

461   Take up   *lift from his knees (by forgiving him).*

Whose Fury not dissembled speaks his Griefs.
Then at my Suit, look graciously on him;
Lose not so noble a Friend on vain Suppose,
Nor with sour Looks afflict his gentle Heart.   445
[*Aside to Saturninus*] My Lord, be rul'd by me,
    be won at last;
Dissemble all your Griefs and Discontents
(You are but newly planted in your Throne),
Lest that the People, and Patricians too,
Upon a just survey take Titus' part,   450
And so supplant you for Ingratitude,
Which Rome reputes to be a heinous Sin.
Yield at entreats, and then let me alone:
I'll find a day to massacre them all,
And race their Faction and their Family,   455
Their cruel Father and his trait'rous Sons,
To whom I sued for my dear Son's Life,
And make them know what 'tis to let a Queen
Kneel in the Streets and beg for Grace in vain.
[*Aloud*] Come, come, sweet Emp'ror. —Come,
    Andronicus.   *Titus kneels.*   460
—Take up this good old Man, and cheer the Heart
That dies in tempest of thy angry Frown.
SATURNINUS   Rise, Titus, rise: my Empress hath
    prevail'd.
TITUS   [*Rising*] I thank your Majesty, and her, my
    Lord.
These Words, these Looks, infuse new Life in me.   465

341

466   incorporate   *incorporated, made part of (as a member of the Roman body politic).*

473   My Word and Promise   *my word of promise.*

474   tractable   *agreeable, flexible.*

479   mildly as we might   *as mildly as we were able to do it.*

480   Tend'ring   *out of a tender concern for.*

481   protest   *profess.*

487   entreats   *entreaties.*

TAMORA   Titus, I am incorporate in Rome,
A Roman now adopted happily,
And must advise the Emp'ror for his good.
This day all Quarrels die, Andronicus.
—And let it be mine Honor, good my Lord,   470
That I have reconcil'd your Friends and you.
—For you, Prince Bassianus, I have pass'd
My Word and Promise to the Emperor
That you will be more mild and tractable.
—And fear not, Lords, and you, Lavinia: 475
By my Advice, all humbled on your Knees,
You shall ask Pardon of his Majesty.
              Marcus, Lucius, Quintus, Martius, Lavinia, and
                                          Bassianus kneel.

LUCIUS   We do, and vow to Heav'n and to his
     Highness,
That what we did was mildly as we might,
Tend'ring our Sister's Honor and our own.   480
MARCUS   That, on mine Honor, here do I protest.
SATURNINUS   [*Turning*] Away and talk not; trouble us
     no more.
TAMORA   Nay, nay, sweet Emp'ror, we must all be
     Friends!
The Tribune and his Nephews kneel for Grace.
I will not be denied: sweet Heart, look back.   485
SATURNINUS   Marcus, for thy sake, and thy Brother's
     here,
And at my lovely Tamora's entreats,

343

488   **remit** *forgive; literally, "send back."*

490   **Churl** *surly boor.*

495   **Love-day** *both (a) a day designated for the settling of disputes, and (b) a day for lovers.*

496   **and** *if.*

498   **Bonjour** *"good day" in French.*

499   **Gramercy** *many thanks (from "grand merci" in French).*

S.D.   **Exeunt all but Aaron.** *From this, and from the stage direction at the beginning of Act II, it is clear that the action is meant to flow uninterrupted from this scene to the next. The act and scene divisions supplied in modern texts of Shakespeare stem from an editorial tradition that commenced with the First Folio; none of the quarto (small paperback) editions published in Shakespeare's lifetime were divided into acts and scenes. The divisions provided here are for the convenience of readers and have nothing to do with the text as a script for actors.*

I do remit these Young Men's heinous Faults:
Stand up.   *Marcus and his Nephews rise.*
—Lavinia, though you left me like a Churl,   490
I found a Friend, and sure as death I swore
I would not part a Bach'lor from the Priest.
Come, if the Emp'ror's Court can feast two
    Brides,
You are my Guest, Lavinia, and your Friends.

                                        She rises.

—This day shall be a Love-day, Tamora.   495
TITUS   Tomorrow and it please your Majesty
    To hunt the Panther and the Hart with me,
    With Horn and Hound we'll give your Grace
        Bonjour.
SATURNINUS   Be it so, Titus, and Gramercy too.
                    Sound Trumpets. Exeunt all but Aaron.

II.i   *Although Aaron has not moved since the end of the "Capitol" scene in Act I, the setting shifts to a site outside the Emperor's Palace (line 46).*

1   Olympus' Top   *Mount Olympus was the home of the Gods.*

2   Safe . . . Shot   *secure from Fortune's aim. Fortune was the force (often personified as a goddess) the Romans thought responsible for all of life's chances and mishaps—its good luck and bad luck. Because Fortune's sway extended only to the lowest of the crystalline spheres (the sphere of the Moon) encircling the Globe, it was assumed that the Gods were "out of Fortune's Shot" or reach.*

3   of   *from.*

7   Zodiac   *the course of the Sun through the Heavens.*
     glist'ring Coach   *glittering chariot.*

10   Wit   *intelligence, cunning.*
     wait   *attend, pay homage.*

346

Act Two

Scene 1

Aaron alone.

AARON   Now climbeth Tamora Olympus' Top
Safe out of Fortune's Shot, and sits aloft,
Secure of Thunder's Crack or Lightning Flash,
Advanc'd above pale Envy's threat'ning Reach:
As when the golden Sun salutes the Morn,   5
And, having gilt the Ocean with his Beams,
Gallops the Zodiac in his glist'ring Coach
And overlooks the highest peering Hills,
So Tamora.
Upon her Wit doth earthly Honor wait,   10
And Virtue stoops and trembles at her Frown.
Then, Aaron, arm thy Heart and fit thy Thoughts

347

14   **mount her Pitch**   *ride her flight to its highest point (an image derived from falconry).*

16   **faster bound**   *more tightly bound.*
        charming   *casting a magical spell.*

17   **Prometheus . . . Caucasus**   *Prometheus was a Titan punished by Zeus for his role in delivering fire to mortals; Zeus chained him to a rock atop the Caucasian Mountains.*

18   **Slavish Weeds**   *the apparel of slaves.*

21   **To wanton with**   *to enjoy sexual abandon with.*

22   **Semiramis**   *The wife of Ninus, founder of the Assyrian empire, Semiramis (pronounced Se-meeŕ-a-miss) was proverbial for her ambition and lust.*

23   **Siren**   *The Sirens were singing goddesses whose voices charmed seamen into treacherous waters and wrecked their ships.*

S.D.   **braving**   *swaggering, challenging one another.*

26   **wants Edge**   *lacks sharpness.*

28   **for ought thou know'st**   *for all you know.*
        affected be   *be found attractive.*

30   **to bear me down with Braves**   *to put me down with boasting and blustering.*

31   **'Tis . . . two**   *no more than a year or two divides us.*

35   **approve**   *prove.*

To mount aloft with thy imperial Mistress,
And mount her Pitch whom thou in triumph long
Hast Pris'ner held, fett'red in amorous Chains,   15
And faster bound to Aaron's charming Eyes
Than is Prometheus tied to Caucasus.
Away with Slavish Weeds and Servile Thoughts!
I will be Bright and shine in Pearl and Gold
To wait upon this new-made Emperess.   20
To wait, said I? To wanton with this Queen,
This Goddess, this Semiramis, this Nymph,
This Siren, that will charm Rome's Saturnine
And see his Shipwrack and his Commonweal's.

Enter Chiron and Demetrius, braving.

Holla, what Storm is this?   25
DEMETRIUS   Chiron, thy Years wants Wit, thy Wits
    wants Edge
And Manners, to intrude where I am grac'd,
And may, for ought thou know'st, affected be.
CHIRON   Demetrius, thou dost overween in all,
And so in this, to bear me down with Braves.   30
'Tis not the diff'rence of a year or two
Makes me less gracious or thee more fortunate:
I am as able and as fit as thou
To serve and to deserve my Mistress' Grace,
And that my Sword upon thee shall approve   35
And plead my Passions for Lavinia's Love.

349

37   Clubs, clubs!   *Aaron alludes to the cry London citizens made when an outbreak of brawling made it necessary to call the Watch to club down the rioters.*

38   unadvis'd   *unadvisedly, unwisely.*

39   Dancing Rapier   *an ornamental sword to wear to dances and other social occasions.*

41   Go to   *away with you (a term of dismissal).*
       Lath   *a type of wooden sword used as a stage property in crude plays of the earlier part of the sixteenth century in England.*

47   And . . . openly   *Dueling was legally forbidden in Shakespeare's England, so gentlemen who wished to indulge their wrath took precautions to do so privately. Shakespeare's audience would probably have assumed that the same constraints on private combat applied in Rome during the waning days of the Empire.*

48   wot the Ground of   *know the basis for.*

49   million   *here pronounced trisyllabically.*

53   put up   *put away your swords.*

54   withal   *thereby.*

AARON   Clubs, clubs! These Lovers will not keep the
      Peace!
DEMETRIUS   Why Boy, although our Mother, unadvis'd,
      Gave you a Dancing Rapier by your side,
      Are you so desp'rate grown to threat your
         Friends?   40
      Go to: have your Lath glu'd within your Sheath
      Till you know better how to handle it.
CHIRON   Mean while, Sir, with the little skill I
      have,
      Full well shalt thou perceive how much I dare.
DEMETRIUS   Ay Boy, grow ye so brave?   *They draw.*
AARON   Why, how now, Lords?   45
      So near the Emp'ror's Palace dare ye draw,
      And maintain such a Quarrel openly?
      Full well I wot the Ground of all this Grudge;
      I would not for a million of Gold
      The cause were known to them it most concerns.   50
      Nor would your noble Mother for much more
      Be so dishonor'd in the Court of Rome.
      For shame, put up.
DEMETRIUS   Not I, till I have sheath'd
      My Rapier in his Bosom, and withal
      Thrust those reproachful Speeches down his Throat   55
      That he hath breath'd in my Dishonor here.
CHIRON   For that I am prepar'd and full resolv'd,
      Foul-spoken Coward, that thund'rest with thy
         Tongue

35¹

62   Brabble   *childish brawling.*

64   jet upon   *challenge or encroach upon.* Jet *had various mean-
        ings and connotations pertinent to the context: (a) strut
        vauntingly, (b) jut forward, and (c) spew out in a stream.*

67   broach'd   *opened up and set flowing.*

68   Without . . . Revenge   *without your incurring arrest
        ("Controlment"), justice, or revenge (from the offended
        Prince).*

70   Ground   *both (a) the reason or basis, and (b) musically, the
        bass notes of a composition upon which the descant (the higher
        notes played in counterpoint) is "raised."* Aaron *also plays on
        a musical sense of* Discord *(a set of notes that do not combine
        to yield harmony).*

71   knew . . . World   *even if she and all the world knew.*

73   meaner   *lower in degree, more in keeping with your station.*

76   How furious . . . be   *In this line the meter calls for "furi-
        ous" to be treated as a two-syllable word and "impatient"
        to be treated as a four-syllable word.*

77   brook   *tolerate.*

81   Why . . . strange?   *Why do you pretend that my desire is so
        surprising?*

And with thy Weapon nothing dar'st perform!

AARON Away, I say!   60

Now by the Gods that warlike Goths adore,
This petty Brabble will undo us all!
Why Lords, and think you not how dangerous
It is to jet upon a Prince's Right?
What, is Lavinia then become so loose,   65
Or Bassianus so degenerate,
That for her Love such Quarrels may be broach'd
Without Controlment, Justice, or Revenge?
Young Lords beware! And should the Empress know
This Discord's Ground, the Music would not
    please.   70

CHIRON I care not, I, knew she and all the World:
I love Lavinia more than all the World.

DEMETRIUS Youngling, learn thou to make some
    meaner Choice:
Lavinia is thine elder Brother's Hope.

AARON Why, are ye mad? Or know ye not in Rome   75
How furious and impatient they be,
And cannot brook Competitors in Love?
I tell you, Lords, you do but plot your Deaths
By this Device.

CHIRON   Aaron, a thousand Deaths
Would I propose, t' achieve her whom I love.   80

AARON T' achieve her! How?

DEMETRIUS   Why makes thou it so strange?
She is a Woman, therefore may be woo'd;

353

86   wots   *knows.*

87   cut Loaf   *here used as a metaphor for a woman who has lost
            her virginity.*
        Shive   *slice (related to* shave, shiver*).*

89   Vulcan's Badge   *the mark of a cuckold. Vulcan's wife, Venus,
            made love to Mars, thus turning her husband into an object of
            ridicule among the Gods.*

90   Ay . . . may!   *Aaron alludes to his own "badge-giving."*

92   Liberality   *free spending.*

93   stroke   *struck.*

94   cleanly   *without getting caught.*
        Keeper   *the warden in a forest preserved for the exclusive use
            of royalty or the nobility.*

95   some certain Snatch   *a catch or a small snack. Here* Snatch
            is also a term for a quick or easy sexual conquest.

96   serve your Turns   *both (a) meet your needs, and (b) service
            your desires.*

97   hit it   *hit the target sexually.*

101   speed   *succeed.*

103   join . . . jar   *cooperate to get what you are quarreling over.*

104   Policy and Stratagem   *cunning and plotting.*

105   affect   *desire.*

She is a Woman, therefore may be won;
She is Lavinia, therefore must be lov'd.
What, Man, more Water glideth by the Mill   85
Than wots the Miller of; and easy 'tis
Of a cut Loaf to steal a Shive, we know.
Though Bassianus be the Emp'ror's Brother,
Better than he have worn Vulcan's Badge.

AARON *[Aside]* Ay, and as good as Saturninus may!   90

DEMETRIUS Then why should he despair that knows to
    court it
    With Words, fair Looks, and Liberality?
    What, hast not thou full often stroke a Doe
    And borne her cleanly by the Keeper's Nose?

AARON Why then it seems some certain Snatch or so   95
    Would serve your Turns.

CHIRON   Ay, so the Turn were served.

DEMETRIUS Aar'n, thou hast hit it.

AARON   Would you had hit it too,
    Then should not we be tir'd with this Ado.
    Why hark ye, hark ye, and are you such Fools
    To square for this? Would it offend you then   100
    That both should speed?

CHIRON 'Faith, not me.

DEMETRIUS   Nor me, so I were one.

AARON For shame, be Friends, and join for that you
    jar:
    'Tis Policy and Stratagem must do
    That you affect; and so must you resolve   105

107   perforce   *here both (a) of necessity, and (b) by force.*

108   Lucrece   *a chaste Roman matron who was raped by Tarquin.*

110   Languishment   *pining with desire.*

115   unfrequented Plots   *unvisited (out-of-the-way) plots of ground.*

116   Fitted by kind   *suited by their nature.*

117   Single you thither   *there single out, as from a herd of deer.*

118   strike her home   *hit her with your "arrows."*

119   stand you in Hope   *do you stand a chance. Like "Wishes' Height" (line 125), "stand you" is a phrase with sexual overtones.*

121   consecrate   *consecrated, dedicated.*

122   withal   *with.*

123   file our Engines   *sharpen our instruments of ingenuity.*

124   suffer   *allow, permit.*
        square   *square off, quarrel with.*

126   House of Fame   *house filled with rumors (because of all the people at Court whispering gossip). Fame meant either "reputation," "renown" (when used positively), or "rumor," "gossip" (when used negatively).*

128   ruthless   *without ruth (sympathy) or pity.*

130   shadow'd   *hidden away.*

That what you cannot as you would achieve,
You must perforce accomplish as you may.
Take this of me: Lucrece was not more chaste
Than this Lavinia, Bassianus' Love.
A speedier Course than ling'ring Languishment   110
Must we pursue, and I have found the Path.
My Lords, a solemn Hunting is in hand;
There will the lovely Roman Ladies troop.
The Forest Walks are wide and spacious,
And many unfrequented Plots there are   115
Fitted by kind for Rape and Villainy:
Single you thither then this dainty Doe,
And strike her home by Force if not by Words.
This way, or not at all, stand you in Hope.
Come, come, our Empress, with her sacred Wit   120
To Villainy and Vengeance consecrate,
Will we acquaint withal what we intend,
And she shall file our Engines with Advice
That will not suffer you to square your selves
But to your Wishes' Height advance you both.   125
The Emp'ror's Court is like the House of Fame,
The Palace full of Tongues, of Eyes and Ears.
The Woods are ruthless, dreadful, deaf, and dull:
There speak, and strike, brave Boys, and take
    your Turns;
There serve your Lust, shadow'd from Heaven's
    Eye,   130
And revel in Lavinia's Treasury.

357

133   Sit fas aut nefas   *Latin for "be it right or wrong."*

135   Per . . . vehor   *Latin for "Through Stygia and through the shades I am carried." Demetrius' meaning is that until he finds relief, he is suffering the torments of one burning in Hell (Stygia being a region of Hades).*

II.ii   *This brief scene occurs on the grounds before the Emperor's residence.*

1   bright and gray   *In Shakespeare's time* gray *was used to describe the color of the pre-dawn sky; here* bright *probably means clear.*

3   Uncouple   *unleash the hounds.*
make a Bay   *have prolonged barking.*

5   ring a Hunter's Peal   *blow a hunter's horn.*

7   Charge   *duty, responsibility, concern.*

8   carefully   *with care and solicitude.*

S.D.   Cry   *loud barking.*
wind   *blow (fill with wind).*

CHIRON Thy Counsel, Lad, smells of no Cowardice.
DEMETRIUS *Sit fas aut nefas,* till I find the Stream
    To cool this Heat, a Charm to calm these Fits,
    Per Stygia, per manes vehor.   *Exeunt.*   135

Scene 2

Enter Titus Andronicus and his three Sons
(making a Noise with Hounds and Horns) and Marcus.

TITUS The Hunt is up, the Morn is bright and gray,
    The Fields are fragrant, and the Woods are green.
    Uncouple here and let us make a Bay
    And wake the Emp'ror and his lovely Bride,
    And rouse the Prince, and ring a Hunter's Peal,   5
    That all the Court may echo with the Noise.
    Sons, let it be your Charge, as it is ours,
    T' attend the Emp'ror's Person carefully.
    I have been troubled in my Sleep this Night,
    But dawning Day new Comfort hath inspir'd.   10

Here a Cry of Hounds, and wind Horns in a peal.
Then enter Saturninus, Tamora, Bassianus, Lavinia,
Chiron, Demetrius, and their Attendants.

359

12   Madam   *Here Titus addresses Tamora.*

15   Somewhat . . . Ladies.   *It is not clear whether Saturninus means this statement literally or facetiously, but it is obvious from Bassianus' response that he regards it as one of his brother's typically ungracious remarks. Bassianus wishes to defend what Titus has done and to prevent a further outbreak of strife.*

18   Horse   *horses.*

21   Chase   *the course to be followed over the grounds during the hunt.*

Many good Morrows to your Majesty;
—Madam, to you as many and as good.
—I promised your Grace a Hunter's Peal.
SATURNINUS   And you have rung it lustily, my Lords:
Somewhat too early for new-married Ladies.   15
BASSIANUS   Lavinia, how say you?
LAVINIA   I say no:
I have been broad awake two hours and more.
SATURNINUS   Come on then, Horse and Chariots let us
    have,
And to our Sport. —Madam, now shall ye see
Our Roman Hunting.
MARCUS   I have Dogs, my Lord,   20
Will rouse the proudest Panther in the Chase
And climb the highest Promontory Top.
TITUS   And I have Horse will follow where the Game
Makes way, and runs like Swallows o'er the Plain.
                    Exeunt all but Demetrius and Chiron.
DEMETRIUS   Chiron, we hunt not, we, with Horse nor
    Hound,   25
But hope to pluck a dainty Doe to Ground.   *Exeunt.*

II.iii   *This scene takes place in the Woods.*

1   Wit   *common sense.*

3   inherit it   *derive any use from it.*

4   thinks of me so abjectly   *has such a low opinion of me.*

5   coin a Stratagem   *devise a trick (with a pun on the use of gold to make coins).*

6   beget   *give birth to.*

8–9   for . . . Chest   *to the undoing of those who take these "Alms" (a word normally referring to gifts for the poor) from the treasury of the Empress.*

S.D.   Enter . . . Moor.   *The phrasing of this stage direction is significant. Tamora enters "alone" because she has come to this secluded setting without her entourage, a fact noted by Bassianus in line 56. It is immediately apparent, in other words, that she is not conducting herself with the decorum expected of an Empress.*

10   Sad   *serious, reflective.*

11   gleeful Boast   *display of gladness.*

17   mocks   *imitates the sound of.*

Scene 3

Enter Aaron, alone, with a Bag of Gold.

AARON   He that had Wit would think that I had none,
       To bury so much Gold under a Tree
       And never after to inherit it;
       Let him that thinks of me so abjectly
       Know that this Gold must coin a Stratagem   5
       Which, cunningly effected, will beget
       A very exc'llent piece of Villainy.
       —And so repose, sweet Gold, for their Unrest
       That have their Alms out of the Empress' Chest.

                                    He buries the Gold.

       Enter Tamora alone to the Moor.

TAMORA   My lovely Aaron, wherefore look'st thou Sad   10
       When ev'ry thing doth make a gleeful Boast?
       The Birds chant Melody on ev'ry Bush,
       The Snake lies rolled in the cheerful Sun,
       The green Leaves quiver with the cooling Wind
       And make a checker'd Shadow on the Ground.   15
       Under their sweet Shade, Aaron, let us sit,
       And, whilst the babbling Echo mocks the Hounds,

   363

19   As . . . once   *as if two hunts were heard simultaneously.*

20   yell'wing   *an onomatopoetic word (one whose sound imitates its sense),* yellowing *is a variant of* yelling *and* yelping *and a close relative of* bellowing, *all of which suggest a chorus of baying hounds.*

21–22   such . . . enjoy'd   *such as Aeneas ("the wand'ring Prince" on his way from fallen Troy to Rome, the city he was to found) and Dido (Queen of Carthage, with whom he spent a sojourn) are said to have enjoyed.*

24   curtain'd . . . Cave   *secluded in a secret-keeping cave. This story is told in Book IV of Vergil's* Aeneid.

30–31   though Venus . . . mine   *Aaron alludes to the view that those born when the planet Venus was ascendant, and thus dominated by her influence, were "Venereal" (line 37) or disposed to the pleasures associated with the Goddess of Love. On the other hand, those born under Saturn were thought to be cold, sullen, and menacing. Much of what Aaron says about himself is also applicable to the Emperor, whose very name is indicative of his "sign."*

32   deadly-standing Eye   *This image suggests a fixed, threatening stare, with analogies to the fabled cockatrice, a creature that was said to be able to kill with a glance from its death-dealing eye.*

35   Adder   *venomous snake.*

43   His Philomel   *This is the first of many allusions to the story of Philomela, who was raped by her brother-in-law Tereus and deprived of her tongue so that she could not disclose his crime.*

Replying shrilly to the well-tun'd Horns
As if a Double Hunt were heard at once,
Let us sit down and mark their yell'wing Noise,   20
And after Conflict such as was suppos'd
The wand'ring Prince and Dido once enjoy'd
When with a happy Storm they were surpris'd
And curtain'd with a Counsel-keeping Cave,
We may, each wreathed in the other's Arms,   25
Our Pastimes done, possess a Golden Slumber,
Whiles Hounds and Horns and sweet melodious
    Birds
Be unto us as is a Nurse's Song
Of Lullaby to bring her Babe asleep.
AARON   Madam, though Venus govern your Desires,   30
Saturn is dominator over mine.
What signifies my deadly-standing Eye,
My Silence and my cloudy Melancholy,
My fleece of woolly Hair that now uncurls
Ev'n as an Adder when she doth unroll   35
To do some fatal Execution?
No, Madam, these are no Venereal Signs:
Vengeance is in my Heart, Death in my Hand,
Blood and Revenge are hamm'ring in my Head.
Hark, Tamora, the Empress of my Soul,   40
Which never hopes more Heav'n than rests in thee,
This is the Day of Doom for Bassianus:
His Philomel must lose her Tongue today,
Thy Sons make pillage of her Chastity,

49   Parcel . . . Booty *part of our hoped-for treasure.*

56   Unfurnish'd of *unaccompanied by.*
      well-beseeming Troop *the kind of entourage befitting an
        Empress.*

57   Dian *Diana, Goddess of Chastity.*
      habited *attired.*

59   Gen'ral Hunting *the hunting available to the general popu-
        lace (as opposed to that reserved for royalty and the nobility in
        private parks or forests). Bassianus is suggesting that there is
        something suspect in the Queen's being in such a "common"
        setting on a day when her husband is hunting in a royal chase.*

60   Controller *warden. Tamora's implication is that Bassianus
        is being "saucy" (sassy, arrogant) in presuming to patrol the
        behavior of his Queen.*

61–65 Had . . . art. *Tamora alludes to the story of Actaeon, a
        hunter who was caught spying on Diana while she and her
        nymphs bathed in a secluded setting. Diana caused horns to
        sprout from his forehead so that his hounds thought him a stag
        and chewed him to death.*

66   Under your patience *with all due respect; begging your
        pardon.*

67   goodly gift in Horning *fine talent for horning (giving the
        horns of a cuckold to your husband by your infidelity).*

68   doubted *suspected.*

And wash their Hands in Bassianus' Blood.   45
Seest thou this Letter? Take it up, I pray thee,
And give the King this fatal plotted Scroll.

He hands her a Letter.

Now question me no more: we are espied.
Here comes a Parcel of our hopeful Booty
Which dreads not yet their Lives' Destruction.   50

TAMORA   Ah my sweet Moor, sweeter to me than Life.

AARON   No more, great Empress: Bassianus comes.
Be cross with him, and I'll go fetch thy Sons
To back thy Quarrels, whatsoe'er they be.   *Exit.*

Enter Bassianus and Lavinia.

BASSIANUS   Who have we here? Rome's royal Emperess   55
Unfurnish'd of her well-beseeming Troop?
Or is it Dian, habited like her,
Who hath abandoned her holy Groves
To see the Gen'ral Hunting in this Forest?

TAMORA   Saucy Controller of my private Steps!   60
Had I the pow'r that some say Dian had,
Thy Temples should be planted presently
With Horns, as was Actaeon's, and the Hounds
Should drive upon thy new-transformed Limbs,
Unmannerly Intruder as thou art.   65

LAVINIA   Under your patience, gentle Empress,
'Tis thought you have a goodly gift in Horning,
And to be doubted that your Moor and you

66   'Tis pity   *it would be a pity if.*

72   Cimm'rian   *In the* Odyssey *the Cimmerians were a race who lived in darkness. Here, with* swarty *(swarthy),* Cimmerian *simply means "black man."*

76   Dismounted . . . Steed   *Bassianus refers to Tamora's husband as well as to her horse. He paints her moral choices in terms of pure black and white.*

81   rated   *berated, scolded.*

83   Raven-color'd   *black. The raven was considered a bird of ill omen, associated with revenge and death.*

84   passing   *surpassingly.*

85   not'ce of   *notice of; here, to be elided into two syllables (notes-of).*

87   abused   *deceived; here the word is probably to be pronounced disyllabically (*abus'd*).*

89   How now   *How are you?*

Are singled forth to try Experiments.
Jove shield your Husband from his Hounds today!   70
'Tis pity they should take him for a Stag.

BASSIANUS   Believe me, Queen, your swarty Cimm'rian
Doth make your Honor of his Body's Hue:
Spotted, detested, and abominable.
Why are you sequest'red from all your Train,   75
Dismounted from your snow-white goodly Steed,
And wand'red hither to an obscure Plot,
Accompanied but with a barb'rous Moor,
If Foul Desire had not conducted you?

LAVINIA   And being intercepted in your Sport,   80
Great reason that my noble Lord be rated
For Sauciness. —I pray you let us hence,
And let her joy her Raven-color'd Love:
This Valley fits the purpose passing well.

BASSIANUS   The King my Brother shall have not'ce of
this.   85

LAVINIA   Ay, for these Slips have made him noted
long:
Good King, to be so mightily abused!

TAMORA   Why I have patience to endure all this?

Enter Chiron and Demetrius.

DEMETRIUS   How now, dear Sovereign and our
gracious Mother!
Why doth your Highness look so pale and wan?   90

369

92   'tic'd   *enticed.*

93   Vale   *valley. In the "moral landscape" of medieval and Renaissance allegory, valleys tend to be associated with confusion, danger, evil, despair, and death.*

95   O'ercome   *both (a) overgrown, and (b) defeated by. The Moss and Mistletoe are presented as indications of the barrenness of the trees. With no vitality of their own, the trees are only able to support these "baleful" (harmful) parasites.*

97   nightly Owl   *The hooting of the owl was widely associated with death.*

101   Urchins   *hedgehogs.*

107   dismal Yew   *Often found in churchyards, yew trees were associated with graves and funerals, and thus with death.*

110   "Lascivious Goth"   *This is probably meant to be a pun on "lascivious goat," an expression derived from the goat's reputation for lechery.*

TAMORA   Have I not Reason, think you, to look Pale?
These two have 'tic'd me hither to this Place.
A barr'n detested Vale you see it is:
The Trees, though Summer, yet Forlorn and Lean,
O'ercome with Moss and baleful Mistletoe;   95
Here never shines the Sun; here nothing breeds,
Unless the nightly Owl or fatal Raven.
And when they show'd me this abhorred Pit,
They told me here at dead time of the Night
A thousand Fiends, a thousand hissing Snakes,   100
Ten thousand swelling Toads, as many Urchins,
Would make such fearful and confused Cries,
As any Mortal Body hearing it
Should straight fall mad, or else die suddenly.
No sooner had they told this hellish Tale   105
But straight they told me they would bind me
    here
Unto the Body of a dismal Yew
And leave me to this miserable Death.
And then they call'd me "Foul Adulteress,"
"Lascivious Goth," and all the bitt'rest Terms   110
That ever Ear did hear to such effect.
And had you not by wondrous Fortune come,
This Vengeance on me they had executed.
Revenge it, as you love your Mother's Life,
Or be ye not henceforth call'd my Children.   115
DEMETRIUS   This is a Witness that I am thy Son!
                                    He stabs Bassianus.

371

117   And . . . Strength!   *Chiron is at pains to prove that he is just as much his Mother's son as is his older brother. The punctuation followed here is that of the First Quarto, which emphasizes "my Strength" and stresses the word* my.

120   Poniard   *dagger.*

122   Stay . . . her   *Wait, Madam, she has more coming to her. As he says* here, *Demetrius probably points to another kind of "Poniard."*

123   First . . . Straw.   *First "thresh" (beat out, flail) the "Corn" (grain) from its husk, then burn the "Straw" (the chaff that remains after removal of the grain). Probably a proverbial expression, here it relates not only to the violence Demetrius and Chiron intend to do in raping Lavinia, but also to the barren stalk they will leave after they have had their way with her.*

124   This . . . Chastity   *This spoiled favorite vaunted her purity.*

132   outlive . . . sting   *survive us and sting back. The word* both *may refer to all three of Tamora's tormentors; alternatively, it may here have the sense of "also," "in addition."*

133   make that sure   *make sure of that.*

135   nice preserved   *The syntax hovers between "nice, preserved" and "nice-preserved." Chiron is making light of the fastidiousness with which Lavinia has maintained her chastity, and is coarsely savoring the chance to gorge on such a delicacy.*

CHIRON   And this for me struck home, to show my
       Strength!   *He too stabs Bassianus.*
LAVINIA   Ay come, Semiramis, nay barb'rous Tamora,
       For no Name fits thy Nature by thy Own!
TAMORA   Give me the Poniard: you shall know, my
       Boys,   120
       Your Mother's Hand shall right your Mother's
       Wrong.
DEMETRIUS   Stay, Madam, here is more belongs to her:
       First thrash the Corn, then after burn the Straw.
       This Minion stood upon her Chastity,
       Upon her Nuptial Vow, her Loyalty,   125
       And with that painted Hope braves your
       Mightiness:
       And shall she carry this unto her Grave?
CHIRON   And if she do, I would I were an Eunuch.
       Drag hence her Husband to some secret Hole,
       And make his dead Trunk pillow to our Lust.   130
TAMORA   But when ye have the Honey we desire,
       Let not this Wasp outlive us both to sting.
CHIRON   I warr'nt you, Madam, we will make that sure.
       —Come, Mistress, now perforce we will enjoy
       That nice preserved Honesty of yours.   135
LAVINIA   O Tamora, thou bear'st a Woman's Face—
TAMORA   I will not hear her speak; away with her!
LAVINIA   Sweet Lords, entreat her hear me but a word!
DEMETRIUS   Listen, fair Madam; let it be your Glory
       To see her Tears; but be your Heart to them   140

373

142   **Dam**   *mother.* Dam *is a term normally applied only to non-human mothers.*

143   **learn**   *teach.*

145   **Tyranny**   *cruelty.*

146   **Sons alike**   *sons who are the same as either (a) herself, or (b) each other. In the next line, Lavinia turns her attention from Demetrius to Chiron, hoping that the younger son will be different from the mother and the older son.*

148   **Bastard**   *Chiron says that if he were not like his mother, he would prove himself to be the son of another woman.*

150   **find it**   *discover it to be true.*

153   **forlorn**   *lost, abandoned by other birds.*

156   **Nothing . . . pitiful**   *not so kind as that, but somewhat pitiful.*

160   **obdurate**   *hard, inflexible.*

161   **Hadst . . . Person**   *had you yourself.*

163–65   **Remember . . . relent.**   *Tamora is drawing a precise parallel with Titus' refusal to hear her pleas when she begged him to preserve her son from the sacrifice prepared by his sons. Just as Titus proved obdurate, she says, so will she.*

As unrelenting Flint to drops of Rain.

LAVINIA   When did the Tiger's young ones teach the
    Dam?
    O do not learn her Wrath: she taught it thee.
    The Milk thou suck'st from her did turn to
        Marble:
    Ev'n at thy Teat thou hadst thy Tyranny.   145
    Yet ev'ry Mother breeds not Sons alike:
    —Do thou entreat her show a Woman's pity.

CHIRON   What, would'st thou have me prove my self a
    Bastard?

LAVINIA   'Tis true the Raven doth not hatch a Lark.
    —Yet have I heard (O could I find it now!)   150
    The Lion mov'd with pity did endure
    To have his princely Paws par'd all away.
    Some say that Ravens foster forlorn Children,
    The whilst their own Birds famish in their Nests.
    O be to me, though thy hard Heart say no,   155
    Nothing so kind, but something pitiful!

TAMORA   I know not what it means; away with her!

LAVINIA   O let me teach thee for my Father's sake,
    That gave thee Life when well he might have
        slain thee:
    Be not obdurate, open thy deaf Ears!   160

TAMORA   Hadst thou in Person ne'er offended me,
    Even for his sake am I pitiless.
    —Remember, Boys, I pour'd forth Tears in vain
    To save your Brother from the Sacrifice,

375

172   Fond *foolish.*

173   present   *immediate.*

178   charitable   *loving, compassionate.*

179   Fee   *payment in compensation for the sacrifice of their brother Alarbus.*

180   satisfice   *satisfy. If* satisfice *is the correct reading here (the First Quarto appears to read* satisfiee, *which could well be a "foul-case" error resulting from an* e *in the* c *tray of the compositor), it is likely that Shakespeare chose that form of the word to echo* sacrifice *and thereby reinforce the parallel with the fate of Alarbus.*

183   gen'ral Name   *The phrase refers to Womankind's good name.*

184   Confusion   *This was a word that carried a much broader range of meanings in Shakespeare's time than it does in our own. In lines 182–84 Lavinia is saying that Tamora's behavior leads to such confusion of genders that it threatens to bring total confusion (devastation, chaos) down on human society.*

But fierce Andronicus would not relent.   165
Therefore away with her, and use her as you will:
The worse to her, the better lov'd of me.

LAVINIA O Tamora, be call'd a gentle Queen,
And with thine own Hands kill me in this place,
                              She clutches Tamora.
For 'tis not Life that I have begg'd so long: 170
Poor I was slain when Bassianus died.

TAMORA What begg'st thou then? Fond Woman, let me
    go!

LAVINIA 'Tis present Death I beg, and one thing
    more
That Womanhood denies my Tongue to tell.
O keep me from their worse than killing Lust,   175
And tumble me into some loathsome Pit,
Where never Man's Eye may behold my Body.
Do this, and be a charitable Murd'rer.

TAMORA So should I rob my sweet Sons of their Fee:
No, let them satisfice their Lust on thee.   180

DEMETRIUS Away! For thou hast stay'd us here too
    long.

LAVINIA No Grace? No Womanhood? Ah, beastly
    Creature,
The Blot and En'my to our gen'ral Name!
Confusion fall—

CHIRON Nay then I'll stop your Mouth. —Bring thou
    her Husband;   185
This is the Hole where Aaron bid us hide him.

377

187   make her sure   *make certain that we are secure against retaliation for what we are doing to her.*

189   made away   *disposed of.*

191   Trull   *slut.*

195   dull   *drowsy.*

196   for Shame   *because of what people would think of me.*

198   subtle   *deceptive.*

Demetrius throws the body of Bassianus into the Pit;
then exeunt Chiron and Demetrius with Lavinia.

TAMORA   Farewell, my Sons; see that you make her
    sure!
Ne'er let my Heart know merry Cheer indeed
Till all th' Andronici be made away.
—Now will I hence to seek my lovely Moor,   190
And let my spleenful Sons this Trull deflow'r.

Exit.

Enter Aaron, with two of Titus' Sons.

AARON   Come on, my Lords, the better foot before:
Straight will I bring you to the loathsome Pit
Where I espied the Panther fast asleep.
QUINTUS   My Sight is very dull, what e'er it bodes.   195
MARTIUS   And mine, I promise you: were 't not for
    Shame,
Well could I leave our Sport to sleep a while.

He falls into the Pit.

QUINTUS   What, art thou fall'n? What subtle Hole is
    this,
Whose Mouth is cover'd with rude-growing Briers,
Upon whose Leaves are drops of new-shed Blood   200
As fresh as Morning Dew distill'd on Flowers?
A very Fatal Place it seems to me.
Speak, Brother, hast thou hurt thee with the
    Fall?

379

210   unhallow'd *unholy.*
        blood-stain'd Hole *In all likelihood Shakespeare expected this bloody cavity to remind his audience of the rape of Lavinia, now occurring offstage.*

211   surprised *overtaken (here pronounced trisyllabically).*
        uncouth *unknown, strange, uncanny.*

214   divining *foretelling.*

217   compassionate *feeling the emotions it would feel if it were in your place (here pronounced trisyllabically: com-pash-nate).*

219   whereat *at which.*
        by Surmise *by inference, by its imaginings.*

222   bereav'd *robbed (bereft) of life, killed. This phrasing is reinforced by the parallel use of "bereft" in line 282.*

223   slaughter'd Lamb *Here Shakespeare offers yet another reminder of the sacrifice of Alarbus, the primal event of this bloody tragedy. The playwright also evokes parallels with Biblical sacrifice, both Hebraic and Christian.*

227   Ring *probably one with a stone of carbuncle, believed to be luminescent.*
        lightens *illuminates.*

228   Taper in some Monument *candle in some burial vault.*

229   earthly *pale; already returning to dust (with a possible reference to the Biblical commonplace first expressed in Genesis 3:19).*

MARTIUS   O Brother, with the dismall'st Object hurt
          That ever Eye with Sight made Heart lament!   205
AARON   [*Aside*] Now will I fetch the King to find
             them here,
          That he thereby may have a likely Guess
          How these were they that made away his Brother.
                                                    Exit.
MARTIUS   Why dost not comfort me, and help me out
          From this unhallow'd and blood-stained Hole?   210
QUINTUS   I am surprised with an uncouth Fear!
          A chilling Sweat o'erruns my trembling Joints;
          My Heart suspects more than mine Eye can see.
MARTIUS   To prove thou hast a true-divining Heart,
          Aaron and thou look down into this Den   215
          And see a fearful Sight of Blood and Death!
QUINTUS   Aaron is gone, and my compassionate Heart
          Will not permit mine Eyes once to behold
          The thing whereat it trembles by Surmise.
          O tell me who it is: for ne'er till now   220
          Was I a Child to fear I know not what.
MARTIUS   Lord Bassianus lies bereav'd in Blood,
          All on a Heap, like to a slaughter'd Lamb,
          In this detested, dark, blood-drinking Pit.
QUINTUS   If it be dark, how dost thou know 'tis he?   225
MARTIUS   Upon his bloody Finger he doth wear
          A precious Ring, that lightens all this Hole,
          Which, like a Taper in some Monument,
          Doth shine upon the Dead-man's earthly Cheeks,

230   ragged Entrails   *Bassianus probably refers to the roots and tubers that break through the soil of the pit, but the phrasing also suggests a womb, an analogy reinforced by line 239. The word* Entrails *is also an echo of I.i.147 in the account of the sacrifice of Alarbus.*

231   Pyramus   *the Greek youth who stabbed himself after he found a bloody garment he thought to be proof that his beloved Thisbe had been devoured by a lion. Shakespeare would have known the story from Book IV of Ovid's* Metamorphoses.

235   fell   *savage.*

236   Cocytus   *(pronounced Co-seé-tus) the River of Lamentations, one of the four rivers of Hades. Here the word is used to symbolize Hell itself.*

238   wanting   *lacking.*

248   lately   *only recently, just now.*

And shows the ragged Entrails of this Pit.   230
So pale did shine the Moon on Pyramus
When he by Night lay bath'd in Maiden Blood.
O Brother, help me with thy fainting Hand,
If Fear hath made thee faint, as me it hath,
Out of this fell devouring Receptacle,   235
As hateful as Cocytus' misty Mouth.

QUINTUS   Reach me thy Hand, that I may help thee
   out,
Or, wanting Strength to do thee so much good,
I may be pluck'd into the swall'wing Womb
Of this deep Pit, poor Bassianus' Grave.   240
I have no Strength to pluck thee to the Brink.

MARTIUS   Nor I no Strength to climb without thy
   Help.

QUINTUS   Thy Hand once more: I will not loose again
Till thou art here aloft or I below.
Thou canst not come to me: I come to thee.   245

                            Quintus falls into the Pit.

        Enter the Emperor and Aaron the Moor.

SATURNINUS   Along with me: I'll see what Hole is
   here,
And what he is that now is leapt into it.
—Say, who art thou that lately didst descend
Into this gaping Hollow of the Earth?

MARTIUS   Th' unhappy Sons of old Andronicus,   250

254 Lodge *hunting lodge.*

255 Chase *hunting park.*

256 hour *here pronounced disyllabically.*

258 out alas *Here* out *is an intensifier (more or less equivalent to* O!) *to reinforce* alas.

262 search *probe.*

264 Writ *piece of writing, letter.*

265 Complot of *plot or conspiracy behind.*
   timeless *untimely.*

266 fold *enfold, conceal.*

268 if . . . handsomely *if we fail to meet him handily (when we are ourselves together).*

Brought hither in a most unlucky Hour,
To find thy Brother Bassianus dead.

SATURNINUS   My Brother dead! I know thou dost but
    jest:
He and his Lady both are at the Lodge
Upon the north side of this pleasant Chase.   255
'Tis not an hour since I left them there.

MARTIUS   We know not where you left them all alive,
But out alas, here have we found him dead!

Enter Tamora with Attendants,
Titus Andronicus, and Lucius.

TAMORA   Where is my Lord the King?

SATURNINUS   Here, Tamora, though griev'd with
    killing Grief.   260

TAMORA   Where is thy brother Bassianus?

SATURNINUS   Now to the bottom dost thou search my
    Wound:
Poor Bassianus here lies murdered.

TAMORA   Then all too late I bring this fatal Writ,
The Complot of this timeless Tragedy,   265
And wonder greatly that Man's Face can fold
In pleasing Smiles such murd'rous Tyranny.

She gives Saturninus a Letter.

SATURNINUS   [*Reading*]
    "And if we miss to meet him handsomely,
    Sweet Huntsman (Bassianus 'tis we mean),

385

270   **dig the Grave for him** *either set him up for the kill or go ahead and kill him yourself. This, "our Meaning" (line 271), is made clear by lines 273–74, in which the letter says that Bassianus will be buried in the pit that has already been dug.*

270–71   **Do . . . Reward** *In this clause the comma in line 271 functions as an implied* **and** *or* **and then.** *In other words, "you may look for your reward if you dig the grave."*

272   **Elder Tree** *According to tradition, Judas hung himself on an elder tree. The elder was also associated, by its name, with all the doings of what St. Paul called "the old man" (Romans 6:6), mankind in its fallen, sinful nature.*

274   **decreed** *decided, agreed.*

279   **should have** *was to have.*

281   **Whelps** *pups.*
    kind *breed, nature.*

284   **bide** *abide, wait.*

285   **tort'ring** *torturing (spelled* tortering *in the early texts).*

286   **What** *who. Shakespeare frequently uses* **what** *when the question elicits an answer defining a person in terms of a category (in this case "murderer").*

287   **discovered** *revealed, disclosed.*

289   **Boon** *special favor.*

292   **apparent** *obvious, completely open to view.*

Do thou so much as dig the Grave for him   270
(Thou know'st our Meaning), look for thy
   Reward
Among the Nettles at the Elder Tree
Which overshades the Mouth of that same Pit
Where we decreed to bury Bassianus.
Do this, and purchase us thy lasting
   Friends."   275
O Tamora, was ever heard the like?
This is the Pit, and this the Elder Tree.
Look, Sirs, if you can find the Huntsman out
That should have murder'd Bassianus here.

AARON My gracious Lord, here is the Bag of Gold.   280
SATURNINUS [*To Titus*] Two of thy Whelps, fell Curs
   of bloody kind,
Have here bereft my Brother of his Life.
[*To Attendants*] Sirs, drag them from the Pit
   unto the Prison;
There let them bide until we have devis'd
Some never-heard-of-tort'ring Pain for them.   285

TAMORA What are they in this Pit? O wondrous thing!
How eas'ly Murder is discovered!

TITUS [*Kneeling*] High Emperor, upon my feeble Knee
I beg this Boon, with Tears not lightly shed,
That this fell Fault of my accursed Sons,   290
Accursed if the Fault be prov'd in them—

SATURNINUS If it be prov'd? You see it is apparent!
   —Who found this Letter? —Tam'ra, was it you?

294   take it up   *pick it up.*

296   Fathers'   *forefathers'.*
reverent   *revered, sacred.*

299   follow   *understand (follow my meaning) and do as I say. Saturninus is telling Titus as firmly as he can that he will hear no further pleading.*

300   murder'd; murd'rers   *spelled* murthered, murtherers *here, and frequently elsewhere in the First Quarto and First Folio. Because the words are also spelled with a* d *at other points in the same texts, the* Guild *edition modernizes them throughout this play. The same practice is followed with a number of other words in which older and more modern spellings are both found in the early texts.*

305   Fear . . . enough.   *Don't worry about your sons; they will be all right.*

388

TAMORA Andronicus himself did take it up.

TITUS I did, my Lord. Yet let me be their Bail;   295
For by my Fathers' rev'rent Tomb I vow
They shall be ready at your Highness' will
To answer their Suspicion with their Lives.

SATURNINUS Thou shalt not bail them; see thou
follow me.
—Some bring the murder'd Body, some the
Murd'rers.   300
Let them not speak a word: the Guilt is plain.
For by my Soul, were there worse end than Death,
That end upon them should be executed.

TAMORA Andronicus, I will entreat the King:
Fear not thy Sons, they shall do well enough.   305

TITUS Come, Lucius, come; stay not to talk with
them.   *Exeunt.*

II.iv   *The setting shifts to an adjacent part of the Forest.*

3   bewray   *reveal.*

5   scrowl   *scrawl, write. Demetrius is taunting Lavinia by sug-*
      gesting that at best she could only scrawl crudely with the
      stumps (handless arms) they have left her.

6   Sweet-water   *perfumed water.*

9   And 'twere   *if it were.*
      Cause   *case, condition.*

Scene 4

Enter the Empress' Sons, with Lavinia,
her hands cut off, her tongue cut out, and ravished.

DEMETRIUS   So now go tell, and if thy Tongue can
    speak,
Who 'twas that cut thy Tongue and ravish'd thee.
CHIRON   Write down thy Mind, bewray thy Meaning so,
And if thy Stumps will let thee play the Scribe.
DEMETRIUS   See how with Signs and Tokens she can
    scrowl.   5
CHIRON   Go home, call for Sweet-water, wash thy
    Hands.
DEMETRIUS   She hath no Tongue to call, nor Hands to
    wash:
And so let's leave her to her silent Walks.
CHIRON   And 'twere my Cause, I should go hang my
    self.
DEMETRIUS   If thou hadst Hands to help thee knit
    the Cord.   *Exeunt Demetrius and Chiron.*   10

13 If . . . me! *If this is only a nightmare, I would give all I own to wake up from it.*

14 some . . . down *Marcus alludes to the assumption that the planets (loosely referred to as "the stars") influence human destiny. Here he invokes the planet that governs his life to strike him dead.*

17 lopp'd and hew'd *These are words associated with pruning trees or chopping wood. We have encountered them before (I.i.132, 146), in connection with the sacrifice of Alarbus.*

19 circling Shadows *the shadows defined by the circles of Lavinia's hugging arms.*
 Kings . . . in *a reminder of Saturninus' suit for Lavinia's hand in I.i.*

26 But sure *surely.*
 Tereus *Philomela's rapist, who cut out her tongue and kept her imprisoned in a hunting lodge to protect himself against detection.*
 deflow'red *violated.*

27 detect him *reveal his identity.*

30 Conduit . . . Spouts *Conduits were fountains, frequently ornamented with sculpted human figures from whose "issuing spouts" water flowed.*

31 Titan's Face *the Sun, whose God was often referred to as Titan.*

32 encount'red with a Cloud *met with a cloud.*

Enter Marcus, from Hunting.

MARCUS   Who's this, my Niece that flies away so
      fast?
   Cousin, a word: where is your Husband?
   —If I do dream, would all my Wealth would wake me!
   If I do wake, some Planet strike me down,
   That I may slumber an eternal Sleep!   15
   —Speak, gentle Niece: what stern ungentle Hands
   Hath lopp'd and hew'd and made thy Body bare
   Of her two Branches, those sweet Ornaments
   Whose circling Shadows Kings have sought to
      sleep in,
   And might not gain so great a Happiness   20
   As half thy Love? Why dost not speak to me?
   Alas, a Crimson River of warm Blood,
   Like to a bubbling Fountain stirr'd with Wind,
   Doth rise and fall between thy Rosed Lips,
   Coming and going with thy Honey Breath.   25
   But sure some Tereus hath deflow'red thee,
   And, lest thou should'st detect him, cut thy
      Tongue.
   Ah now thou turn'st away thy Face for Shame,
   And, notwithstanding all this loss of Blood,
   As from a Conduit with their issuing Spouts,   30
   Yet do thy Cheeks look red as Titan's Face
   Blushing to be encount'red with a Cloud.
   Shall I speak for thee? Shall I say 'tis so?

393

36   like an Oven stopp'd   *If an oven's door were closed tightly for too long, the food being prepared would burn to cinders.*

39   tedious Sampler   *This image associates the sampler with the long and laborious ("tedious") hours Philomela spent embroidering an account of the crime committed against her. As Ovid notes in Book VI of his* **Metamorphoses,** *Philomela had the sampler delivered to Procne, her sister and the wife of Tereus, the man who had raped Philomela and cut out her tongue. In revenge against her husband, Procne killed their son Itys and served his remains to Tereus for supper. Tereus then attempted to kill both sisters, but eventually they escaped by being transformed into birds: Philomela a tongueless swallow, and Procne a nightingale.*

40   Mean   *means.*

45   Tremble   *move tremulously over (to create delicately tremulous notes).*

51   As . . . Feet   *When Orpheus entered the Underworld to plead for the return of his dead wife Eurydice, he used his skill on the lute to charm the three-headed dog Cerberus to fall asleep. This allowed "the Thracian Poet" to pass through the entrance to Hades without interference.*

54   Hour's   *here pronounced disyllabically.*
       Meads   *meadows.*

56   Do . . . back   *Evidently Marcus' words have so disheartened Lavinia that she starts to turn back rather than inflict further pain on her uncle.*

O that I knew thy Heart, and knew the Beast,
That I might rail at him to ease my Mind.   35
Sorrow concealed, like an Oven stopp'd,
Doth burn the Heart to cinders where it is.
Fair Philomel, why she but lost her Tongue,
And in a tedious Sampler sew'd her Mind;
But lovely Niece, that Mean is cut from thee!   40
A craftier Tereus, Cousin, hast thou met,
And he hath cut those pretty Fingers off
That could have better sew'd than Philomel.
O had the Monster seen those Lily Hands
Tremble like Aspen-leaves upon a Lute,   45
And make the silken Strings delight to kiss them,
He would not then have touch'd them for his Life.
Or had he heard the heav'nly Harmony
Which that sweet Tongue hath made,
He would have dropp'd his Knife and fell asleep,   50
As Cerb'rus at the Thracian Poet's Feet.
Come let us go, and make thy Father blind:
For such a Sight will blind a Father's Eye.
One Hour's Storm will drown the fragrant Meads;
What will whole Months of Tears thy Father's
    Eyes?   55
Do not draw back, for we will mourn with thee.
O could our Mourning ease thy Misery!   *Exeunt.*

III.i   *This scene takes place on a street or square before the Capitol.*

1   grave   *solemn, dignified.*

4   my Blood   *the blood of my slain sons.*

5   watch'd   *stayed awake protecting Rome's security.*

9   Souls is   *souls are. Grammar in Elizabethan times was much more relaxed than modern usage tends to be.*

10   two and twenty   *Evidently Titus is now reconciled to including Mutius among his honorable sons.*

Act Three

Scene 1

*Enter the Judges, Senators, and Tribunes, with Titus' two
Sons, bound, passing on the Stage to the place of Execution,
and Titus going before, pleading.*

TITUS   Hear me, grave Fathers! Noble Tribunes, stay!
    For pity of mine Age, whose Youth was spent
    In dang'rous Wars whilst you securely slept:
    For all my Blood in Rome's great Quarrel shed,
    For all the frosty Nights that I have watch'd,   5
    And for these bitter Tears which now you see,
    Filling the aged Wrinkles in my Cheeks,
    Be pitiful to my condemned Sons,
    Whose Souls is not corrupted as 'tis thought.
    For two and twenty Sons I never wept,   10

13   Languor   *heaviness, weariness.*

14–15   Let . . . blush.   *Let my tears quench the dry earth's thirst,
            because the blood of my sons would shame it so deeply that it
            would blush.*

17   That . . . Ruins   *that shall flow out from these two old eyes.
        The "Ruins" Titus refers to are probably stone cisterns or
        reservoirs, which would fill with water during April's showers
        (line 18), and then provide water for "Summer's Drought"
        (line 19). Modern editions normally emend "ruins" to
        "urns." The word to be found in all the early texts offers a
        richer complex of implications.*

19   still   *continually, without interruption.*

22   So thou refuse   *on the condition that you refuse.*

23   reverent   *revered.*

24   Unbind   *release from prison.*
        Doom   *judgment, penalty.*

26   Orators   *pleaders. Titus refers to legal or judicial proceedings.*

28   by   *here.*

29   recount   *tell, repeat.*

398

Because they died in Honor's lofty Bed;

Titus lies down, and the Judges pass by him,
leading the Prisoners to execution.

For these, Tribunes, in the Dust I write
My Heart's deep Languor and my Soul's sad Tears.
Let my Tears staunch the Earth's dry Appetite:
My Sons' sweet Blood will make it shame and
   blush.   15
O Earth, I will befriend thee more with Rain
That shall distill from these two ancient Ruins
Than youthful April shall with all his Show'rs;
In Summer's Drought I'll drop upon thee still;
In Winter with warm Tears I'll melt the Snow,   20
And keep eternal Springtime on thy Face:
So thou refuse to drink my dear Sons' Blood.

Enter Lucius, with his Weapon drawn.

O reverent Tribunes! O gentle aged Men!
Unbind my Sons, reverse the Doom of Death,
And let me say, that never wept before,   25
My Tears are now prevailing Orators.
LUCIUS   O noble Father, you lament in vain:
The Tribunes hear you not, no Man is by,
And you recount your Sorrows to a Stone.
TITUS   Ah Lucius, for thy Brothers let me plead.   30
   —Grave Tribunes, once more I entreat of you—

34 mark me *pay attention to me.*

36 bootless *without hope of success.*

38 answer my Distress *provide the answer to my problems.*

39 in some sort *in some respects.*

40 intercept *cut off, interrupt.*

43 attired in grave Weeds *dressed in sober apparel. Titus is probably also thinking of the weeds that would be watered by his tears falling on the ground. If so, he may be thinking specifically of the weeds that attire gravestones.*

44 afford *provide.*

48 wherefore *why.*

51 Doom *penalty, sentence.*

LUCIUS   My gracious Lord, no Tribune hears you
       speak.
TITUS   Why 'tis no matter, Man: if they did hear,
       They would not mark me, or if they did mark,
       They would not pity me; yet plead I must,   35
       And bootless, unto them.
       Therefore I tell my Sorrows to the Stones,
       Who, though they cannot answer my Distress,
       Yet in some sort they're better than the
          Tribunes,
       For that they will not intercept my Tale.   40
       When I do weep, they humbly at my Feet
       Receive my Tears, and seem to weep with me;
       And were they but attired in grave Weeds,
       Rome could afford no Tribunes like to these.
       A Stone is soft as Wax, Tribunes more hard than
          Stones;   45
       A Stone is silent and offendeth not,
       And Tribunes with their Tongues doom Men to
          Death.
       But wherefore stand'st thou with thy Weapon
          drawn?
LUCIUS   To rescue my two Brothers from their Death,
       For which attempt the Judges have pronounc'd   50
       My everlasting Doom of Banishment.
TITUS   [*Rising*] O Happy Man, they have befriended
       thee!
       Why foolish Lucius, dost thou not perceive

54   Wilderness of Tigers   *Titus' disillusionment has increased to the point where he now sees Rome as worse than even the most barbarous of human societies. What had been the epitome of human civilization has become for Titus a "Wilderness," a state of nature as bestial and primitive as the jungle.*

55   affords   *provides, offers.*

61   consuming   *all-consuming, devouring.*

62   Will . . . me?   *Titus is now so despondent that he wishes for the relief that death would bring him.*

64   Object   *sight, object of vision.*

66   Speak . . . Hand   *This is an example of Shakespeare's use of a headless line (an iambic pentameter line lacking its initial unstressed syllable) to vary the rhythm of his verse.*

69   Fagot   *a bundle of branches. Titus' image in this line focuses primarily on the idea of heaping one trouble on top of another. But members of Shakespeare's audience might also have been reminded of the* fasces *(the bundle of rods bound about an axe with a projecting blade) carried before Roman magistrates as a symbol of their authority over a diverse population.*

71   Nilus   *the Nile River.*
        disdaineth Bounds   *shows contempt for its banks.*

74   nurs'd . . . Life   *nurtured this suffering as a consequence of nurturing the life of the one who endures it.*

76   to effectless use   *to no avail.*

That Rome is but a Wilderness of Tigers?
Tigers must prey, and Rome affords no Prey   55
But me and mine: how happy art thou then
From these Devourers to be banished!
But who comes with our Brother Marcus here?

Enter Marcus with Lavinia.

MARCUS   Titus, prepare thy aged Eyes to weep,
   Or if not so, thy noble Heart to break: 60
   I bring consuming Sorrow to thine Age.
TITUS   Will it consume me? Let me see it then.
MARCUS   This was thy Daughter.
TITUS   Why Marcus, so she is!
LUCIUS   Ay me, this Object kills me!   *He falls down.*
TITUS   Faint-hearted Boy, arise and look upon her.   65
   —Speak, Lavinia, what accursed Hand
   Hath made thee Handless in thy Father's sight?
   What Fool hath added Water to the Sea,
   Or brought a Fagot to bright-burning Troy?
   My Grief was at the Height before thou cam'st,   70
   And now like Nilus it disdaineth Bounds.
   Give me a Sword, I'll chop off my Hands too:
   For they have fought for Rome and all in vain,
   And they have nurs'd this Woe in feeding Life;
   In bootless Prayer have they been held up,   75
   And they have serv'd me to effectless use.
   Now all the Service I require of them

403

82   **Engine of her Thoughts** *instrument to express her thoughts: namely, her tongue.*

83   **blabb'd** *chattered. This term conveys affection for the innocence and fragility of this poor "Bird" (line 85).*

84   **pretty hollow Cage** *a metaphor for Lavinia's mouth.*

88   **Park** *deer park, the preserve set aside for royal hunting.*

90   **unrecuring** *incurable.*

91   **Dear** *Both this word and the word* **Deer** *are spelled the same way (***Deare***) in the Quarto and Folio texts; it is clear that we are to think of the two together in both lines 89 and 91.*

94   **Environ'd** *surrounded.*

       Wilderness *wild expanse.*

96   **envious** *malign.*

98   **This way** *As he speaks these words, Titus probably points toward the place of execution to which his sons have been led.*

101   **Spurn** *painful blow, as from a kick in the stomach.*

Is that the one will help to cut the other.
'Tis well, Lavinia, that thou hast no Hands,
For Hands to do Rome service is but vain.   80
LUCIUS   Speak, gentle Sister, who hath martyr'd
    thee?
MARCUS   O that delightful Engine of her Thoughts,
    That blabb'd them with such pleasing Eloquence,
    Is torn from forth that pretty hollow Cage,
    Where like a sweet melodious Bird it sung   85
    Sweet varied Notes, enchanting ev'ry Ear.
LUCIUS   O say thou for her, who hath done this
    Deed?
MARCUS   O thus I found her straying in the Park,
    Seeking to hide her self, as doth the Deer
    That hath receiv'd some unrecuring Wound.   90
TITUS   It was my Dear, and he that wounded her
    Hath hurt me more than had he kill'd me dead:
    For now I stand as one upon a Rock
    Environ'd with a Wilderness of Sea,
    Who marks the waxing Tide grow wave by wave,   95
    Expecting ever when some envious Surge
    Will in his brinish Bowels swallow him.
    This way to Death my wretched Sons are gone,
    Here stands my other Son, a Banish'd Man,
    And here my Brother, weeping at my Woes;   100
    But that which gives my Soul the greatest Spurn
    Is dear Lavinia, dearer than my Soul.
    —Had I but seen thy Picture in this Plight

405

105   **lively**   *living, as distinguished from her "Picture" (line 103).*

107   **mart'red**   *martyred; tortured and mutilated, as were many of the early Christians who suffered for their faith.* **Martyr** *derives from a Greek word that originally meant "witness."*

109   **by this**   *by now, by this time.*

112   **honey Dew**   *sweet dew.*

113   **gath'red**   *enfolded. Lavinia, in her humiliation, is probably gathering her body into a ball to hide the injuries she has suffered.*

121   **do thee Ease**   *comfort you, make you feel better.*

123   **Fountain**   *spring.*

128   **taken**   *removed.*

129   **Brine-pit**   *pit of salty water.*

It would have madded me; what shall I do
Now I behold thy lively Body so?   105
Thou hast no Hands to wipe away thy Tears,
Nor Tongue to tell me who hath mart'red thee.
Thy Husband he is dead, and for his Death
Thy Brothers are condemn'd, and dead by this.
—Look, Marcus! —Ah Son Lucius, look on her!   110
When I did name her Brothers, then fresh Tears
Stood on her Cheeks, as doth the honey Dew
Upon a gath'red Lily almost withered.
MARCUS   Perchance she weeps because they kill'd her
    Husband,
Perchance because she knows them innocent.   115
TITUS   If they did kill thy Husband, then be joyful,
    Because the Law hath ta'en revenge on them.
—No, no, they would not do so foul a Deed:
Witness the Sorrow that their Sister makes.
—Gentle Lavinia, let me kiss thy Lips,   120
Or make some Sign how I may do thee Ease.
Shall thy good Uncle and thy Brother Lucius
And thou and I sit round about some Fountain,
Looking all downwards to behold our Cheeks
How they are stain'd like Meadows yet not dry,   125
With miry Slime left on them by a Flood?
And in the Fountain shall we gaze so long
Till the fresh Taste be taken from that
    Clearness
And made a Brine-pit with our bitter Tears?

407

131   bite our Tongues *bite off our tongues.*
Dumb Shows *pantomimes; silent gestures imitating stage action.*

134   Plot some Device *plan some scheme. Ironically, one is being plotted even as Titus speaks.*

139   wot *know.*

140   Napkin *handkerchief.*
drink *absorb.*

141   drown'd *saturated.*

148   Sympathy of Woe *sharing of sorrows.* Sympathy *literally means "to feel with."*

149   as Limbo is from Bliss *as far as Hell is from Heaven. Limbo was an outlying region of Hell reserved for the souls of the unbaptized (such as the virtuous pagans who never had an opportunity to become Christians) who were neither sinful enough to deserve damnation nor qualified for admission to Heaven.*

Or shall we cut away our Hands like thine? 130
Or shall we bite our Tongues, and in Dumb Shows
Pass the remainder of our hateful Days?
What shall we do? Let us that have our Tongues
Plot some Device of further Misery
To make us wonder'd at in Time to come. 135

LUCIUS Sweet Father, cease your Tears: for at your
    Grief
See how my wretched Sister sobs and weeps.

MARCUS Patience, dear Niece. Good Titus, dry thine
    Eyes.

TITUS Ah Marcus, Marcus! Brother, well I wot
Thy Napkin cannot drink a Tear of mine, 140
For thou, poor Man, hast drown'd it with thine
    own.

LUCIUS Ah my Lavinia, I will wipe thy Cheeks.

TITUS Mark, Marcus, mark! I understand her Signs:
Had she a Tongue to speak, now would she say
That to her Brother which I said to thee: 145
His Napkin, with his true Tears all bewet,
Can do no service on her sorrowful Cheeks.
O what a Sympathy of Woe is this:
As far from Help as Limbo is from Bliss.

Enter Aaron the Moor, alone.

AARON Titus Andronicus, my Lord the Emperor 150
Sends thee this Word: that if thou love thy Sons,

156 Ransom *Aaron requests yet one more propitiatory sacrifice.*

158 Did . . . Lark *The raven's cacophonous croaking was frequently contrasted with the lark's mellifluous melodies.*

159 Sun's uprise *This traditional symbol of hope and renewal is given special poignance here: Titus contemplates the miracle of his sons' uprising from apparently certain death.*

160 With . . . Hand *This line, with six iambic feet, is an example of Shakespeare's use of alexandrines (twelve-syllable lines) at points of special emphasis in this play. The lengthened metrical line helps to convey the overflowing of Titus' heart at this moment of exultation.*

164 serve the Turn *supply the occasion. The presence of the mutilated Lavinia would help to remind the audience of an earlier use of this expression in II.i.96. There, of course, a less ennobling kind of sacrifice was under discussion.*

170 O . . . Desert. *O, there is no hand of either of you that is not of high deserving.*

177 with'red Herbs *wilted plants.*

Let Marcus, Lucius, or thy self, old Titus,
Or any one of you, chop off your Hand
And send it to the King. He for the same
Will send thee hither both thy Sons alive,   155
And that shall be the Ransom for their Fault.

TITUS   O gracious Emperor! O gentle Aaron!
Did ever Raven sing so like a Lark
That gives sweet Tidings of the Sun's uprise?
With all my Heart I'll send the Emperor my Hand.   160
Good Aaron, wilt thou help to chop it off?

LUCIUS   Stay, Father, for that noble Hand of thine,
That hath thrown down so many Enemies,
Shall not be sent; my Hand will serve the Turn,
My Youth can better spare my Blood than you,   165
And therefore mine shall save my Brothers' Lives.

MARCUS   Which of your Hands hath not defended Rome
And rear'd aloft the bloody Battleaxe
Writing Destruction on the En'my's Castle?
O none of both but are of high Desert.   170
My Hand hath been but idle: let it serve
To ransom my two Nephews from their Death,
Then have I kept it to a worthy End.

AARON   Nay come, agree whose Hand shall go along,
For fear they die before their Pardon come.   175

MARCUS   My Hand shall go.

LUCIUS   By Heav'n, it shall not go!

TITUS   Sirs, strive no more: such with'red Herbs as
    these

411

178   meet   *suitable.*

179–   Sweet . . . thee.   *This passage offers a telling contrast to an*
82   *earlier exchange of parallel sentiments in II.iii.114–17.*

192   stay your Strife   *cease your quarreling.*
       dispatch'd   *both (a) completed, and (b) prepared for ship-*
          ment.

194   warded   *guarded, protected.*

197   account of them   *account them, consider them.*

198   easy   *manageable, affordable.*

Are meet for plucking up, and therefore mine.

LUCIUS   Sweet Father, if I shall be thought thy Son,
    Let me redeem my Brothers both from Death.   180

MARCUS   And for our Father's Sake, and Mother's
    Care,
    Now let me show a Brother's Love to thee.

TITUS   Agree between you: I will spare my Hand.

LUCIUS   Then I'll go fetch an Axe.

MARCUS   But I will use the Axe.   *Exeunt.*   185

TITUS   Come hither, Aaron: I'll deceive them both.
    Lend me thy Hand, and I will give thee mine.

AARON   *[Aside]* If that be call'd Deceit, I will be
    Honest,
    And never whilst I live deceive Men so!
    But I'll deceive you in another sort,   190
    And that you'll say ere half an hour pass.
                    He cuts off Titus' Hand.

    Enter Lucius and Marcus again.

TITUS   Now stay your Strife: what shall be is
    dispatch'd.
    —Good Aaron, give his Majesty my Hand:
    Tell him it was a Hand that warded him
    From thousand Dangers. Bid him bury it: 195
    More hath it merited, that let it have.
    As for my Sons, say I account of them
    As Jewels purchas'd at an easy Price,

199 **Dear** *Titus puns on two senses of the word: (a) expensive, and (b) precious.*

201 **Look** *expect.*

203 **fat me** *feed me; feast me till I grow fat.*

211 **with . . . dim** *The Welkin (sky) was the innermost of the crystalline spheres thought to house the planets and stars in concentric globes around the world. Titus suggests that the sighs of Lavinia and himself will be enough to mist the Welkin's glass as one's breath fogs a mirror.*

212 **stain** *obscure, discolor.*

213 **melting Bosoms** *a marvelously precise way of describing both the softness and the melting away of clouds in a partly sunny sky.*

214 **speak with Possibility** *confine your speech to the realm of the possible.*

217 **Passions** *emotions, feelings.*

218 **govern** *control.*

221 **When . . . o'erflow?** *a poetic way of saying "when it rains, doesn't the Earth have floods?"*

And yet Dear too, because I bought mine Own.

AARON I go, Andronicus; and for thy Hand   200
Look by and by to have thy Sons with thee.
[Aside] Their Heads, I mean. O how this
    Villainy
Doth fat me with the very Thoughts of it!
Let Fools do Good, and Fair Men call for Grace;
Aaron will have his Soul Black like his Face.   205

                                                   Exit.

TITUS O here I lift this one Hand up to Heaven,
And bow this feeble Ruin to the Earth.
If any Power pities wretched Tears,
To that I call. *[To Lavinia, kneeling beside him]*
                What, would'st thou kneel with me?
Do then, dear Heart, for Heav'n shall hear our
    Prayers,   210
Or with our Sighs we'll breathe the Welkin dim,
And stain the Sun with Fog, as sometime Clouds
When they do hug him in their melting Bosoms.

MARCUS O Brother, speak with Possibility,
And do not break into these deep Extremes.   215

TITUS Is not my Sorrows deep, having no Bottom?
Then be my Passions bottomless with them.

MARCUS But yet let Reason govern thy Lament.

TITUS If there were Reason for these Miseries,
Then into Limits could I bind my Woes.   220
When Heav'n doth weep, doth not the Earth
    o'erflow?

415

222   wax   *grow.*

223   big-swoll'n Face   *surging waves and high tides.*

224   Coil   *turmoil.*

230   For why   *And why?*
       Bowels   *The intestines were considered to be the seat of
       compassion.*

232   Losers   *Titus refers to those about to lose their meals through
       vomiting. In doing so, however, he echoes a proverbial saying:
       "Give losers leave to speak."*
       leave   *permission, pardon.*

233   To . . . Tongues   *Titus seems to be referring to induced
       vomiting. What he says also reflects the terminology of Eliza-
       bethan psychology: to ease one's stomach was to give vent to
       one's anger, since the stomach was thought to be the seat of
       valor.*

239   That Woe is me   *so that I am overcome with grief.*

241   Etna   *a volcano in Sicily. Among other things, Mount Etna
       was associated with the ancient Greek philosopher Empedo-
       cles, an aristocrat who played a role in the rise of democratic
       institutions in pre-Socratic Athens, and who, after being exiled
       as the result of a shift in the political winds, committed suicide
       by throwing himself into the volcano's crater.*

244   some deal   *somewhat.*

245   flouted at   *scoffed at, treated contemptuously.*

If the Winds rage, doth not the Sea wax mad,
Threat'ning the Welkin with his big-swoll'n Face?
And wilt thou have a Reason for this Coil?
I am the Sea. Hark, how her Sighs doth flow!   225
She is the weeping Welkin, I the Earth:
Then must my Sea be moved with her Sighs;
Then must my Earth with her continual Tears
Become a Deluge, overflow'd and drown'd.
For why, my Bowels cannot hide her Woes,   230
But like a Drunkard must I vomit them.
Then give me leave, for Losers will have leave
To ease their Stomachs with their bitter Tongues.

Enter a Messenger with two Heads and a Hand.

MESSENGER   Worthy Andronicus, ill art thou repaid
For that good Hand thou sent'st the Emperor: 235
Here are the Heads of thy two noble Sons,
And here's thy Hand, in Scorn to thee sent back,
Thy Grief their Sports, thy Resolution mock'd,
That Woe is me to think upon thy Woes,
More than Remembrance of my Father's Death. *Exit.*   240
MARCUS   Now let hot Etna cool in Sicily,
And be my Heart an ever-burning Hell!
These Miseries are more than may be borne.
To weep with them that weep doth ease some deal,
But Sorrow flouted at is double Death.   245

417

247   shrink thereat   *slip or cower as a result of that; die.*

249   no . . . breathe   *nothing more at stake than breathing.*

251   starved   *benumbed with cold. The expression "starved Snake"
       was a common metaphor for misery. Here* starved *is disyl-
       labic.*

252   fearful Slumber   *nightmarish sleep.*

253   Flatt'ry   *pleasing deception.*

256   this dear Sight   *this sight that costs so much in grief.*

258   stony Image   *lifeless statue.*

259   control   *restrain.*

260   Rent   *rend, tear.*

261   Gnawing   *Pronounced glidingly, so as to constitute one sylla-
       ble metrically.*

268   usurp upon   *take over the functions of.*

269   tributary   *both (a) demanded as a tribute for an enemy
       usurper, Sorrow, and (b) flowing like a stream to feed Sorrow.*

LUCIUS   Ah that this Sight should make so deep a
     Wound,
     And yet detested Life not shrink thereat;
     That ever Death should let Life bear his Name,
     Where Life hath no more int'rest but to breathe!
                              Lavinia kisses Titus.
MARCUS   Alas, poor Heart, that Kiss is comfortless   250
     As frozen Water to a starved Snake.
TITUS   When will this fearful Slumber have an End?
MARCUS   Now farewell, Flatt'ry; die, Andronicus!
     Thou dost not slumber: see thy two Sons' Heads,
     Thy warlike Hand, thy mangled Daughter here,   255
     Thy other banish'd Son with this dear Sight
     Struck pale and bloodless, and thy Brother, I,
     Ev'n like a stony Image, cold and numb.
     Ah now no more will I control thy Griefs:
     Rent off thy silver Hair, thy other Hand   260
     Gnawing with thy Teeth, and be this dismal Sight
     The closing up of our most wretched Eyes.
     Now is a time to Storm; why art thou Still?
TITUS   Ha, ha, ha!
MARCUS   Why dost thou Laugh? It fits not with this
     Hour.   265
TITUS   Why, I have not another Tear to shed;
     Besides, this Sorrow is an Enemy,
     And would usurp upon my wat'ry Eyes
     And make them blind with tributary Tears.
     Then which way shall I find Revenge's Cave?   270

419

271   **these two Heads**   *Titus probably gestures toward the severed heads of his two sons.*

272   **threat**   *warn.*

276   **heavy**   *grieving, disconsolate.*

277–78   **That . . . Wrongs.**   *Stage action is indicated in the words Titus speaks here.*

281–82   **And . . . Teeth.**   *Line 281 is awkwardly hypermetrical, and many editors assume that it is corrupt and emend it. Since no proposed emendation is completely satisfying, however, it seems best to leave the passage as it is found in the First Quarto. The grotesque image of Lavinia carrying Titus' hand in her mouth, supported by her stumps, is one that epitomizes how far Roman civilization has degenerated, and it may be that the length of line 281 is meant to help convey the overwrought condition of its speaker at this moment.*

291   **his Pledges**   *both (a) his vows, and (b) those to whom he has pledged love.*

293   **to fore**   *heretofore, previously.*

294   **nor . . . nor**   *neither . . . nor.*

295   **Oblivion**   *the state of one who has been forgotten or removed from present consideration.*

For these two Heads do seem to speak to me,
And threat me I shall never come to Bliss
Till all these Mischiefs be return'd again
Ev'n in their Throats that hath committed them.
Come let me see what Task I have to do.   275
—You heavy People, circle me about,
That I may turn me to each one of you
And swear unto my Soul to right your Wrongs.
The Vow is made. —Come, Brother, take a Head,
And in this Hand the other will I bear.   280
—And Lavinia, thou shalt be employed in these
    Arms:
Bear thou my Hand, sweet Wench, between thy
    Teeth.
—As for thee, Boy, go get thee from my Sight;
Thou art an Exile, and thou must not stay.
Hie to the Goths and raise an Army there;   285
And if ye love me as I think you do,
Let's kiss and part, for we have much to do.
                                Exeunt all but Lucius.
LUCIUS Farewell, Andronicus, my noble Father;
The woefull'st Man that ever liv'd in Rome.
Farewell, proud Rome, till Lucius come again;   290
He loves his Pledges dearer than his Life.
Farewell, Lavinia, my noble Sister;
O would thou wert as thou to fore hast been!
But now nor Lucius nor Lavinia lives
But in Oblivion and hateful Griefs.   295

421

298   Tarquin   *Tarquinus Superbus, the last of the kings of Rome, who was expelled by Lucius Junius Brutus in 509 B.C. after his son raped the matron Lucrece.*

299   Pow'r   *power; an army to fight the Romans.*

III.ii   *This scene takes place in Titus' house.*

S.D.   Banquet   *a light meal. Often in the Quarto and Folio texts the word is spelled* Banket, *and was probably so pronounced.*

1   look you   *see that you.*

4   unknit . . . Knot   *Marcus is apparently sitting with his arms folded, a posture that connoted melancholy.*
Sorrow-wreathen   *wrapped or folded in sorrow.*

5   want   *lack.*

6   passionate   *give expression to.*

9   Who   *which (referring to "my Breast," line 8).*

10   this hollow Prison of my Flesh   *my chest cavity.*

12   Map of Woe   *image of misery. The metaphor of Lavinia as a map is continued a few words later with the reference to "Signs" (symbolic representations).*

If Lucius live, he will requite your Wrongs
And make proud Saturnine and his Empress
Beg at the Gates like Tarquin and his Queen.
Now will I to the Goths, and raise a Pow'r
To be reveng'd on Rome and Saturnine.   *Exit Lucius.*   300

Scene 2

A Banquet. Enter Titus Andronicus, Marcus, Lavinia,
and Lucius' Son.

TITUS   So, so, now sit, and look you eat no more
Than will preserve just so much Strength in us
As will revenge these bitter Woes of ours.
Marcus, unknit that Sorrow-wreathen Knot:
Thy Niece and I, poor Creatures, want our Hands,   5
And cannot passionate our tenfold Grief
With folded Arms. This poor right Hand of mine
Is left to tyrannize upon my Breast,
Who, when my Heart, all mad with Misery,
Beats in this hollow Prison of my Flesh,   10
Then thus I thump it down. *[To Lavinia]*
Thou Map of Woe, that thus dost talk in Signs,

15   Wound it with Sighing   *It was commonly believed that every sigh resulted in the heart's loss of a drop of blood.*

22   tender   *This word is probably meant to carry several connotations: (a) young, like a tender sapling; (b) fragile, delicate; and (c) dear.*

23   dote   *grow foolish (frequently used to describe old people).*

25   What violent Hands   *Titus takes Marcus' figure of speech literally.*

27–28   To . . . mis'rable   *In Book II of the* Aeneid *the hero heaves a sigh of grief when Dido asks him to recount the story of the fall of Troy. Titus says that to use the word* Hands *in Lavinia's presence is to make her just as miserable as it made Aeneas to "tell the Tale twice o'er."*

31   I square my Talk   *I restrict what I say (limiting my frame of reference as would one who tried to remain within a square).*

34   let's fall to   *let's start eating.*

36   martyr'd Signs   *tortured signals.*

38   Brew'd . . . Cheeks   *The metaphor is drawn from the process of brewing tea. The word* mesh'd *is related to* mashed *and* mixed, *and refers to the action of combining tea leaves with water to produce a brew.*

39   Complainet   *complainant, complainer. Many editors believe that the* t *in the First Folio printing of this word is the compositor's misreading of a proof correction.*

When thy poor Heart beats with outrageous beating
Thou canst not strike it thus to make it still.
Wound it with Sighing, Girl, kill it with Groans;   15
Or get some little Knife between thy Teeth
And just against thy Heart make thou a Hole,
That all the Tears that thy poor Eyes let fall
May run into that Sink and, soaking in,
Drown the lamenting Fool in Sea-salt Tears.   20
MARCUS   Fie, Brother, fie! Teach her not thus to lay
Such violent Hands upon her tender Life!
TITUS   How now! Has Sorrow made thee dote already?
Why Marcus, no Man should be mad but I.
What violent Hands can she lay on her Life?   25
Ah wherefore dost thou urge the name of "Hands,"
To bid Aeneas tell the Tale twice o'er,
How Troy was burnt and he made mis'rable?
O handle not the Theme, to talk of Hands,
Lest we remember still that we have none.   30
—Fie, fie, how franticly I square my Talk,
As if we should forget we had no Hands
If Marcus did not name the word of "Hands"!
Come let's fall to. —And gentle Girl, eat this.
Here is no Drink? —Hark, Marcus, what she says.   35
I can interpret all her martyr'd Signs:
She says she drinks no other drink but Tears,
Brew'd with her Sorrow, mesh'd upon her Cheeks.
—Speechless Complainet, I will learn thy
   Thought;

40 dumb Action *pantomimed gestures.*
   perfect *faithful in interpreting and executing holy orders. The expression "word-perfect" captures the sense intended: to know a set of words by heart.*

43 wink *close one's eyes.*

44 wrest *extract, pull out.*

45 still *constant.*

46 leave *cease.*

50–51 thou . . . away. *Titus seems to be thinking of the power of warm water to melt a block of ice.*

55 cloy'd . . . Tyranny *clogged with images of wanton cruelty.*

56 A deed of Death *an act of execution, as by a wicked tyrant.*

58 art . . . Company *are not a fit companion for me.*

61 he *It is not clear whether this refers to the dead fly or to its father.*

In thy dumb Action will I be as perfect   40
As begging Hermits in their holy Prayers.
Thou shalt not sigh, nor hold thy Stumps to
     Heaven,
Nor wink, nor nod, nor kneel, nor make a Sign,
But I of these will wrest an Alphabet
And by still practice learn to know thy Meaning.   45
BOY   Good Grandsire, leave these bitter deep
     Laments:
Make my Aunt merry with some pleasing Tale.
MARCUS   Alas, the tender Boy, in passion mov'd,
Doth weep to see his Grandsire's Heaviness.
TITUS   Peace, tender Sapling: thou art made of
     Tears,   50
And Tears will quickly melt thy Life away.
               Marcus strikes the Dish with a Knife.
What dost thou strike at, Marcus, with thy
     Knife?
MARCUS   At that that I have kill'd, my Lord: a Fly.
TITUS   Out on thee, Murderer! Thou kill'st my Heart!
Mine Eyes are cloy'd with view of Tyranny: 55
A deed of Death done on the Innocent
Becomes not Titus' Brother. Get thee gone:
I see thou art not for my Company.
MARCUS   Alas, my Lord, I have but kill'd a Fly.
TITUS   "But"? How if that Fly had a Father and a
     Mother?   60
How would he hang his slender gilded Wings

427

66   ill-favor'd   *ugly.*

69   reprehending   *condemning.*

70   a Charitable Deed   *a loving deed.*

71   insult on him   *treat him disrespectfully (as do soldiers who exult over fallen adversaries and mutilate their corpses).*

72   Flatt'ring my self   *pretending to myself.*

74   There's . . . Tamora.   *This line is addressed to the fly as if it were Aaron the Moor.*

79   wrought on him   *deformed his mind.*

81   take away   *clear away the dishes.*

82   Closet   *private chamber.*

83   chanced   *that took place.*

85   when . . . dazzle   *when my eyes begin to daze or blur.*

428

And buzz lamenting doings in the Air.
Poor harmless Fly,
That with his pretty buzzing Melody
Came here to make us merry, and thou hast kill'd
    him.   65

MARCUS   Pardon me, Sir. It was a black, ill-favor'd
    Fly
Like to the Empress' Moor: therefore I kill'd
    him.

TITUS   O, O, O!
Then pardon me for reprehending thee,
For thou hast done a Charitable Deed.   70
Give me thy Knife: I will insult on him,
Flatt'ring my self as if it were the Moor
Come hither purposely to poison me.
—There's for thy self, and that's for Tamora.
—Ah, Sirrah,   75
Yet I think we are not brought so low
But that between us we can kill a Fly
That comes in likeness of a coal-black Moor.

MARCUS   Alas, poor Man! Grief has so wrought on him
He takes false Shadows for true Substances.   80

TITUS   Come take away. Lavinia, go with me:
I'll to thy Closet and go read with thee
Sad Stories chanced in the Times of Old.
Come, Boy, and go with me: thy Sight is young,
And thou shalt read when mine begin to dazzle.   85

Exeunt.

IV.i   *The setting remains in Titus' house.*

5   Stand by me   *Come to me and stand here: I'll protect you.*

9   somewhat   *something.*

Act Four

Scene 1

Enter Lucius' Son, and Lavinia running after him.
The Boy flies from her with his Books under his arm.
Enter Titus and Marcus.

BOY   Help, Grandsire, help! My Aunt Lavinia
Follows me every where, I know not why.
    —Good Uncle Marcus, see how swift she comes!
    —Alas, sweet Aunt, I know not what you mean!
MARCUS   Stand by me, Lucius; do not fear thine Aunt.   5
TITUS   She loves thee, Boy, too well to do thee
    harm.
BOY   Ay, when my Father was in Rome she did.
MARCUS   What means my Niece Lavinia by these Signs?
TITUS   Fear her not, Lucius: somewhat doth she mean.

11   Some whither   *somewhere.*

12   Cornelia   *mother of the Tribunes Tiberius and Gaius Gracchi, who lost their lives in noble efforts to broaden participatory citizenship in the Roman republic of the second century* B.C.

14   Tully's Orator   *Marcus refers to the rhetorical treatise* De Oratore, *by Marcus Tullius Cicero (106–43* B.C.*), a contemporary of Julius Caesar.*

15   wherefore she plies thee   *why she pleads with you to come with her.*

17   Frenzy   *seizure or distracted state.*

18   full oft   *frequently.*

20–21   Hecuba . . . Sorrow   *Hecuba, Queen of Troy and wife of King Priam, suffered deep grief over the death of her son Hector, whose defeat foreshadowed the fall of Troy.*

24   Fury   *madness (not anger).*

26   Causeless   *without reason.*

28   attend   *do the bidding of.*

33   skill'd   *schooled, educated.*

35   beguile thy Sorrow   *put your sorrow out of mind (by deceiving your mind into believing that it has no reason to feel sad).*

MARCUS   See, Lucius, see how much she makes of thee: 10
    Some whither would she have thee go with her.
    Ah Boy, Cornelia never with more care
    Read to her Sons than she hath read to thee
    Sweet Poetry and Tully's Orator.
    Canst thou not guess wherefore she plies thee
       thus?   15
BOY   My Lord, I know not, I, nor can I guess,
    Unless some Fit or Frenzy do possess her:
    For I have heard my Grandsire say full oft,
    Extremity of Griefs would make Men mad.
    And I have read that Hecuba of Troy   20
    Ran mad for Sorrow. That made me to fear,
    Although, my Lord, I know my noble Aunt
    Loves me as dear as e'er my Mother did,
    And would not, but in Fury, fright my youth;
    Which made me down to throw my Books and fly,   25
    Causeless perhaps. —But pardon me, sweet Aunt;
    And Madam, if my Uncle Marcus go,
    I will most willingly attend your Ladyship.
MARCUS   Lucius, I will.
               Lavinia uses her Stump to point to a Book.
TITUS   How now, Lavinia? —Marcus, what means this?   30
    Some Book there is that she desires to see.
    —Which is it, Girl, of these? —Open them, Boy.
    —But thou art deeper read, and better skill'd:
    Come and take choice of all my Library,
    And so beguile thy Sorrow till the Heav'ns   35

433

36   Contriver *doer.*

37   in sequence *in quick succession.*

39   Confed'rate in the fact *involved in the deed.*

42   Metamorphosis *Young Lucius refers, of course, to the* Meta-
     morphoses.

44   cull'd *selected.*

45   Soft *Be quiet, pay attention.*

46   what would she find? *what does she want to find?*

49   root of thy Annoy *at the bottom of your troubles.*

50   cotes *notes, carefully scrutinizes or examines. Here spelled*
     coats *in the First Quarto and* quotes *in the First Folio, this*
     word was normally spelled cotes *and was almost certainly*
     pronounced with a k *rather than a* kw *sound.*

51   surpris'd *seized by surprise.*

53   vast *This word probably means "waste" (desolate) as well as*
     unfathomably large.

57   Pattern'd by *of the same pattern as. This phrasing suggests*
     that the setting in the "Woods" (line 53) is patterned after the
     setting in Ovid's tale of Philomela in the Metamorphoses.
     This is yet another instance of Shakespeare's heavy dependence
     on Ovid for so many of the details of a drama that remains
     extraordinarily "literary," at least when compared with the
     playwright's later tragedies.

Reveal the damn'd Contriver of this Deed.
—Why lifts she up her Arms in sequence thus?
MARCUS   I think she means that there were more than
     one
     Confed'rate in the fact. Ay, more there was,
     Or else to Heav'n she heaves them for Revenge.   40
TITUS   Lucius, what Book is that she tosseth so?
BOY   Grandsire, 'tis Ovid's Metamorphosis;
     My Mother gave it me.
MARCUS   For love of her that's gone,
     Perhaps, she cull'd it from among the rest.
TITUS   Soft, so busily she turns the Leaves!   45
     Help her; what would she find? —Lavinia, shall
       I read?
     This is the tragic Tale of Philomel,
     And treats of Tereus' Treason and his Rape;
     And Rape, I fear, was root of thy Annoy!
MARCUS   See, Brother, see! Note how she cotes the
     Leaves.   50
TITUS   Lavinia, wert thou thus surpris'd, sweet
       Girl,
     Ravish'd and wrong'd as Philomela was,
     Forc'd in the ruthless, vast, and gloomy Woods?
     See, see!
     Ay, such a Place there is, where we did hunt   55
     (O had we never, never hunted there!)
     Pattern'd by that the Poet here describes,
     By Nature made for Murders and for Rapes.

435

59–60 O why . . . Tragedies? *Marcus' question anticipates the kind of cosmic query Shakespeare will treat with more profundity in later tragedies such as* King Lear. *It is the classic question of a theodicy, a work (such as the Book of Job in the Old Testament) whose purpose is to probe human suffering and attempt, in Milton's words, "to justify God's ways to man."*

63 as Tarquin erst *as did the last of the Roman kings long ago.*

67 this Treason find *discover the perpetrator of this treachery.*

72 Shift *makeshift device, expedient.*

78 Stuprum *rape (Latin).*

MARCUS   O why should Nature build so foul a Den
    Unless the Gods delight in Tragedies? 60
TITUS   Give Signs, sweet Girl, for here are none
      but Friends,
    What Roman Lord it was durst do the Deed;
    Or slunk not Saturnine, as Tarquin erst,
    That left the Camp to sin in Lucrece' Bed?
MARCUS   Sit down, sweet Niece. —Brother, sit down
    by me. 65
    —Apollo, Pallas, Jove, or Mercury,
    Inspire me that I may this Treason find!
    —My Lord, look here! —Look here, Lavinia!
    This Sandy Plot is plain: guide, if thou canst,
    This after me.   *He writes his name with his Staff*
                    and guides it with his Feet and Mouth.
           I have writ my Name 70
    Without the help of any Hand at all.
    Curs'd be that Heart that forc'd us to this
      Shift!
    Write thou, good Niece, and here display at last
    What God will have discover'd for Revenge.
    Heav'n guide thy Pen to print thy Sorrows plain, 75
    That we may know the Traitors and the Truth!
          She takes the Staff in her Mouth and, guiding it
                with her Stumps, writes in the Sand.
    —O do ye read, my Lord, what she hath writ?
TITUS   "*Stuprum.* Chiron, Demetrius."
MARCUS   What, what! The lustful Sons of Tamora

437

81–82 "Magni . . . vides?" *"Great Ruler of the Heavens, are you so slow to hear crimes, so slow to see them?" Titus quotes from* Phaedra, *a Senecan tragedy.*

88 Roman Hector's Hope *As the son and namesake of Lucius, the "Roman Hector" has a mission like that of Troy's "hope."*

89 Fere *husband (from the Anglo-Saxon word for* farer, *companion).*

89–91 And . . . Rape *After the rape of Lucrece, her husband and father learned from her that her assailant was Sextus Tarquinus, son of the King, Lucius Tarquinus. At this, Junius Brutus, nephew of the King, vowed with them to rid Rome of the Tarquins forever.*

92 prosecute by good Advice *accomplish through careful planning.*

95 'Tis . . . how *It would be a sure plan if you knew how to execute it.*

97 and if she wind ye once *if she once gets wind of you.*

98 She's . . . league *She's still in deep union with the King.*

101 let alone *let it be (with the implication "leave it to me").*

103 gad of Steel *a sharp spike, here one to engrave letters.*

105 Sibyl's Leaves *In Book IV of the* Aeneid *Aeneas fears that the leaf that bears the prophecy the Cumaean Sibyl means for him will blow away before he reads it.*

438

Performers of this heinous, bloody deed? 80

TITUS   "*Magni dominator poli,*
         Tam lentis audis scelera? tam lentus vides?"

MARCUS   O calm thee, gentle Lord, although I know
         There is enough written upon this Earth
         To stir a Mut'ny in the mildest Thoughts 85
         And arm the Minds of Infants to Exclaims.
         My Lord, kneel down with me. —Lavinia, kneel.
         —And kneel, sweet Boy, the Roman Hector's Hope.
         And swear with me, as with the woeful Fere
         And Father of that chaste dishonor'd Dame 90
         Lord Junius Brutus sware for Lucrece' Rape,
         That we will prosecute by good Advice
         Mortal Revenge upon these trait'rous Goths,
         And see their Blood, or die with this Reproach.

TITUS   'Tis sure enough and you knew how, 95
         But if you hunt these Bear-whelps, then beware:
         The Dam will wake, and if she wind ye once.
         She's with the Lion deeply still in league,
         And lulls him whilst she playeth on her Back;
         And when he sleeps will she do what she list. 100
         You are a young Huntsman, Marcus, let alone.
         And come, I will go get a Leaf of Brass,
         And with a gad of Steel will write these Words
         And lay it by: the angry Northern Wind
         Will blow these Sands like Sibyl's Leaves abroad, 105
         And where's our Lesson then? —Boy, what say you?

BOY   I say, my Lord, that if I were a Man

439

110   full oft   *very frequently.*

114   I'll . . . withal   *I'll equip you, and therewith.*

120   look to   *take care of.*

121   brave it   *swagger.*

122   marry   *indeed. This mild interjection originally referred to the Virgin Mary.*
       waited on   *attended, taken seriously.*

123   groan   *agonize.*

124   compassion him   *take pity on him.*

125   Ecstasy   *madness. The word is of Greek origin and literally means to "stand outside" or be beside oneself.*

127   Foemen's Marks   *the nicks and gashes from enemy swords.*

129   Revenge the Heav'ns   *May the Heavens take revenge.*

Their Mother's Bedchamber should not be safe
For these base Bondmen to the Yoke of Rome.
MARCUS   Ay, that's my Boy! Thy Father hath full oft   110
For his ungrateful Country done the like.
BOY   And Uncle, so will I and if I live.
TITUS   Come go with me into mine Armory.
Lucius, I'll fit thee, and withal my Boy
Shall carry from me to the Empress' Sons   115
Presents that I intend to send them both.
Come, come: thou'lt do my Message, wilt thou
not?
BOY   Ay, with my Dagger in their Bosoms, Grandsire.
TITUS   No, Boy, not so: I'll teach thee another
Course.
—Lavinia, come. —Marcus, look to my House: 120
Lucius and I'll go brave it at the Court,
Ay marry will we, Sir, and we'll be waited on!
                              Exeunt all but Marcus.
MARCUS   O Heavens, can you hear a Good Man groan
And not relent, or not compassion him?
—Marcus, attend him in his Ecstasy,   125
That hath more Scars of Sorrow in his Heart
Than Foemen's Marks upon his batt'red Shield,
But yet so just that he will not revenge.
—Revenge the Heav'ns for old Andronicus!   *Exit.*

441

TITUS ANDRONICUS ACT IV, SCENE 2

IV.ii   *This scene takes place in a room of the King's Palace.*

6   confound   *overthrow, destroy.*

7   Gramercy   *many thanks.*

8   decipher'd   *found out. This verb precisely describes the means of detection we have witnessed in the previous scene.*

10   well-advis'd   *fully aware of what he was doing.*

12   gratify   *to please, pay homage to.*

442

Scene 2

*Enter Aaron, Chiron, and Demetrius at one Door,
and at the other Door young Lucius and another,
with a Bundle of Weapons, and Verses writ upon them.*

CHIRON   Demetrius, here's the Son of Lucius;
   He hath some Message to deliver us.
AARON   Ay, some mad Message from his mad
     Grandfather.
BOY   My Lords, with all the Humbleness I may,
   I greet your Honors from Andronicus   5
   [*Aside*] And pray the Roman Gods confound you
     both.
DEMETRIUS   Gramercy, lovely Lucius: what's the News?
BOY   [*Aside*] That you are both decipher'd, that's
     the News,
   For Villains mark'd with Rape. [*Aloud*] May it
     please you,
   My Grandsire, well-advis'd, hath sent by me   10
   The goodliest Weapons of his Armory
   To gratify your honorable Youth,
   The Hope of Rome, for so he bid me say.
   And so I do, and with his Gifts present
   Your Lordships, that whenever you have need,   15

443

16   appointed   *equipped.*

20–21   Integer . . . arcu.   *"The man who is upright in his life and pure of crime has no need of the arrows or the bow of the Moor"—a passage from Horace's* Odes.

23   Grammar   *Shakespeare and his audience would probably have known the above verse from Horace in William Lily's Latin Grammar, which was widely used in schools of his time.*

24   Ay just   *Yes, precisely.*

26   Here's no sound Jest!   *With conscious irony Aaron appears to be speaking for Demetrius and Chiron, who lack the wit to realize that this "Jest" shows Titus' mind to be "sound" indeed.*
    'th   *hath. Elided here for metrical purposes.*

28   beyond their Feeling   *beyond what their victims perceive.*
    to the Quick   *to the pulse of life itself.*

29–30   But . . . Conceit   *If the witty Tamora were secure in her footing, she would appreciate Andronicus' clever device.*

34   to this Height   *In this speech Aaron is playing a game with Tamora's sons, puffing up their pride by reminding them of how far they have risen in fortune, while privately savoring his own intellectual superiority over these barbarians.*

35–36   It . . . hearing.   *Aaron refers to an occasion when he taunted Marcus within Titus' hearing in front of the Palace gate. Aaron's purpose is to evoke a comment (lines 37–38) that proves Demetrius to be just as naive as his brother.*

444

You may be armed and appointed well.
And so I leave you both, [*aside*] like bloody
    Villains.   *Exeunt Boy and Attendant.*

DEMETRIUS   What's here? A Scroll, and written round
    about.

    Let's see:

        Integer vitae, sclerisque purus,   20
        Non eget Mauri iaculis, nec arcu.

CHIRON   O 'tis a verse in Horace. I know it well:
    I read it in the Grammar long ago.

AARON   [*Aside*] Ay just: a verse in Horace! Right,
    you have it!

    Now what a thing it is to be an Ass!   25
    Here's no sound Jest! The Old Man 'th found
      their Guilt,
    And sends them Weapons wrapp'd about with Lines
    That wound beyond their Feeling, to the Quick.
    But were our witty Empress well afoot,
    She would applaud Andronicus' Conceit;   30
    But let her rest in her Unrest a while.
    —And now, young Lords, was't not a happy Star
    Led us to Rome, Strangers and, more than so,
    Captives, to be advanced to this Height?
    It did me good before the Palace Gate   35
    To brave the Tribune in his Brother's hearing.

DEMETRIUS   But me more good to see so great a Lord
    Basely insinuate and send us Gifts.

AARON   Had he not Reason, Lord Demetrius?

445

40   **Did . . . friendly?** *Aaron uses* friendly *facetiously here. In the next line, Demetrius fails to observe that Titus' gifts are "friendly" in the same way that their treatment of his daughter has been.*

42   **At such a Bay** *like an animal cornered by baying dogs; at our mercy.*

48   **Pray . . . over.** *Aaron's implication is that if these young Goths are Rome's hope, then there is little that prayer to the Roman Gods can do to save the situation.*

50   **Belike** *In all likelihood, probably.*

S.D.   **Blackamoor** *black Moor.*

51   **God morrow** *a contraction of the phrase "God give you good morrow."*

53   **more . . . all** *Aaron puns on* Moor/more *and* whit/(white).

55   **undone** *brought down.*

56   **betide** *befall.*

57   **Caterwauling** *an onomatopoetic word referring to the quarreling of cats in mating season.*
        keep *maintain.*

58   **fumble** *bundle, bounce.*

Did you not use his Daughter very friendly?   40
DEMETRIUS   I would we had a thousand Roman Dames
    At such a Bay, by turn to serve our Lust.
CHIRON   A Charitable Wish and full of Love.
AARON   Here lacks but your Mother for to say "Amen."
CHIRON   And that would she for twenty thousand more.   45
DEMETRIUS   Come let us go and pray to all the Gods
    For our beloved Mother in her Pains.
AARON   [*Aside*] Pray to the Dev'ls: the Gods have
        giv'n us over.   *Trumpets sound within.*
DEMETRIUS   Why do the Emp'ror's Trumpets flourish
    thus?
CHIRON   Belike for joy the Emp'ror hath a Son.   50
DEMETRIUS   Soft, who comes here?

Enter Nurse, with a Blackamoor Child.

NURSE   God morrow, Lords.
    O tell me, did you see Aaron the Moor?
AARON   Well, more or less, or ne'er a whit at all:
    Here Aaron is, and what with Aaron now?
NURSE   O gentle Aaron, we are all undone!   55
    Now help, or Woe betide thee evermore!
AARON   Why what a Caterwauling dost thou keep!
    What dost thou wrap and fumble in thy Arms?
NURSE   O that which I would hide from Heaven's Eye:
    Our Empress' Shame, and stately Rome's Disgrace.   60
    She is deliver'd, Lords, she is delivered.

447

62   **brought a-bed**   *brought to bed for labor and childbirth.*

64–65   **Why . . . Issue!**   *Aaron's meaning is that if she has given birth to a devil, Tamora must be the Devil's Dam (the Devil's mother); from his point of view, that would be a delightful outcome ("issue") of such a birth ("issue"), both because it would link Tamora with Aaron (in his role as the character who plays the Devil in the world of this play) and because it would rebuke those who use "Devil's Dam" solely as a term of contempt.*

68   **fair-fac'd . . . Clime**   *the light-complexioned men and women of our region.*

70   **Point**   *Shakespeare may intend a verbal echo of* font, *the baptismal basin used for christenings.*

71   **'Zounds**   *a contraction for "God's wounds," a mild oath pronounced to rhyme with* wounds.

72   **Blowse**   *a fat, red-cheeked wench; totally unlike a "beauteous Blossom," notwithstanding the aural similarities with "bloss" or "blossom."*

76   **done**   *enjoyed sexually.*

AARON   To whom?

NURSE   I mean she's brought a-bed.

AARON   Well, God give her good rest! What hath he
     sent her?

NURSE   A Dev'l!

AARON   Why then she is the Devil's Dam:
     A joyful Issue!   65

NURSE   A joyless, dismal, black, and sorr'wful
          Issue!
     Here is the Babe, as loathsome as a Toad
     Amongst the fair-fac'd Breeders of our Clime.
     The Empress sends it thee, thy Stamp, thy Seal,
     And bids thee christ'n it with thy Dagger's
          Point.   70

AARON   'Zounds, ye Whore! Is Black so base a Hue?
     Sweet Blowse, you are a beauteous Blossom, sure!

DEMETRIUS   Villain, what hast thou done?

AARON   That which thou canst not undo.

CHIRON   Thou hast undone our Mother.   75

AARON   Villain, I have done thy Mother.

DEMETRIUS   And therein, hellish Dog, thou hast
          undone her.
     Woe to her Chance, and damn'd her loathed Choice!
     Accurs'd the Offspring of so foul a Fiend!

CHIRON   It shall not live.   80

AARON   It shall not die.

NURSE   Aaron, it must: the Mother wills it so.

AARON   What, must it, Nurse? Then let no Man but I

449

85   broach   *impale (as in skewering meat on a spit to roast it).*

87   Sooner . . . up. *Aaron's use of this agricultural metaphor is a grotesque inversion of the prophets' image of the peace to come when men beat their "swords into plowshares" (Isaiah 2:4, Micah 4:3).*

89–90 Now . . . got *Aaron swears by the "Tapers" (the stars and planets) that were in the ascendant when his child was conceived ("got").*

91   Scimitar *a short curved sword associated with the Turks and Moors.*

93–94 not . . . Brood *Enceladus was one of the Titans (all sons of Typhon) who ruled the Universe before they were overthrown by Zeus and the Olympian Gods in a war so fierce that it threatened to destroy creation.*

95   Alcides *Hercules, a descendant of Alcaeus.*

97   sanguine *Aaron refers both to Demetrius' and Chiron's pink complexions (as contrasted with his own dark one) and to what he scornfully dismisses as their "sanguine" (here compliant and cowardly) natures.*

98   White-lim'd Walls *Aaron is speaking of Demetrius' and Chiron's white faces, but the image (echoing Matthew 23:27) also suggests hypocrisy.*
       Alehouse-painted Signs *Aaron is probably thinking of the white backgrounds of such crudely painted signs.*

103   lave them hourly in the Flood *wash them hourly in the sea.*

Do execution on my Flesh and Blood.

DEMETRIUS   I'll broach the Tadpole on my Rapier's
    Point.   85
    Nurse, give it me: my Sword shall soon dispatch
    it.

Aaron seizes the Child and brandishes his Sword.

AARON   Sooner this Sword shall plough thy Bowels up.
    Stay, murd'rous Villains! Will you kill your
        Brother?
    Now by the burning Tapers of the Sky
    That shone so brightly when this Boy was got,   90
    He dies upon my Scimitar's sharp Point
    That touches this my first-born Son and Heir!
    I tell you, Younglings, not Enceladus,
    With all his threat'ning band of Typhon's Brood,
    Nor great Alcides, nor the God of War,   95
    Shall seize this prey out of his Father's Hands!
    What, what, ye sanguine, shallow-hearted Boys!
    Ye White-lim'd Walls! Ye Alehouse-painted Signs!
    Coal-black is better than another Hue
    In that it scorns to bear another Hue: 100
    For all the Water in the Ocean
    Can never turn the Swan's black Legs to white,
    Although she lave them hourly in the Flood.
    Tell the Emperess from me, I am of Age
    To keep mine own, excuse it how she can.   105

DEMETRIUS   Wilt thou betray thy noble Mistress
    thus?

451

110   mauger   *notwithstanding, in spite of.*

111   smoke for it   *die by the sword for it.*

113   Escape   *escapade, transgression, breach of the normal bounds of propriety.*

114   doom her Death   *sentence her to death.*

115   Ignomy   *ignominy, shame.*

116   Why . . . bears!   *Why, there's one of the "privileges" of being of a "beautiful" hue: that you can blush!*

118   The . . . Heart   *the secret deeds and purposes you harbor in your heart.*

119   fram'd . . . Leer   *made for another look.*

122–   sensibly fed . . . you   *his vitality drawing from the same*
23   *blood that gave you life.*

125   enfranchised   *set free.*

126   by the surer side   *by the more certain side (the mother's, which is more easily established than the father's side).*

130   subscribe to   *agree to support.*

133   My . . . you   *Here Aaron is telling Demetrius and Chiron where to sit. Aaron is taking no chances about his child's protection, and he intends to keep a close watch on his young "allies."*

452

AARON   My Mistress is my Mistress, this my Self,
   The Vigor and the Picture of my Youth.
   This before all the World do I prefer;
   This mauger all the World will I keep safe,   110
   Or some of you shall smoke for it in Rome.
DEMETRIUS   By this our Mother is for ever sham'd.
CHIRON   Rome will despise her for this foul Escape.
NURSE   The Emp'ror in his rage will doom her Death.
CHIRON   I blush to think upon this Ignomy.   115
AARON   Why there's the Privilege your Beauty bears!
   Fie, Treach'rous Hue, that will betray with
      Blushing
   The close Enacts and Counsels of thy Heart!
   Here's a young Lad fram'd of another Leer:
   Look how the black Slave smiles upon the Father,   120
   As who should say "Old Lad, I am thine own!"
   He is your Brother, Lords, sensibly fed
   Of that self Blood that first gave Life to you;
   And from that Womb where you imprison'd were
   He is enfranchised and come to Light.   125
   Nay, he is your Brother by the surer side,
   Although my Seal be stamped in his Face.
NURSE   Aaron, what shall I say unto the Empress?
DEMETRIUS   Advise thee, Aaron, what is to be done,
   And we will all subscribe to thy Advice: 130
   Save thou the Child so we may all be safe.
AARON   Then sit we down, and let us all consult.
   My Son and I will have the Wind of you:

453

136–37   Why . . . Lamb. *Aaron's response to Demetrius' question (directed to the Nurse, and implying that "we're all in this together") is a taunting reminder that the young Lords will be well advised to recognize that Aaron is now in complete control. If they cooperate, he will be as gentle as a lamb.*

138   chafed   *irritated (and thus, unusually vicious).*

144   "Two . . . away." *Aaron's meaning is that a secret can be shared with no more than one person. A variant of this proverb is quoted by the Nurse in* Romeo and Juliet, *II.iv.206: "Two may keep counsel, putting one away."*

146   "Weeke, weeke!" *Aaron is imitating the squealing of a pig being slaughtered.*

148   Policy *political wisdom of the sort associated with ethical pragmatists like the Italian writer Niccolo Machiavelli, whose treatise* The Prince *(published in 1532) advised political leaders to do anything necessary to establish and maintain a strong, stable state.*

152–53   Muliteus . . . Wife *This construction means "the wife of Muliteus, my fellow-countryman."*

155   pack with him *make a compact with him, seal a deal with him.*

156   the Circumstance of all *all the circumstances.*

157   advanc'd *elevated in social standing.*

454

Keep there! Now talk at pleasure of your Safety.

They sit.

DEMETRIUS   How many women saw this Child of his?   135
AARON   Why so, brave Lords! When we join in League
    I am a Lamb. But if you brave the Moor,
    The chafed Boar, the mountain Lioness,
    The Ocean swells not so as Aaron storms.
    —But say again, how many saw the Child?   140
NURSE   Cornelia the Midwife, and my self,
    And no one else but the deliver'd Empress.
AARON   The Emperess, the Midwife, and your self:
    "Two may keep counsel when the third's away."
    Go to the Empress; tell her this I said.   145

He kills her.

    "Weeke, weeke!" So cries a Pig prepar'd to th'
        Spit.
DEMETRIUS   What mean'st thou, Aaron? Wherefore
        didst thou this?
AARON   O Lord, Sir, 'tis a deed of Policy.
    Shall she live to betray this Guilt of ours,
    A long-tongu'd babbling Gossip? No, Lords, no.   150
    And now be 't known to you my full Intent.
    Not far one Muliteus, my Countryman,
    His Wife but yesternight was brought to Bed;
    His Child is like to her, fair as you are.
    Go pack with him, and give the Mother Gold,   155
    And tell them both the Circumstance of all,
    And how by this their Child shall be advanc'd,

455

161   **And . . . own** *This image of the Emperor suggests that he is so gullible as to be little better than a child himself.*

162   **I've giv'n her Physic** *As the "doctor," I have given the nurse her "medicine."*

163–   **And . . . Grooms.** *Now you must take care of burying her,*
64   *like the grooms (servingmen) you are. Aaron is now treating Demetrius and Chiron with undisguised contempt.*

169–   **Aaron . . . thee.** *Chiron's comment suggests that he now*
71   *feels his own life to be in danger. If Aaron won't trust the air with secrets, why should these two feel that he will trust them? Following Chiron's observation, Demetrius' statement sounds so cautious as to be obsequious.*

176   **puts us to our Shifts** *forces us to resort to these devices.*

178   **Curds and Whey** *Curds are the coagulated particles of soured milk from which cheese is made;* **whey** *is the watery liquid that remains.*

179   **cabin** *reside. The use of this verb is effective not only for its alliteration with* **Cave** *but also for its conformity with the imagery of pristine nature in Aaron's description of how his son will be reared (lines 177–80). Aaron's phrasing echoes the legends of such mythical heroes as Romulus and Remus (who were nursed by a she-wolf before they grew up to found the city of Rome). It is clear that Aaron is now beginning to think of himself as the father of a new nation, one that will supplant the Goths in the same way that the Goths are now bidding to supplant the Romans.*

And be received for the Emp'ror's Heir,
And substituted in the place of mine,
To calm this Tempest whirling in the Court,   160
And let the Emp'ror dandle him for his own.
Hark ye, Lords, [*pointing to the dead Nurse*]
                    you see I've giv'n her Physic,
And you must needs bestow her Funeral:
The Fields are near, and you are gallant Grooms.
This done, see that you take no longer days,   165
But send the Midwife presently to me.
The Midwife and the Nurse well made away,
Then let the Ladies tattle what they please.
CHIRON   Aaron, I see thou wilt not trust the Air
    With Secrets.
DEMETRIUS   For this care of Tamora,   170
    Her self and hers are highly bound to thee.
        Exeunt Demetrius and Chiron with the Nurse's body.
AARON   Now to the Goths, as swift as Swallow flies,
    There to dispose this Treasure in mine Arms,
    And secretly to greet the Empress' Friends.
    —Come on, you thick-lipp'd Slave, I'll bear you
        hence: 175
    For it is you that puts us to our Shifts.
    I'll make you feed on Berries and on Roots,
    And feed on Curds and Whey, and suck the Goat,
    And cabin in a Cave, and bring you up
    To be a Warrior and command a Camp.   *Exit.*   180

457

IV.iii   *This scene is set in an unspecified public place in Rome.*

3   Look . . . straight!   *Take care to draw the bow to its full extent, and the arrow will be there on target.*

4   "Terras Astraea reliquit"   *"Justice has left the Earth." This quotation, from Book I of the* Metamorphoses, *occurs in a passage where Ovid says that man's wickedness during the Iron Age was so horrible that Astraea, the Goddess of Justice, fled to the Heavens and formed the constellation Virgo. This scene finds Titus in such desperation that he is lofting arrows into the air in an attempt to reach Astraea with the message that she must return to Earth and help him.*

4–5   be you / Remember'd   *remember.*

7   sound   *probe the depths of.*

8   Happily   *haply, perhaps.*

9   there's   *there there is. Titus means that at sea there is as little justice as there is on land.*

11   Mattock   *a tool combining features of the pick-axe and the grubbing hoe.*

13   Pluto's Region   *Hades. Pluto was ruler of the Underworld.*

14   d'liver 'im   *deliver him. Both words are here elided for metrical reasons.*
     Petition   *plea for assistance (here pronounced as a four-syllable word).*

458

Scene 3

*Enter Titus, old Marcus, young Lucius, and other Gentlemen
(Publius, Sempronius, and Caius) with Bows; and Titus bears
the Arrows with Letters on the ends of them.*

TITUS   Come, Marcus, come; Kinsmen, this is the way.
   —Sir Boy, let me see your Archery:
   Look ye draw home enough and 'tis there straight!
   —*"Terras Astraea reliquit,"* be you
   Rememb'red, Marcus: she is gone, she's fled.   5
   —Sirs, take you to your Tools. You, Cousins, shall
   Go sound the Ocean and cast your Nets.
   Happily you may catch her in the Sea;
   Yet there's as little Justice as at Land.
   —No, Publius and Sempronius, you must do it: 10
   'Tis you must dig with Mattock and with Spade
   And pierce the inmost Center of the Earth.
   Then when you come to Pluto's Region,
   I pray you d'liver 'im this Petition:
   Tell him it is for Justice and for Aid,   15
   And that it comes from old Andronicus,
   Shaken with Sorrows in ungrateful Rome.
   —Ah Rome! Well, well, I made thee mis'rable

459

19 What time *at the time when.*
   Suffrages *votes.*

22 Man of War *warship.*

24 pipe *whistle (that is, look in vain).*

25 a heavy Case *a sad situation.*

26 distract *distracted, out of his wits.*

29 feed his Humour *humor him, give him what he needs to maintain the illusions that are now giving his mind some relief from direct contemplation of his woes.*

30 careful *caring, merciful.*

33 Take wreak *take vengeance, provide a day of reckoning.*

36 her *Astraea.*

37–41 No . . . time. *Publius is humoring Titus by attributing to Pluto the advice that if Titus waits for Justice, he'll wait forever; Titus had best invoke the spirit of Revenge, then, and summon it from Hell, where it resides.*

42 feed me *put me off.*

43 burning Lake *Phlegethon, the burning river of Hades.*

44 Ach'ron *Acheron, the river of woe in Hades.*

What time I threw the People's Suffrages
On him that thus doth tyrannize o'er me. 20
—Go get you gone, and pray be careful all,
And leave you not a Man of War unsearch'd:
This wicked Emp'ror may have shipp'd her
    hence,
And, Kinsmen, then we may go pipe for Justice.
MARCUS   O Publius, is not this a heavy Case, 25
  To see thy noble Uncle thus distract?
PUBLIUS   Therefore, my Lords, it highly us concerns
  By Day and Night t' attend him carefully
  And feed his Humour kindly as we may
  Till Time beget some careful Remedy. 30
MARCUS   Kinsmen, his Sorrows are past Remedy.
  Join with the Goths, and with revengeful War
  Take wreak on Rome for this Ingratitude,
  And Vengeance on the traitor Saturnine.
TITUS   Publius, how now! —How now, my Masters! 35
  What, have you met with her?
PUBLIUS   No, my good Lord; but Pluto sends you word
  If you will have Revenge from Hell, you shall,
  Marry, for Justice she is so employ'd,
  He thinks, with Jove in Heav'n, or some where
    else, 40
  So that perforce you must needs stay a time.
TITUS   He doth me wrong to feed me with Delays.
  I'll dive into the burning Lake below
  And pull her out of Ach'ron by the Heels.

461

46   Cyclops   *one-eyed giants who worked at Vulcan's forge.*

49   sith   *since.*

52   Gear   *equipment.*

53   Ad Jovem   *To Jove (Jupiter), ruler of the Gods.*
         Ad Apollinem   *To Apollo, the God who presided over music, poetry, prophecy, and medicine.*

54   Ad Martem   *To Mars, God of War.*

55   Pallas   *Pallas Athena, Goddess of Wisdom (called Minerva in Roman mythology).*
         Mercury   *messenger of the Gods, who also presided over eloquence and commerce.*

56   Saturn   *the original ruler of the Gods, who presided over agriculture.*

58   loose when I bid   *shoot when I say to.*

59   to effect   *effectively, well.*

63   well said   *well done. Titus is probably thinking of the shot as a message.*

64   in Virgo's Lap   *in the lap of Astraea.*

66   Jubiter   *a variant spelling and pronunciation of* Jupiter, *used throughout this scene in the First Quarto, probably to set up the joke that occurs in line 79.*

—Marcus, we are but Shrubs, no Cedars we,   45
No big-bon'd Men fram'd of the Cyclops' size,
But Metal, Marcus: Steel to th' very Back,
Yet wrung with Wrongs more than our Backs can
    bear.
And sith there's no Justice in Earth nor Hell,
We will solicit Heav'n and move the Gods   50
To send down Justice for to wreak our Wrongs.
Come to this Gear.   *He distributes the Arrows.*
              You are a good Archer, Marcus:
"*Ad Jovem,*" that's for you. —Here, "*Ad Apollinem.*"
—"*Ad Martem,*" that's for my self.
—Here, Boy, "To Pallas." —Here, "To Mercury."   55
—"To Saturn," Caius, not to Saturnine:
You were as good to shoot against the Wind.
—To it, Boy! —Marcus, loose when I bid.
—Of my word, I have written to effect:
There's not a God left unsolicited.   60
MARCUS   Kinsmen, shoot all your Shafts into the
    Court:
We will afflict the Emp'ror in his Pride.
TITUS   Now, Masters, draw.   *They shoot.*
              —O well said, Lucius!
Good Boy, in Virgo's Lap; give it Pallas.
MARCUS   My Lord, I aim a Mile beyond the Moon: 65
Your Letter is with Jubiter by this.
TITUS   Ha, ha! —Publius, Publius, what hast thou
    done?

463

68 Taurus' Horns   *Taurus (the Bull) is both a constellation and a sign of the Zodiac.*

69–70 This . . . Knock   *Marcus says that the object of the game was to chafe ("gall") the Bull so that he would bump Aries (the Ram of the Zodiac).*

71–74 That . . . Present.   *Getting into the spirit of the occasion, Marcus tells Titus a story to suggest that their arrows are, in fact, making things happen in the Emperor's Court. Marcus suggests that it was because of Publius' shots to Heaven that the Moor gave the Emperor his horns (the sign of a cuckold) for a present.*

75 Why there it goes   *This was the cry a hunter shouted to indicate that the prey had been spotted in a chase.*

76 Post   *In his distracted state, Titus mistakes the Clown (a name applied to both rustics and Court fools) for the post delivering mail. He assumes that the Clown has come with replies from the Gods who have received messages.*

80 them   *The Clown refers to the gibbet (pronounced jibbet), the scaffold used to display to public scorn the corpses of executed criminals.*

86 Ay, of my Pigeons   *The joke, which may or may not be intended by the Clown, is in the wordplay on the word* Carrier, *which means (a) postman (in line 85), (b) one who carries (as applied to the Clown), and (c) carrier pigeons, pigeons who carry messages and thus serve as posts.*

See, see, thou hast shot off one of Taurus' Horns!

MARCUS This was the Sport, my Lord: when Publius
    shot,
    The Bull, being gall'd, gave Aries such a Knock   70
    That down fell both the Ram's Horns in the Court;
    And who should find them but the Empress'
    Villain?
    She laugh'd, and told the Moor he should not
    choose
    But give them to his Master for a Present.

TITUS Why there it goes: God give his Lordship joy!   75

Enter the Clown, with a Basket,
and two Pigeons in it.

    News, news from Heaven! —Marcus, the Post is
    come!
    —Sirrah, what Tidings? Have you any Letters?
    Shall I have Justice? What says Jubiter?

CLOWN Ho, the Gibbet-maker? He says that he hath
    taken them down again, for the Man must not be   80
    hang'd till the next week.

TITUS But what says Jubiter, I ask thee?

CLOWN Alas, Sir, I know not Jubiter: I never drank
    with him in all my life.

TITUS Why Villain, art thou not the Carrier?   85

CLOWN Ay, of my Pigeons, Sir; nothing else.

TITUS Why, did'st thou not come from Heaven?

89–90   God . . . days.   *The Clown replies as if he thought Titus believed him to be one who would "press" or rush to Heaven by committing suicide.*

91   Tribunal Plebs   *the* tribunus plebis *or People's Tribunal, a court of ten officials who heard complaints from the plebeians.*

93   Emperal's   *the Clown's mispronunciation of* Emperor's.

98   with a grace   *Titus means "with due courtesy," but the Clown understands him to mean "with the saying of grace," a prayer of thanksgiving before a meal.*

104   Hold, hold   *This seems to be an order for the Clown to stay for a moment while Titus finishes preparing the scroll he plans to have the Clown deliver.*

107   Supplication   *a humble request.*

CLOWN   From Heaven? Alas, Sir, I never came there.
God forbid I should be so bold to press to
Heaven in my young days. Why, I am going with   90
my Pigeons to the Tribunal Plebs, to take up a
matter of Brawl betwixt my Uncle and one of the
Emperal's Men.

MARCUS   —Why, Sir, that is as fit as can be to serve
for your Oration; and let him deliver the   95
Pigeons to the Emperor for you.

TITUS   —Tell me, can you deliver an Oration to the
Emperor with a grace?

CLOWN   Nay truly, Sir, I could never say Grace in
all my life.   100

TITUS   Sirrah, come hither: make no more ado,
But give your Pigeons to the Emperor.
By me thou shalt have Justice at his Hands.
Hold, hold; meanwhile here's Money for thy
  Charges.   *Titus gives the Clown Money.*
—Give me Pen and Ink.   105
—Sirrah, can you with a grace deliver up
A Supplication?

CLOWN   Ay Sir.

TITUS   Then here is a Supplication for you.
       Titus gives the Clown a Scroll.
And when you come to him, at the first approach
you must Kneel, then kiss his Foot, then deliver   110
up your Pigeons, and then look for your Reward.

112 bravely *with boldness and style.*

113 let me alone *leave it to me; it will be taken care of.*

114 Sirrah *a word normally used to address a social inferior, such as a rustic lacking in the sophistication of court or city life.*

114–16 hast thou . . . Suppliant. *Titus does not want the "Oration" or "Supplication" to come across as merely that of "an humble Suppliant." With the knife included, it will carry a veiled threat.*

IV.iv *This scene takes place at Saturninus' Court.*

1 Wrongs *insults.*

2 overborne *treated overbearingly, contemptuously.*

3–4 for th' . . . Justice *as a result of extending equal ("egal") justice, of showing restraint in the exercise of the Emperor's authority.*

5 mightful *powerful.*

I'll be at hand, Sir; see you do it bravely.

CLOWN   I warrant you, Sir, let me alone.

TITUS   Sirrah, hast thou a Knife? Come, let me see
it.

—Here Marcus, fold it in th' Oration: 115
For thou hast made it like an humble Suppliant.
—And when thou hast giv'n it to the Emperor,
Knock at my Door, and tell me what he says.

CLOWN   God be with you, Sir; I will.   *Exit.*

TITUS   Come, Marcus, let us go. —Publius, follow me.   120

Exeunt.

Scene 4

*Enter Emperor and Empress and her two Sons and others; the
Emperor brings the Arrows in his hand that Titus shot at him.*

SATURNINUS   Why Lords, what Wrongs are these! Was
ever seen
An Emperor in Rome thus overborne,
Troubled, confronted thus? And, for th' extent
Of egal Justice, us'd in such Contempt?
My Lords, you know, as know the mightful Gods,   5
How ever these disturbers of our Peace

7   Buzz   *whisper suspicions.*

7–8   there . . . Law   *nothing has happened but what is in conformity with law.*

9   and if   *if.*

10   overwhelm'd his Wits   *overcome his mental faculties.*

11   Wreaks   *vindictive gestures.*

13   for his Redress   *for the righting of his wrongs.*

18   blaz'ning   *blazoning, proclaiming. A* blazon *was a coat of arms or heraldic shield.*

20   As who would say   *as if one were to say.*

21   feigned Ecstasies   *pretended fits of madness.*

22   Shelter to   *excuse for, protection against penalty for.*

23–24 Justice . . . Health   *Justice is dependent on Saturninus' health and happiness.*

24   whom . . . he   *Both pronouns refer to Justice, but with the implication that Justice and Saturninus are one and the same; so also with* He'll *and* he *in line 25.*

25   as   *that.*

29   bear   *put up with, overlook.*

Buzz in the People's Ears, there nought hath
    pass'd
But ev'n with Law against the willful Sons
Of old Andronicus. And what and if
His Sorrows have so overwhelm'd his Wits?   10
Shall we be thus afflicted in his Wreaks,
His Fits, his Frenzy, and his Bitterness?
And now he writes to Heav'n for his Redress:
See, here's "To Jove," and this "To Mercury,"
This "To Apollo," this "To the God of War";   15
Sweet Scrolls to fly about the Streets of Rome!
What's this but libeling against the Senate
And blaz'ning our Injustice every where?
A goodly Humour, is it not, my Lords?
As who would say, in Rome no Justice were.   20
But if I live, his feigned Ecstasies
Shall be no Shelter to these Outrages,
But he and his shall know that Justice lives
In Saturninus' Health, whom, if he sleep,
He'll so awake as he in fury shall   25
Cut off the proud'st Conspirator that lives!
TAMORA   My gracious Lord, my lovely Saturnine,
    Lord of my Life, Commander of my Thoughts,
    Calm thee, and bear the Faults of Titus' Age,
    Th' effects of Sorrow for his valiant Sons,   30
    Whose Loss hath pierc'd him deep and scarr'd his
        Heart,
    And rather comfort his distressed Plight

47¹

33   prosecute the Meanest or the Best   *punish either the lowest (Titus' servants and messengers) or the highest (Titus himself) people involved.*

34   Contempts   *insults and accusations.*

35   gloze   *gloss over, tell plausible lies.*

36   touch'd thee to the Quick   *pierced to your very heart.*

37   Thy Lifeblood out   *once your lifeblood has all flown out.*
if Aaron now be wise   *if Aaron now succeeds in his schemes.*

40   be Emperial   *be the Emperor. It is difficult to tell whether this is a naive malapropism or the intended jest of a witty clown pretending to be a bumpkin.*

43   god-den   *good evening.*

45   hang him presently   *hang him immediately. The Clown's next line indicates that he understands the Emperor to say "thank him" rather than "hang him."*

48–49 By'r Lady . . . end.   *The Clown puns on two senses of* brought up *(reared; lifted to the top of a scaffold) and* fair End *(happy fortune; end of a hangman's rope). As elsewhere, the Clown's words make it difficult for us to see him either as a simple bumpkin or as a "wise fool." The price he pays for his services is no laughing matter, and yet it appears that the audience is expected to find his comic turn funny. Perhaps it is best to think of him as a kind of "cartoon" figure who performs a brief interlude in what is otherwise a "real" world.*

Than prosecute the Meanest or the Best
For these Contempts. [*Aside*] Why thus it shall
   become
High-witted Tamora to gloze with all.   35
—But Titus, I have touch'd thee to the Quick;
Thy Lifeblood out, if Aaron now be wise,
Then is all safe, the Anchor in the Port.

Enter Clown.

[*Aloud*] How now, good Fellow! Would'st thou
   speak with us?
CLOWN   Yea forsooth, and your Mistress-ship be
   Emperial.   40
TAMORA   Empress I am, but yonder sits the Emperor.
CLOWN   'Tis he. God and Saint Stephen give you
   god-den. I have brought you a Letter and a
   couple of Pigeons here.   *Saturninus reads the Letter.*
SATURNINUS   Go take him away, and hang him
   presently.   45
CLOWN   How much Money must I have?
TAMORA   Come, Sirrah, you must be hang'd.
CLOWN   Hang'd? By'r Lady, then I have brought up a
   Neck to fair End.   *Exit in the hands of Attendants.*
SATURNINUS   Despiteful and intolerable Wrongs!   50
Shall I endure this monstrous Villainy?
I know from whence this same Device proceeds.
May this be borne as if his trait'rous Sons

473

57   Nor . . . Privilege.   *Neither his age nor his honor shall make him immune.*

58   Slaughterman   *executioner.*

59   Sly frantic Wretch   *crafty, inflamed villain.*
       holp'st   *helped.*

S.D.   Nuntius   *Messenger, Latin for one who announces news.*

63   gather'd Head   *assembled forces.*

64   bent to the Spoil   *intent on victory. Originally* spoil *referred to that which the victor stripped from the loser in the aftermath of battle.*

65   amain   *forcefully and rapidly.*

68   Coriolanus   *a legendary hero from the earliest days of the Roman Empire. After being exiled, he formed an army of Rome's enemies and threatened to destroy his native city. If* Titus Andronicus *was Shakespeare's first tragedy, it is interesting that it refers to the hero of* Coriolanus, *destined to be his last.*

70   nip me   *both (a) catch me by surprise, and (b) wilt me (as frost surprises early buds in the spring).*

474

That died by Law for murder of our Brother
Have by my means been butcher'd wrongfully? 55
Go, drag the Villain hither by the Hair:
Nor Age nor Honor shall shape Privilege.
—For this proud Mock I'll be thy Slaughterman,
Sly frantic Wretch, that holp'st to make me great
In hope thy self should govern Rome and me! 60

Enter Nuntius Aemilius.

—What News with thee, Aemilius?
AEMILIUS   Arm, my Lords! Rome never had more
    Cause.
The Goths have gather'd Head, and with a Power
Of high-resolved Men, bent to the Spoil,
They hither march amain, under conduct 65
Of Lucius, Son to old Andronicus,
Who threats in course of his Revenge to do
As much as ever Coriolanus did.
SATURNINUS   Is warlike Lucius Gen'ral of the Goths?
These Tidings nip me, and I hang the Head 70
As Flow'rs with Frost, or Grass beat down with
    Storms.
Ay, now begins our Sorrows to approach.
'Tis he the Common People love so much:
My self hath often heard them say,
When I have walked like a Private Man, 75
That Lucius' Banishment was wrongfully,

80   succour   *help, support.*

82   Is . . . it?   *Does it dim the Sun itself when gnats fly in front of it?*

83   suffers   *allows.*

84   is not careful   *does not care, is not concerned.*

86   at pleasure   *when it pleases him.*
      stint   *stop.*

87   giddy   *unsteady, fickle.*

91   Honey-stalks   *stalks of clover.*

92   When as   *when.*

93   rotted with delicious Seed   *overcome with a surfeit of overly sweet delicacies. Modern editions normally emend to "feed" (following the Third Quarto of 1611) or "food" (following the 1623 First Folio), but "Seed" seems more appropriate to the food consumed by sheep.*

96   smooth   *smooth-talk, speak seductively.*

98   impregnable   *impenetrable, unreachable.*

And they have wish'd that Lucius were their
    Emperor.
TAMORA   Why should you fear? Is not your City
    strong?
SATURNINUS   Ay, but the Cit'zens favor Lucius,
And will revolt from me to succour him.   80
TAMORA   King, be thy Thoughts imperious like thy
    Name!
    Is the Sun dimm'd that Gnats do fly in it?
    The Eagle suffers little Birds to sing
    And is not careful what they mean thereby,
    Knowing that with the shadow of his Wings   85
    He can at pleasure stint their Melody:
    Ev'n so may'st thou the giddy Men of Rome.
    Then cheer thy Spirit, for know thou, Emperor,
    I will enchant the old Andronicus
    With Words more sweet, and yet more dangerous,   90
    Than Baits to Fish, or Honey-stalks to Sheep,
    When as the one is wounded with the Bait,
    The other rotted with delicious Seed.
SATURNINUS   But he will not entreat his Son for us.
TAMORA   If Tamora entreat him, then he will: 95
    For I can smooth and fill his aged Ears
    With golden Promises that, were his Heart
    Almost impregnable, his old Ears deaf,
    Yet should both Ear and Heart obey my Tongue.
    [*To Aemilius*] Go thou before t' be our
    Ambassador: 100

101–2   Parley / Of   *meeting with, conversation with.*

105   stand . . . Safety   *insist on conditions to secure his safety. Saturninus probably refers to the practice of demanding a high-ranking person ("Pledge") to be held hostage during the parley to guarantee good-faith negotiations.*

109   temper him   *bring him under control.*

111   blithe   *cheerful.*

112   bury . . . Devices   *put away your fear in the awareness of the devices I have planned.*

113   successantly   *This word probably means "in fulfillment of your plan."*

478

Say that the Emperor requests a Parley
Of warlike Lucius, and appoint the meeting
Ev'n at his Father's House, the old Andronicus.

SATURNINUS   Aemilius, do this Message honorably,
And if he stand in Hostage for his Safety,   105
Bid him demand what Pledge will please him best.

AEMILIUS   Your Bidding shall I do effectually.   *Exit.*

TAMORA   Now will I to that old Andronicus,
And temper him with all the Art I have
To pluck proud Lucius from the warlike Goths.   110
And now, sweet Emperor, be blithe again,
And bury all thy Fear in my Devices.

SATURNINUS   Then go successantly, and plead to him.

Exeunt.

479

V.i *This scene takes place in the field with Lucius' army.*

1 Approved *both (a) proven, and (b) meeting approval.*

4 desirous of our Sight *eager to see us.*

5 as your Titles witness *as your names and honors signify.*

6 Imperious . . . Wrongs *proud and unwilling to tolerate any wrongs you have been done.*

7 Scathe *injury.*

8 treble *three-fold, triple.*

Act Five

Scene 1

Flourish. Enter Lucius with an Army of Goths,
signified by Drums and Soldiers.

LUCIUS Approved Warriors and my faithful Friends,
  I have received Letters from great Rome
  Which signifies what hate they bear their
    Emperor
  And how desirous of our Sight they are.
  Therefore, great Lords, be as your Titles
    witness,   5
  Imperious and impatient of your Wrongs,
  And wherein Rome hath done you any Scathe,
  Let him make treble Satisfaction.

481

9   **Slip**   *offshoot, scion.*

12   **Ingrateful**   *ungrateful.*
       requites   *repays.*

13   **Be bold in us**   *have confidence in us.*

21   **ruinous Monastery**   *either a decaying monastery or, more likely, the ruins of what was once a monastery.*

22   **earnestly**   *attentively.*

24   **underneath**   *behind.*

26   **controll'd**   *quieted.*

28   **bewray**   *reveal, betray.*

29   **Look**   *appearance.*

FIRST GOTH   Brave Slip sprung from the great
    Andronicus,
    Whose Name was once our Terror, now our Comfort,   10
    Whose high Exploits and honorable Deeds
    Ingrateful Rome requites with foul Contempt,
    Be bold in us: we'll follow where thou lead'st,
    Like stinging Bees in hottest Summer's Day
    Led by their Master to the flow'red Fields,   15
    And be aveng'd on cursed Tamora.
OTHER GOTHS   And as he saith, so say we all with
    him.
LUCIUS   I humbly thank him, and I thank you all.
    But who comes here, led by a lusty Goth?

*Enter a Goth, leading Aaron with his Child
in his arms.*

SECOND GOTH   Renowned Lucius, from our Troops I
    stray'd   20
    To gaze upon a ruinous Monastery;
    And as I earnestly did fix mine Eye
    Upon the wasted Building, suddenly
    I heard a Child cry underneath a Wall.
    I made unto the Noise when soon I heard   25
    The crying Babe controll'd with this Discourse:
    "Peace, Tawny Slave, half me and half thy Dame!
    Did not thy Hue bewray whose Brat thou art,
    Had Nature lent thee but thy Mother's Look,

483

32   **beget** *give birth to.*

33   **rates** *berates.*

36   **hold thee dearly** *value you highly.*

38   **Surpris'd** *apprehended.*

40   **incarnate Devil** *Devil made flesh, Devil in human form.*

42   **Pearl** *Lucius probably alludes to the proverb "A black man is a pearl in a fair woman's eye."*

44   **wall-ey'd** *probably "white-eyed," glaring.*
        whither *to where.*

45   **Image** *likeness.*

47   **Halter** *hangman's noose.*

50   **Too like the Sire . . . good.** *Too like the father in always being good (spoken scornfully). Lucius picks up on the concept of "Royal" (line 49) as a term epitomizing quality and virtue, but he uses the word* Sire *to suggest that the child is of royal blood in the sense that applies to thoroughbred horses. Here as elsewhere, Aaron is defined either as subhuman (a beast or a slave) or as a devil (even as an incarnation of the Devil himself). It seldom occurs to anyone that a man of his complexion might be merely human—though we see some humanizing touches in Aaron's affection for his son.*

51   **sprawl** *struggle in the throes of death.*

Villain, thou might'st have been an Emperor.   30
But where the Bull and Cow are both Milk-white,
They never do beget a Coal-black Calf.
Peace, Villain, peace!" Ev'n thus he rates the
   Babe,
"For I must bear thee to a trusty Goth,
Who, when he knows thou art the Empress' Babe,   35
Will hold thee dearly for thy Mother's sake."
With this, my Weapon drawn, I rush'd upon him,
Surpris'd him suddenly, and brought him hither
To use as you think needful of the Man.

LUCIUS   O worthy Goth, this is th' incarnate Devil   40
That robb'd Andronicus of his good Hand;
This is the Pearl that pleas'd your Empress' Eye,
And here's the base Fruit of her burning Lust.
—Say, wall-ey'd Slave, whither would'st thou
   convey
This growing Image of thy Fiend-like Face?   45
Why dost not speak? What, deaf? Not a word?
—A Halter, Soldiers: hang him on this Tree
And by his side his Fruit of Bastardy.

AARON   Touch not the Boy, he is of Royal Blood.

LUCIUS   Too like the Sire for ever being good.   50
—First hang the Child, that he may see it
   sprawl,
A sight to vex the Father's Soul withal.

AARON   Get me a Ladder.

                    Aaron is brought a Ladder.

485

66 Ruthful *lamentable.*
    piteously *so ruthless as to excite the most extreme pity.*

69 Tell on thy Mind *Say what is on your mind.*

71 Thou . . . God *You believe in no God.*

74 for *because.*

Lucius, save the Child,
And bear it from me to the Emperess.
If thou do this, I'll show thee wondrous things   55
That highly may advantage thee to hear;
If thou wilt not, befall what may befall,
I'll speak no more but "Vengeance rot you all!"
LUCIUS   Say on, and if it please me which thou
    speak'st,
Thy Child shall live, and I will see it
    nourish'd.   60
AARON   And if it please thee! Why, assure thee,
    Lucius,
'Twill vex thy Soul to hear what I shall speak:
For I must talk of Murders, Rapes, and Massacres,
Acts of black Night, abominable Deeds,
Complots of Mischief, Treason, Villainies,   65
Ruthful to hear, yet piteously performed;
And this shall all be buri'd in my Death,
Unless thou swear to me my Child shall live.
LUCIUS   Tell on thy Mind: I say thy Child shall
    live.
AARON   Swear that he shall, and then I will begin.   70
LUCIUS   Who should I swear by? Thou believ'st no
    God;
That granted, how canst thou believe an Oath?
AARON   What if I do not? as indeed I do not!
Yet, for I know thou art religious,
And hast a thing within thee called Conscience,   75

4⁸7

76 Popish Tricks *Papist deceptions (an anti-Catholic slur).*

77 careful to observe *conscientious about observing.*

79 An . . . God *The idiot was conventionally depicted as a boy carrying a long stick with an inflated bladder (a bauble) bobbing from its end. Professional court fools were often called idiots, and their baubles were long sticks crowned with jester's heads and coxcombs. Aaron puns on the word* holds, *which here refers both to (a) what the idiot holds in his hands, and (b) what he holds or believes to be true.*

85 discover nought *disclose nothing.*

88 insatiate and luxurious *insatiably lecherous.*

95 wash'd . . . trimm'd *Aaron's imagery suggests a butcher or cook's preparation of a fowl for cooking. But the phrasing also alludes to the steps a barber undergoes in trimming a beard or a head of hair, an implication reinforced by Lucius' use of the word* barb'rous *in line 97.*

96 Trim *neat, proper (as with the sporting activities of young aristocrats who have private tutors).*

99 Coddling Spirit *Aaron uses this term with overt verbal irony, referring to behavior that illustrates anything but a nurturing, overly affectionate spirit. Shakespeare probably also had a sexual implication in mind:* cod *was another word for testicles, and* spirit *for semen.*

100 As . . . Set *Aaron depicts Tamora as a "sure" (certain, game-winning) card in a "Set" (game).*

488

With twenty Popish Tricks and Ceremonies,
Which I have seen thee careful to observe,
Therefore I urge thy Oath: for that I know
An Idiot holds his Bauble for a God,
And keeps the Oath which by that God he swears;   80
To that I'll urge him. Therefore thou shalt vow
By that same God, what God soe'er it be,
That thou ador'st and hast in reverence,
To save my Boy, to nour'sh and bring him up,
Or else I will discover nought to thee.   85
LUCIUS   Ev'n by my God I swear to thee I will.
AARON   First know thou, I begot him on the Empress.
LUCIUS   O most insatiate and luxurious Woman!
AARON   Tut, Lucius, this was but a deed of Charity
To that which thou shalt hear of me anon.   90
'Twas her two Sons that murd'red Bassianus:
They cut thy Sister's Tongue and ravish'd her,
And cut her Hands and trimm'd her as thou saw'st.
LUCIUS   O detestable Villain! Call'st thou that
Trimming?
AARON   Why, she was wash'd, and cut, and trimm'd,
and 'twas   95
Trim Sport for them which had the doing of it.
LUCIUS   O barb'rous beastly Villains like thy self!
AARON   Indeed, I was their Tutor to instruct them.
That Coddling Spirit had they from their Mother,
As sure a Card as ever won the Set;   100
That Bloody Mind I think they learn'd of me,

489

---

102   As . . . Head *Aaron compares himself to one of the dogs used to bait bulls and bears in amphitheatres similar to the playhouses in which Shakespeare's works were performed publicly in the London suburbs. A good dog went straight for the head of the bull or bear staked for the baiting.*

104   train'd *led, lured.*
       guileful *deceptive, concealed.*

109   And . . . rue *and what has not been done, which you have cause to grieve.*

111   the Cheater *both (a) rule-breaker, deceiver, and (b) escheater, officer assigned to take care of property forfeited to the Crown.*

114   I pried me *I peered.*

119   sounded *swooned; a contraction of* swounded *(rhymes with* wounded*).*

126   compass *reach, range.*

As true a Dog as ever fought at Head.
Well, let my Deeds be witness of my Worth.
I train'd thy Brethren to that guileful Hole
Where the dead Corpse of Bassianus lay;   105
I wrote the Letter that thy Father found,
And hid the Gold within that Letter mentioned,
Confed'rate with the Queen and her two Sons.
And what not done, that thou hast cause to rue,
Wherein I had no stroke of Mischief in it?   110
I play'd the Cheater for thy Father's Hand,
And when I had it, drew my self apart,
And almost broke my Heart with extreme Laughter.
I pried me though the crevice of a Wall
When for his Hand he had his two Sons' Heads,   115
Beheld his Tears, and laugh'd so heartily
That both mine Eyes were rainy like to his.
And when I told the Empress of this Sport,
She sounded almost at my pleasing Tale,
And for my Tidings gave me twenty Kisses.   120
FIRST GOTH   What, canst thou say all this, and
      never blush?
AARON   Ay, like a black Dog, as the saying is.
LUCIUS   Art thou not sorry for these heinous Deeds?
AARON   Ay, that I had not done a thousand more.
Ev'n now I curse the Day, and yet I think   125
Few come within the compass of my Curse,
Wherein I did not some notorious Ill,
As kill a Man, or else devise his Death,

130   forswear *perjure.*

133   Haystalks *haystacks.*

134   quench *extinguish.*

138   their Skins *the skins of the corpses.*

150   But *solely.*

151   stop his Mouth *This order is probably carried out immediately, by placing a gag over Aaron's mouth.*

Ravish a Maid, or plot the way to do it,
Accuse some Inn'cent, and forswear my self,   130
Set deadly Enmity between two Friends,
Make Poor-men's Cattle break their Necks,
Set fire on Barns and Haystalks in the Night,
And bid the Owners quench them with their Tears.
Oft have I digg'd up Dead-men from their Graves,   135
And set them upright at their dear Friends' Door,
Ev'n when their Sorrows almost was forgot,
And on their Skins, as on the Bark of Trees,
Have with my Knife carved in Roman Letters
"Let not your Sorrow die, though I am dead."   140
But I have done a thousand dreadful things
As willingly as one would kill a Fly,
And nothing grieves me heartily indeed
But that I cannot do ten thousand more.

LUCIUS   Bring down the Devil, for he must not die   145
So sweet a Death as Hanging presently.

Aaron is forced to descend the Ladder.

AARON   If there be Devils, would I were a Devil,
To live and burn in everlasting Fire,
So I might have your company in Hell
But to torment you with my bitter Tongue!   150

LUCIUS   Sirs, stop his Mouth, and let him speak no
more.

Enter Aemilius.

493

154   Let him come near   *Here the short line probably indicates a pause (equivalent to the time it would take to speak the six missing syllables) to allow the messenger to come forward. "Gaps" in Shakespeare's verse are often indications of stage business to be conducted; at other times they indicate pauses to allow reaction time, as in line 162 below.*

158   for   *because.*

159   Parley   *meeting.*

160   Willing . . . Hostages   *willing to have you state your conditions.*

V.ii   *This scene takes place in Titus' house, with Titus above in his study.*

1   sad Habiliment   *somber apparel.*

2   encounter with   *meet with.*

5   keeps   *keeps himself.*

494

GOTH My Lord, there is a Messenger from Rome
     Desires to be admitted to your presence.
LUCIUS Let him come near.
     Welcome Aemilius; what's the News from Rome?   155
AEMILIUS Lord Lucius, and you Princes of the Goths,
     The Roman Emp'ror greets you all by me;
     And, for he understands you are in Arms,
     He craves a Parley at your Father's House,
     Willing you to demand your Hostages,   160
     And they shall be immediately delivered.
FIRST GOTH What says our General?
LUCIUS Aemilius, let the Emp'ror give his Pledges
     Unto my Father and my Uncle Marcus,
     And we will come. March away.   *Exeunt.*   165

Scene 2

Enter Tamora and her two Sons, disguised.

TAMORA Thus, in this strange and sad Habiliment,
     I will encounter with Andronicus
     And say I am Revenge, sent from below
     To join with him and right his heinous Wrongs.
     —Knock at his Study, where they say he keeps,   5

495

6   strange   *exotic, secret.*

8   Confusion   *destruction.*

9   molest my Contemplation   *disturb my concentration on my thoughts.*

10   Trick   *stratagem, cunning device.*

11   sad Decrees   *serious decisions and resolutions.*

17–18 how . . . Accord?   *how can I give my speech eloquence [and thus make it effectual] without a hand to supply gestures in accordance with my words?*

19   Thou . . . me   *You have the advantage over me.*

22   Crimson Lines   *Titus probably refers to the lines he has written in blood (line 14).*

23   Trenches   *furrows and wrinkles (probably spoken as Titus points to his brow).*

To ruminate strange Plots of dire Revenge;
Tell him Revenge is come to join with him
And work Confusion on his Enemies.

They knock, and Titus opens his Study Door above.

TITUS Who doth molest my Contemplation?
Is it your Trick to make me ope the Door, 10
That so my sad Decrees may fly away
And all my Study be to no effect?
You are deceiv'd: for what I mean to do
See here in Bloody Lines I have set down,
And what is written shall be executed. 15

TAMORA Titus, I am come to talk with thee.

TITUS No, not a Word: how can I grace my Talk,
Wanting a Hand to give it that Accord?
Thou hast the Odds of me, therefore no more.

TAMORA If thou didst know me, thou would'st talk
with me. 20

TITUS I am not mad, I know thee well enough:
Witness this wretched Stump, witness these
Crimson Lines,
Witness these Trenches made by Grief and Care,
Witness the tiring Day and heavy Night,
Witness all Sorrow that I know thee well 25
For our proud Empress, mighty Tamora.
Is not thy coming for my other Hand?

TAMORA Know, thou Sad Man, I am not Tamora;
She is thy Enemy, and I thy Friend.
I am Revenge, sent from th' Infernal Kingdom 30

497

31 gnawing Vulture *This is probably an allusion to the story of Prometheus, whose punishment was to be bound to a rock in the Caucasian Mountains while vultures gnawed at his liver.*

32 wreakful Vengeance *well-deserved vengeance.*

36 Obscurity *darkness, shadow.*
    misty Vale *foggy valley.*

38 couch *crouch, hide.*

46 'surance *assurance, proof.*

49 Globes *This is the reading of all the early texts of the play, with "Globes" probably referring to the spheres surrounding the Earth.*

50 proper Palfreys *fine horses.*

51 hale *haul, draw.*
    Wagon *chariot.*

52 find . . . Cares *The Quarto and Folio texts read* murder *in this line; since the eighteenth century most editors have emended to* murderers, *and this edition follows suit. But this edition does not follow most editions and emend* Cares *to* Caves.

55 Footman *a man who walked alongside his master's horse or carriage.*

56 Hyperion's *the Sun's. Hyperion was one of the names for the Sun God.*

57 downfall *setting, descent.*

To ease the gnawing Vulture of thy Mind
By working wreakful Vengeance on thy Foes.
Come down and welcome me to this World's Light;
Confer with me of Murder and of Death.
There's not a hollow Cave or Lurking-place,   35
No vast Obscurity or misty Vale,
Where bloody Murder or detested Rape
Can couch for fear, but I will find them out
And in their Ears tell them my dreadful Name,
Revenge, which makes the foul Offender quake.   40

TITUS   Art thou Revenge? And art thou sent to me
    To be a torment to mine Enemies?

TAMORA   I am, therefore come down and welcome me.

TITUS   Do me some Service ere I come to thee.
    Lo by thy side where Rape and Murder stands,   45
    Now give some 'surance that thou art Revenge.
    Stab them, or tear them on thy Chariot Wheels,
    And then I'll come and be thy Wagoner
    And whirl along with thee about the Globes.
    Provide two proper Palfreys, black as jet,   50
    To hale thy vengeful Wagon swift away,
    And find out Murd'rers in their guilty Cares;
    And when thy Car is loaden with their Heads,
    I will dismount and by thy Wagon Wheel
    Trot like a servile Footman all day long,   55
    Ev'n from Hyperion's rising in the East
    Until his very downfall in the Sea;
    And day by day I'll do this heavy Task,

59   Rapine   *Rape.*

60   Ministers   *agents.*

65   worldly Men   *mortal men, men whose perspectives are limited to this world.*

68   one Arm's Embracement   *an embrace with one arm.*

70   Closing   *agreement, conclusion.*

71   forge   *invent.*

74   being . . . Thought   *his being easily deceived in this delusion (that I am Revenge).*

76   hold him sure   *keep him secure (from interfering with what is going on elsewhere).*

77   out of hand   *This phrase is usually interpreted as meaning "on the spur of the moment." But Tamora also seems to be drawing a contrast between what will be happening at the Banquet and what will be happening elsewhere (perhaps in someone else's hands) to "scatter and disperse the giddy Goths" (line 78).*

80   ply my Theme   *execute my plan. Tamora puns on* ply/play, *with the word* theme *functioning as a reference to a musical passage or motif.*

81   forlorn   *lost, lonely.*

So thou destroy Rapine and Murder there.

TAMORA   These are my Ministers, and come with me.   60

TITUS   Are they thy Ministers? What are they
    call'd?

TAMORA   Rape and Murder: therefore called so
    'Cause they take Vengeance of such kind of Men.

TITUS   Good Lord, how like the Empress' Sons they
    are,
    And you the Empress! But we worldly Men   65
    Have miserable, mad, mistaking Eyes.
    O sweet Revenge, now do I come to thee;
    And if one Arm's Embracement will content thee,
    I will embrace thee in it by and by.   *Exit above.*

TAMORA   This Closing with him fits his Lunacy.   70
    What e'er I forge to feed his Brain-sick Humours,
    Do you uphold and maintain in your Speeches:
    For now he firmly takes me for Revenge,
    And, being credulous in this mad Thought,
    I'll make him send for Lucius his Son,   75
    And whilst I at a Banquet hold him sure,
    I'll find some cunning Practice out of hand
    To scatter and disperse the giddy Goths,
    Or at the least make them his Enemies.
    See, here he comes, and I must ply my Theme.   80

Enter Titus below.

TITUS   Long have I been forlorn, and all for thee.

85   fitted   *appareled and supplied.*

87   wot   *know.*
         wags   *travels (related to both* wagon *and* way*).*

89   aright   *correctly.*

90   convenient   *fitting (literally, "coming together").*

98–   Look . . . Ravisher.   *Given Titus' knowledge of the identi-*
103   *ties of Murder and Rapine, these lines are ironic in the way*
         they take a fictional premise (that Tamora's sons are actually
         allegorical personifications) and apply it to statements that are
         literally true (such as the fact that a murderer on the streets,
         such as Chiron, is "like to" the figure, Murder, being sent
         forth to stab such a man).

107   up and down   *from top to bottom.*

Welcome, dread Fury, to my woeful House.
—Rapine and Murder, you are welcome too;
—How like the Empress and her Sons you are!
Well are you fitted, had you but a Moor;   85
Could not all Hell afford you such a Devil?
For well I wot the Empress never wags
But in her company there is a Moor,
And would you represent our Queen aright
It were convenient you had such a Devil.   90
But welcome as you are: what shall we do?
TAMORA   What would'st thou have us do, Andronicus?
DEMETRIUS   Show me a Murderer, I'll deal with him.
CHIRON   Show me a Villain that hath done a Rape,
And I am sent to be reveng'd on him.   95
TAMORA   Show me a thousand that hath done thee
   Wrong,
And I will be revenged on them all.
TITUS   Look round about the wicked Streets of Rome,
And when thou find'st a Man that's like thy self,
Good Murder, stab him: he's a Murderer.   100
—Go thou with him, and when it is thy hap
To find another that is like to thee,
Good Rapine, stab him: he's a Ravisher.
—Go thou with them, and in the Emp'rors Court
There is a Queen attended by a Moor;   105
Well shalt thou know her by thine own Proportion,
For up and down she doth resemble thee.
I pray thee do on them some violent Death:

503

110   lesson'd   *instructed.*

113   towards   *here pronounced as a single syllable.*

115   solemn   *formal, stately.*

120   Device   *scheme, plan.*

124   repair   *come.*

They have been violent to me and mine.

TAMORA Well hast thou lesson'd us; this shall we
    do.   110
    But would it please thee, good Andronicus,
    To send for Lucius, thy thrice-valiant Son,
    Who leads towards Rome a band of warlike Goths,
    And bid him come and banquet at thy House,
    When he is here, ev'n at thy solemn Feast,   115
    I will bring in the Empress and her Sons,
    The Emperor himself, and all thy Foes,
    And at thy mercy shall they stoop and kneel,
    And on them shalt thou ease thy angry Heart.
    What says Andronicus to this Device?   120

TITUS Marcus, my Brother! 'Tis sad Titus calls.

Enter Marcus.

    Go, gentle Marcus, to thy Nephew Lucius
    (Thou shalt inquire him out among the Goths);
    Bid him repair to me and bring with him
    Some of the chiefest Princes of the Goths.   125
    Bid him encamp his Soldiers where they are;
    Tell him the Emp'ror and the Empress too
    Feast at my House, and he shall feast with them.
    This do thou for my Love; and so let him,
    As he regards his aged Father's Life.   130

MARCUS This will I do, and soon return again.   *Exit.*

TAMORA Now will I hence about thy Business

136 And . . . Lucius *and cling to no revenge but that which Lucius is already engaged in bringing about.*

137 abide *remain.*

139 govern'd *managed.*

140 smooth *flatter.*

141 turn *return.*

145 ' at pleasure *at your pleasure.*

147 Complot *plot, conspiracy.*

149 employ'd *put to use.*

And take my Ministers along with me.

TITUS   Nay, nay, let Rape and Murder stay with me,
 Or else I'll call my Brother back again   135
 And cleave to no Revenge but Lucius.

TAMORA   [*Aside to her Sons*] What say you, Boys?
  Will you abide with him,
 Whiles I go tell my Lord the Emperor
 How I have govern'd our determin'd Jest?
 Yield to his Humour, smooth and speak him fair, 140
 And tarry with him till I turn again.

TITUS   [*Aside*] I knew them all, though they
  suppos'd me mad,
 And will o'erreach them in their own Devices:
 A pair of cursed Hellhounds and their Dame.

DEMETRIUS   Madam, depart at pleasure; leave us here. 145

TAMORA   Farewell, Andronicus; Revenge now goes
 To lay a Complot to betray thy Foes.

TITUS   I know thou dost; and sweet Revenge,
  farewell.   *Exit Tamora.*

CHIRON   Tell us, Old Man, how shall we be employ'd?

TITUS   Tut, I have work enough for you to do. 150
 —Publius, come hither! —Caius and Valentine!

Enter Publius, Caius, and Valentine.

PUBLIUS   What is your will?

TITUS   Know you these two?

155   Fie . . . deceiv'd!   *Titus speaks this line sardonically, in such a way as to let Publius know that he is not deceived.*

161   cry   *cry out.*

163   therefore   *for that very reason. Ironically, the identification that Chiron discloses on the assumption that it will set him free ("we are the Empress' Sons!") is precisely the one that seals his fate.*

165   sure   *securely.*
       fast   *tightly.*

170   Spring   *Titus uses this word first to refer to a wellspring of pure water; but in the next line he plays on a second sense, the season that initiates the summer of the year.*

PUBLIUS   The Empress' Sons, I take them, Chiron and
          Demetrius.
TITUS   Fie, Publius, fie: thou art much deceiv'd!   155
       The one is Murd'r, and Rape's the other's Name;
       And therefore bind them, gentle Publius;
       Caius and Valentine, lay Hands on them.
       Oft have you heard me wish for such an Hour,
       And now I find it: therefore bind them sure,   160
       And stop their Mouths if they begin to cry.
                    Exit Titus while Publius, Caius, and Valentine
                              bind Chiron and Demetrius.
CHIRON   Villains, forbear: we are the Empress' Sons!
PUBLIUS   And therefore do we what we are commanded.
        Stop close their Mouths; let them not speak a
          Word.
        Is he sure bound? Look that you bind them fast.   165

              Enter Titus Andronicus with a Knife, and
                    Lavinia with a Basin.

TITUS   Come, come, Lavinia: look, thy Foes are
          bound.
       —Sirs, stop their Mouths; let them not speak to
          me,
       But let them hear what fearful Words I utter.
       —O Villains, Chiron and Demetrius,
       Here stands the Spring whom you have stain'd
          with Mud,   170

509

175   dear   *precious, infinite in value.*

177   constrain'd   *compelled.*

179   for Shame   *because of the shame you bear.*

180   martyr   *murder in a ritual fashion. What Titus goes on to describe is yet another sacrificial offering, this one a grotesque parody of the Christian Communion service and one that will turn out to be Tamora's last supper.*

188   Coffin   *both a burial coffin and a pie crust.*
      rear   *erect, make.*

189   Pasties   *meat pies.*

190   Strumpet   *whore.*
      unhallow'd Dam   *unholy Mother.*

191   Increase   *offspring.*

193   surfeit   *feed to excess.*

195   Progne   *Procne, who served her son Itys to her husband Tereus in revenge for his rape of Philomela.*

This goodly Summer with your Winter mix'd.
You kill'd her Husband, and for that vile Fault
Two of her Brothers were condemn'd to Death,
My Hand cut off and made a merry Jest.
Both her sweet Hands, her Tongue, and that more
   dear   175
Than Hands or Tongue, her spotless Chastity,
Inhuman Traitors, you constrain'd and forc'd.
What would you say if I should let you speak?
Villains, for Shame you could not beg for Grace.
Hark, Wretches, how I mean to martyr you.   180
This one Hand yet is left to cut your Throats,
Whiles that Lavinia 'tween her Stumps doth hold
The Basin that receives your guilty Blood.
You know your Mother means to feast with me,
And calls her self Revenge, and thinks me mad. 185
Hark, Villains, I will grind your Bones to Dust,
And with your Blood and it I'll make a Paste,
And of the Paste a Coffin I will rear,
And make two Pasties of your shameful Heads,
And bid that Strumpet, your unhallow'd Dam, 190
Like to the Earth swallow her own Increase.
This is the Feast that I have bid her to,
And this the Banquet she shall surfeit on:
For worse than Philomel you us'd my Daughter,
And worse than Progne I will be reveng'd.   195
And now prepare your Throats. —Lavinia, come,
Receive the Blood; and when that they are dead,

203   stern   *grim and unyielding in its harsh justice.*

       Centaurs' Feast   *Titus refers to the marriage feast following the wedding of Hippodamia to Pirithous, King of the Lapithae. When one of the guests, the Centaur Eurution, attempted to abduct the bride and the other Centaurs tried to steal away the remaining Lapithae women, the Lapithae defeated the Centaurs in a bloody battle and drove them out of the country. (The story is detailed in Book XII of Ovid's* Metamorphoses.) *The Centaurs were mythical creatures, horses from the waist down and men from the waist up; they were thus apt symbols of unbridled lust.*

205   'gainst their Mother comes   *in preparation for the arrival of their Mother.*

V.iii   *This scene takes place in Titus' house.*

2   repair   *return.*

3   ours   *our minds. The Goths are saying that just as Lucius' will is in accord with that of his Father, so theirs are in accord with his.*

6   fetter him   *shackle him.*

Let me go grind their Bones to Powder small,
And with this hateful Liquor temper it,
And in that Paste let their vile Heads be bak'd.   200
—Come, come, be ev'ry one officious
To make this Banquet, which I wish may prove
More stern and bloody than the Centaurs' Feast.

He cuts their throats.

So; now bring them in, for I'll play the Cook,
And see them ready 'gainst their Mother comes.   205

Exeunt.

Scene 3

Enter Lucius, Marcus, and the Goths.

LUCIUS   Uncle Marcus, since 'tis my Father's mind
    That I repair to Rome, I am content.
GOTHS   And ours with thine, befall what Fortune
        will.
LUCIUS   Good Uncle, take you in this barb'rous Moor,
    This rav'nous Tiger, this accursed Devil;   5
    Let him receive no Sust'nance, fetter him,
    Till he be brought unto the Empress' Face

9   Ambush   *an arrangement of forces in preparation for a surprise attack.*

17   What . . . one?   *Saturninus greets Lucius as a rebel, asking him if the Heavens have more than one Sun—an implicit challenge for Lucius to show how Rome can have more than one Emperor.*

18   What boots it thee   *How does it help you?*

19   break the Parle   *Cut the talk.*

21   careful   *both (a) considerate, and (b) troubled over Rome's present difficulties.*

22   Hath . . . End   *has planned for an honorable purpose.*

23   League   *alliance, fellowship.*

24   draw nigh   *draw near. Marcus is probably saying "Come to the table."*

For Testimony of her foul Proceedings.
And see the Ambush of our Friends be strong:
I fear the Emp'ror means no good to us.   10
AARON   Some Devil whisper Curses in my Ear,
And prompt me that my Tongue may utter forth
The ven'mous Malice of my swelling Heart!
LUCIUS   Away, inhuman Dog, unhallow'd Slave!
Sirs, help our Uncle to convey him in.   15
          Exeunt Goths with Aaron. Sound Trumpets within.
The Trumpets show the Emp'ror is at hand.

          Flourish. Enter Emperor and Empress, with
          Aemilius, Tribunes, and Others.

SATURNINUS   What, hath the Firmament moe Suns
     than one?
LUCIUS   What boots it thee to call thy self a Sun?
MARCUS   Rome's Emperor, and Nephew, break the
     Parle:
These Quarrels must be quietly debated.   20
The Feast is ready which the careful Titus
Hath ordain'd to an honorable End:
For Peace, for Love, for League, and Good to
     Rome.
Please you therefore draw nigh and take your
     places.
SATURNINUS   Marcus, we will.   25

515

26   **dread**   *awesome. The term was frequently used in reference to one's superiors as a sign of respect.*

28   **the Cheer**   *the fare being offered. Titus is manifesting the self-deprecation expected of a gracious host.*

33   **beholding**   *indebted.*

36   **rash Virginius**   *Virginius was a Roman centurion of the fifth century B.C. who killed his daughter Virginia before she could be raped ("enforc'd," line 38) by her abductor, the wicked judge Apius Claudius. The story was originally told in Book III of Livy's* Roman History; *it was retold in the "Physician's Tale" of Chaucer's* Canterbury Tales. *The oddity in Titus' use of the story here is that in lines 38–45 he implies that Virginius killed Virginia after she was raped, whereas in fact he killed her because she was about to be raped and he wished to prevent it. Perhaps at this point in the action Shakespeare simply wanted to draw a parallel between Titus' plight and that of Virginius. In lines 50–52, Titus quite rightly observes that he has "a thousand times more Cause" than Virginius to slay his daughter.*

41–42   **Because . . . Sorrows.**   *Neither Titus nor Saturninus considers the issue of Lavinia's shame from her point of view. Her sole function in life would seem to be to please and glorify her father. She bears "Shame" even if she has had nothing to do with the loss of her virginity. She must die or "by her presence still [constantly] renew his Sorrows."*

44   **lively Warrant**   *powerful justification.*

Trumpets sounding, enter Titus like a Cook
placing the Dishes, Lavinia with a Veil
over her face, young Lucius, and Others.

TITUS   Welcome, my Lord; welcome, dread Queen;
 Welcome, ye warlike Goths; welcome Lucius;
 And welcome all. Although the Cheer be poor,
 'Twill fill your Stomachs; please you eat of it.
SATURNINUS   Why art thou thus attir'd, Andronicus?   30
TITUS   Because I would be sure to have all well
 To entertain your Highness and your Empress.
TAMORA   We are beholding to you, good Andronicus.
TITUS   [*Aside*] And if your Highness knew my Heart,
  you were.
 [*Aloud*] My Lord the Emperor, resolve me this: 35
 Was it well done of rash Virginius
 To slay his Daughter with his own right Hand
 Because she was enforc'd, stain'd, and
  deflow'r'd?
SATURNINUS   It was, Andronicus.
TITUS   Your Reason, mighty Lord?   40
SATURNINUS   Because the Girl should not survive her
  Shame,
 And by her Presence still renew his Sorrows.
TITUS   A Reason mighty, strong, and effectual;
 A Pattern, Precedent, and lively Warrant
 For me, most wretched, to perform the like.   45
 —Die, die, Lavinia, and thy Shame with thee;

517

48   unkind   *here, another word for "unnatural."*

61   Whereof   *of which.*
       daintily   *Titus uses this word to draw a contrast between the formality of a "solemn Feast" and the barbarity of Tamora's unwitting cannibalism.*

And with thy Shame thy Father's Sorrow die!

He kills her.

SATURNINUS   What hast thou done, unnatural and
  unkind?

TITUS   Kill'd her for whom my Tears have made me
  blind.

I am as woeful as Virginius was,   50
And have a thousand times more Cause than he
To do this Outrage, and it now is done.

SATURNINUS   What, was she ravish'd? Tell who did
  the Deed.

TITUS   Will 't please you eat? Will 't please your
  Highness feed?   *They eat.*

TAMORA   Why hast thou slain thine only Daughter
  thus?   55

TITUS   Not I, 'twas Chiron and Demetrius:
They ravish'd her, and cut away her Tongue,
And they, 'twas they, that did her all this
  Wrong.

SATURNINUS   Go fetch them hither to us presently!

TITUS   Why, there they are, both baked in this Pie,   60
Whereof their Mother daintily hath fed,
Eating the Flesh that she her self hath bred.
'Tis true, 'tis true; witness my Knive's sharp
  Point.   *He stabs the Empress.*

SATURNINUS   Die, frantic Wretch, for this accursed
  Deed!   *He stabs Titus.*

LUCIUS   Can the Son's Eye behold his Father bleed?   65

519

66 **Meed for Meed** *payment for payment.*

71 **Corn** *grain, here represented as still on its stalk.*
  one mutual Sheaf *one united bundle of stalks. This image,
  like that of the "Fagot" in III.i.69, is probably intended to
  remind the audience of the* fasces, *the bundle of rods that
  symbolized Roman unity and power.*

72 **These . . . Body** *This line reminds us of the "Body" image
  with which the play began (I.i.190–91), but it calls to mind
  even more forcibly the lopping off of limbs that has dominated
  so much of the play's action.*

73–95 ROMAN LORD . . . speak. *With one exception, this passage
  is here rendered as it appears in the First Quarto. The sole
  emendation occurs at line 77, where a speaker designation has
  been added to assign lines 77–95 to Marcus. These lines
  sound like a reply to the Roman Lord's sardonic comments,
  and they pave the way for Lucius to speak.*

77 **my . . . Age** *my gray hair and my sagging cheeks.*

80 **as erst our Ancestor** *as on an earlier occasion our ancestor
  Aeneas did.*

85 **Sinon** *the crafty Greek who persuaded the Trojans to accept
  the wooden horse that let the Greeks get into Troy.*

87 **our Troy, our Rome** *Since a Trojan, Aeneas, had founded
  Rome, the Romans felt a close connection between their history
  and that of Troy. The British claimed as their founder another
  Trojan (Brutus, the great grandson of Aeneas).*

There's Meed for Meed: Death for a bloody Deed!
He stabs Saturninus.

After the Tumult settles, Marcus addresses
the Survivors.

MARCUS   You sad-fac'd Men, People and Sons of Rome,
By Uproars sever'd, as a flight of Fowl
Scatter'd by Winds and high tempestuous Gusts,
O let me teach you how to knit again   70
This scatter'd Corn into one mutual Sheaf,
These broken Limbs again into one Body.
ROMAN LORD   Let Rome her self be Bane unto her self,
And she whom mighty Kingdoms cur'sy to,
Like a forlorn and desp'rate Castaway,   75
Do shameful Execution on her self!
MARCUS   But if my Frosty Signs and Chaps of Age,
Grave Witnesses of true Experience,
Cannot induce you to attend my Words,
[*To Lucius*] Speak, Rome's dear Friend, as erst
    our Ancestor,   80
When with his solemn Tongue he did discourse
To love-sick Dido's sad-attending Ear
The story of that baleful burning Night
When subtle Greeks surpris'd King Priam's Troy.
Tell us what Sinon hath bewitch'd our Ears,   85
Or who hath brought the fatal Engine in
That gives our Troy, our Rome, the civil Wound.

521

88   compact *composed.*
       Flint nor Steel *Flint and steel were both common metaphors for hard hearts.*

90   But *or.*

91   break my Utt'rance *interrupt my remarks.*

93   Commiseration *pity. The word* commiseration *was often applied to that part of an oration designed to move the audience to sympathy with the speaker and his cause.*

96   Auditory *audience.*

100   fell Faults *savage crimes.*

101   cozen'd *cheated.*

104   unkindly *unmercifully, in a way that was unnatural.*

107   Who . . . Tears *whose hate was overcome by their pity of my genuine tears.*

108   op'd *opened.*

109   Turn'd-forth *exile.*

110   in my Blood *Lucius means two things: (a) in my noble heritage as a son of Titus Andronicus, and (b) in the blood I've shed in Rome's defense.*

113   Vaunter *boaster, braggart.*

114   dumb *silent, unspeaking.*

—My Heart is not compact of Flint nor Steel,
Nor can I utter all our bitter Grief,
But Floods of Tears will drown my Oratory,   90
And break my Utt'rance, ev'n in the time
When it should move ye to attend me most
And force you to Commiseration.
Here's Rome's young Captain: let him tell the
    Tale,
While I stand by and weep to hear him speak.   95
LUCIUS   Then, gracious Auditory, be it known to you,
That Chiron and the damn'd Demetrius
Were they that murdered our Emp'ror's Brother;
And they it were that ravished our Sister;
For their fell Faults our Brothers were beheaded,   100
Our Father's Tears despis'd, and basely cozen'd
Of that true Hand that fought Rome's Quarrel out
And sent her Enemies unto the Grave;
Lastly, my self unkindly banished,
The Gates shut on me, and turn'd weeping out,   105
To beg relief among Rome's Enemies,
Who drown'd their Enmity in my true Tears
And op'd their Arms t' embrace me as a Friend.
I am the Turn'd-forth, be it known to you,
That hath preserv'd her Welfare in my Blood   110
And from her Bosom took the En'my's Point,
Sheathing the Steel in my advent'rous Body.
Alas, you know I am no Vaunter, I;
My Scars can witness, dumb although they are,

116   soft   *hush.*

119   Behold the Child   *At this moment Marcus probably gestures
toward the baby, who may be in an attendant's arms or who
may even be in the arms of Marcus himself. The early texts
provide us no stage direction to indicate when or how the Child
appears.*

125   what . . . revenge   *either (a) what course was available to
Titus to obtain revenge, or (b) what course was forced upon
Titus to take revenge.*

129   ought   *anything.*

137–   Come . . . Hand   *Aemilius appears to address these words
38   to the Romans as an exhortation for them to accept Lucius as
their new Emperor. If on the word "fall" (line 136) Marcus
and Lucius have bowed reverently to offer their lives to their
fellow Romans, Aemilius probably lifts them up. He may also
offer Lucius' hands to some nearby Roman citizens. Aemilius'
words and gestures probably elicit their "Common Voice" (line
140) as they assent to the proposal that Lucius be acclaimed
as Rome's new Emperor.*

That my Report is just and full of Truth. 115
But soft, methinks I do digress too much,
Citing my worthless Praise. O pardon me,
For when no Friends are by, Men praise
    themselves.
MARCUS   Now is my turn to speak. Behold the Child:
Of this was Tamora delivered, 120
The issue of an irreligious Moor,
Chief Architect and Plotter of these Woes.
The Villain is alive in Titus' House,
And as he is to witness, this is true.
Now judge what course had Titus to revenge 125
These Wrongs unspeakable, past Patience,
Or more than any living Man could bear.
Now have you heard the Truth: what say you,
    Romans?
Have we done ought amiss? Show us wherein,
And, from the place where you behold us pleading, 130
The poor remainder of Andronici
Will Hand in Hand all headlong hurl our selves,
And on the ragged Stones beat forth our Souls
And make a mutual Closure of our House.
Speak, Romans, speak, and if you say we shall, 135
Lo, Hand in Hand, Lucius and I will fall.
AEMILIUS   Come, come, thou reverent Man of Rome,
And bring our Emp'ror gently in thy Hand,
Lucius our Emperor: for well I know
The Common Voice do cry it shall be so. 140

141   MARCUS . . . Emperor! *As in the early texts of* Titus Andronicus, *this line and line 146 are attributed to Marcus. Given the parallel with the way the play began, it seems altogether fitting that Marcus should be the person to proclaim Lucius Rome's true Emperor, and to do so again on behalf of all the People.*

143   hither hale   *haul here.*

147   SO   *so as.*

149   give me Aim a while   *give me a while to get my bearings (my "aim").*

152   obsequious Tears   *tears appropriate to obsequies (funeral rites).*

154   blood slain   *The wording of this phrase seems to hover between two closely associated meanings: "bloody, slain" or "slain in a bloody fashion." Modern editions normally print* blood-stain'd, *following the emendation in the Third Folio of 1663.*

157   tenders on   *lays tenderly on.*

MARCUS   Lucius! All hail Rome's royal Emperor!
  [*To Attendants*] Go, go into old Titus' sorr'wful
     House,
  And hither hale that misbelieving Moor,
  To be adjudg'd some direful slaught'ring Death
  As punishment for his most wicked Life.   145
                              Exeunt Attendants.
  Lucius! All hail Rome's gracious Governor!
LUCIUS   Thanks, gentle Romans. May I govern so
  To heal Rome's Harms and wipe away her Woe.
  But, gentle People, give me Aim a while,
  For Nature puts me to a heavy Task.   150
  Stand all aloof. —But Uncle, draw you near
  To shed obsequious Tears upon this Trunk.
  —O take this warm Kiss on thy pale cold Lips,
  These sorr'wful Drops upon thy blood slain Face,
  The last true Duties of thy noble Son.   155
                              He kisses Titus.
MARCUS   Tear for Tear, and loving Kiss for Kiss
  Thy Brother Marcus tenders on thy Lips:
  O were the Sum of these that I should pay
  Countless and infinite, yet would I pay them.
LUCIUS   Come hither, Boy; come, come, and learn of
     us   160
  To melt in Show'rs. Thy Grandsire lov'd thee
     well:
  Many a time he danc'd thee on his Knee,
  Sung thee asleep, his loving Breast thy Pillow;

527

---

165   **pretty Tales**   *simple tales told with affection.*

169   **latest**   *final.*

178   **Breeder**   *originator (with a reference as well to Aaron's role as a "sire").*

179   **famish**   *starve.*

182   **Doom**   *sentence.*

184   **dumb**   *silent.*

Many a Story hath he told to thee,
And bid thee bear his pretty Tales in mind, 165
And talk of them when he was dead and gone.
MARCUS How many thousand times hath these poor
    Lips,
When they were living, warm'd themselves on
    thine!
O now, sweet Boy, give them their latest Kiss.
Bid him farewell; commit him to the Grave; 170
Do them that Kindness, and take leave of them.
BOY O Grandsire, Grandsire, ev'n with all my Heart
Would I were dead, so you did live again!
—O Lord, I cannot speak to him for weeping;
My Tears will choke me if I ope my Mouth. 175

Re-enter Attendants, with Aaron.

ROMANS You sad Andronici, have done with Woes:
Give Sentence on this execrable Wretch
That hath been Breeder of these dire Events.
LUCIUS Set him Breast-deep in Earth and famish
    him;
There let him stand and rave and cry for Food. 180
If any one relieves or pities him,
For the Offense he dies. This is our Doom.
Some stay to see him fast'ned in the Earth.
AARON Ah why should Wrath be mute, and Fury
    dumb?

529

185 base *abject, demeaning.*

193 forthwith *immediately.*

194 closed *sealed.*

195 rav'nous *fiercely devouring.*

196 Weed *clothes.*

198 to prey *to prey upon.*

199– Her life . . . take pity. *Let birds take pity on Tamora in*
200 *the same way that she took pity on others during her lifetime.*
The First Folio printing of the play adds four additional lines
that may or may not be authentically Shakespearean. Modern-
ized, they read as follows: "See Justice done on Aaron, that
damned Moor, / From whom our heavy Haps had their
beginning; / Then afterwards, to order well the State, / That
like Events may ne'er it ruinate." Because of their doubts
about the authenticity of these lines, most editors omit them
from modern editions. This edition follows suit. The first two
lines appear redundant in light of the sentence Lucius has
already pronounced on Aaron (lines 179–83). And the last
two lines, though characteristic of Shakespeare in their at-
tempt to tie up loose ends and provide a political resolution to
the action, seem too pat and banal to attribute to the play-
wright even in one of the earliest plays of his career.

I am no Baby, I, that with base Prayers   185
I should repent the Evils I have done:
Ten thousand worse than ever yet I did
Would I perform if I might have my will.
If one good Deed in all my Life I did,
I do repent it from my very Soul.   190
LUCIUS   Some loving Friends convey the Emp'ror
    hence,
And give him Burial in his Father's Grave.
My Father and Lavinia shall forthwith
Be closed in our Household's Monument.
As for that rav'nous tiger Tamora,   195
No Fun'ral Rite, nor Man in Mourning Weed;
No Mournful Bell shall ring her Burial;
But throw her forth to Beasts and Birds to prey.
Her Life was beastly and devoid of Pity,
And, being dead, let Birds on her take pity.   200

Exeunt.

FINIS